BURT FRANKLIN: RESEARCH & SOURCE WORKS SERIES 598
Selected Essays in History, Economics, & Social Science 199

HISTORY AND PROCEDURE OF
THE HOUSE OF REPRESENTATIVES

HISTORY AND PROCEDURE
OF THE
HOUSE OF REPRESENTATIVES

BY

De ALVA STANWOOD ALEXANDER, A.M., LL.D.

BURT FRANKLIN
NEW YORK

Published by LENOX HILL Pub. & Dist. Co. (Burt Franklin)
235 East 44th St., New York, N.Y. 10017
Originally Published: 1916
Reprinted: 1970
Printed in the U.S.A.

S.B.N.: 8337-00375
Library of Congress Card Catalog No.: 78-136044
Burt Franklin: Research and Source Works Series 598
Selected Essays in History, Economics, and Social Science 199

Reprinted from the original edition in the Princeton University
Library.

PREFACE

WHEN the writer entered Congress, Speaker Reed, whom he had known for several years, advised him to prepare a series of lectures upon the history and procedure of the House for use when invited to address clubs and other social organizations in the writer's district. In proof of his sincerity he offered his assistance, and the notes made at that time and afterward frequently used in unwritten addresses form the basis of this volume.

Speaker Reed's articles in the *North American Review* and other publications, including the little treatise on *Parliamentary Rules*, advertised the thoroughness of his study of the House procedure from its earliest beginnings; but long before he began to publish, his ready explanations of apparently conflicting precedents, disclosing the history of their origin and the difference in their parliamentary status, proclaimed his familiarity with the various rulings of a long line of Speakers. Indeed, he gained his authority in the House as much by his knowledge of things hidden in a mass of parliamentary proceedings, which others rarely disturbed, as by his ability felicitously to express and apply them when brought to the surface. His remarkable memory may be called the prototype of Hinds's *Precedents*, for he knew and could cite them offhand as readily as the average student of parliamentary proceedings now refers to the *Precedents*.

In his friendly talks on the evolution of the House procedure, Mr. Reed delighted to dwell upon the idiosyncrasies of the past. The indisposition of early legislators to aid in the expedition of business amused him. Members loved to exploit their opinions then as much as now, he said, and the only reason why we are not as overloaded with their speeches is because Congress wisely refused to pay for their publication. Even when business and membership increased, they preferred to jog along in the old stage-coach fashion. Few knew anything of the *Code*. When things got into a tangle it was easier to suspend the rules than to untie the knots. It provoked his criticism that the House, rather than give up the selfish habit of making long speeches, reversed the Speaker's ruling cutting off all debate after the previous question had been ordered. Even after the principle was fully established in 1811, the speech-loving members invoked its relief only four times in the next twenty years. In fact, the House had existed over half a century before it limited the length of speeches to one hour.

The disposition of the House to conserve the minority's alleged right to delay and even to stop business greatly diverted him. The majority seemed to be afraid of itself, he declared, with his usual sarcastic drawl. It acted as if it needed a guardian; otherwise why did it insist upon having two thirds, a quorum voting, before it dared to suspend the rules to limit dilatory motions, or to adopt a special order for any purpose, or to take a Senate bill from the Speaker's table and send it to conference? Even more ridiculous was its insistence that

to pass a bill a quorum must answer to a roll-call, even
though every member entitled to vote was in his seat.
In fact, the unwritten law of the House, he said, in-
trenched the minority's power to check the majority,
and rather than depart from such alleged legislative
safeguards a partisan majority, although trembling with
anger, preferred accepting a humiliating compromise
or a stinging defeat. As late as 1880, he recalled, the
Committee on Rules, charged with a revision of the
Code, boasted that it had not "invaded the powers of a
minority to check temporarily, if not permanently, the
action of a majority believed to be improper or unconstitutional." When a conservative and well-inten-
tioned party, reduced to desperate straits and backed
by the ruling of a bold Speaker, fearlessly adopted a
special order by a majority vote, it caused such a
tempest of dismay that forty-one years elapsed before
such a thing occurred again. And yet, he mused, within
less than a generation this view has become so obsolete
as to make the sober maintenance of it seem incredible.
So with the "disappearing quorum," once debated
with extreme bitterness as affecting the very existence
of parliamentary government, now abandoned if not
entirely forgotten. The yea and nay vote, he added,
was based upon the assumption that no other count
could be as accurate, and thus the roll-call continued
to be the test of the presence of a quorum until the
silence of members became so intolerable that it could
no longer be endured without dishonor. The trouble
was we identified safety with numbers rather than with
adherence to the principle that true progress is sure to

make for good. The conservative, in every department
of life, is always open to the attack of the progressive,
and is always eventually defeated.

Mr. Reed might have added, if not prevented by the
modesty that made his intellectual power the more
marked, that back of every movement for the expedition
of business in the House stood an able, courageous
leader, who dared to think new thoughts and find new
ways. The history of those progress-making innovations
is as interesting to-day to every lover of the forensic duel
as the events themselves were exciting at the time of
their occurrence. Mr. Reed enjoyed telling of John W.
Eppes, of Virginia, who established the practice that
ordering the previous question ended all debate. It
occurred at two o'clock in the morning, while John
Randolph, whom Eppes had challenged, was hunting for
a second, and when only four days remained in which
to pass a bill that deeply interested President Madison
and the backers of his Administration. No less sensational was the adoption for the first time of a special
order by a majority vote, which released a bill from the
Committee of the Whole after a minority had held it in
captivity all winter. Speaker White, of Kentucky, who
engineered the *coup d'état*, came in for as much condemnation as if he had been concerned in a Gunpowder Plot.
Indeed, so violent was the scene that the staid old clerk
turned newsmonger, entering in the *Journal* the fact that
the great uproar within made members unmindful of a
terrific thunder storm without. A scene equally boisterous, if not as threateningly vehement, occurred when
Alexander H. Stephens, of Georgia, played a cunning

trick — "a parliamentary fraud," Speaker Blaine pronounced it — that passed the bill repealing the Missouri Compromise, which Free Soilers had held up for five months. But the tumult which attended the counting of a quorum exceeded all former scenes of disorder. The House became a perfect bedlam. At the mention of each member's name, to be counted as present and not voting, an explosion occurred more violent than its predecessor. Even when the deafening noise attending a roll-call would subside, the older weapons, dragged from the arsenal of obstruction, filled the great chamber with hot denunciations of a revolutionary and anarchistic type. Thus for three days business was halted and the vocabulary of passionate remonstrance exhausted.

Some of these new ways did not change the thought or the parliamentary practice of the House. For the moment Speaker White's device seemed like the beginning of a new order of things; but the leaders, although claiming to believe in majority rule, would give not so much as a hearing to the idea of allowing the Speaker to suppress dilatory motions, or of permitting a majority to clear the way for a special order. In fact, the situation in the Forty-seventh Congress (1881–83) seemed to imply the final failure of a majority to accomplish anything opposed by a minority of more than one third. The rules seemed wholly out of accord, not only with the age, but with the spirit of parliamentary progress.

It was at this crisis that Thomas B. Reed, declaring that the protection of the minority did not mean the destruction of the majority, began to inflict the blows that destroyed dilatory motions, limited the passage of special orders to a majority vote, exterminated the "disappearing quorum," and then crystallized the results into rules which have become the accepted law of the House. As, in his time, Henry Clay freed the House from the control of the President, so Reed, for all time, freed it from the restraints of a minority. Clay governed by enforcing the old rules; Reed dominated by creating new rules. Clay made the House a power by managing men; Reed made it a power by establishing the majority's right to rule.

The story of subsequent changes in the House procedure, no less drastic if not yet vindicated by results, is equally interesting. Mr. Reed had a profound regard for the dignity and importance of the Speakership. To him it spoke the aspirations of the Fathers to give initiative and force to policies demanded by a majority of the people at each biennial election. In his opinion the Speaker was chosen not simply to preside over the deliberations of his fellow members, but to carry out party pledges and round up a successful legislative session. This involved committee appointments, for legislation derives its character in large part from the complexion of committees, and the fairer, more experienced, and better fitted is their membership, the more satisfactory must be their work. Properly to select appointees in a House membership running up into the hundreds requires an intimate personal knowledge of individual ambitions, characteristics, achievements, and peculiar fitness for service, and in Mr. Reed's judgment no one would so patiently and certainly acquire such

information as the Speaker, — not because the right
of appointment belonged to the office, but because upon
him rested the whole responsibility of choosing men who
would loyally write party pledges into legislation and
give conscientious study, guided by an open mind, to all
other measures. Moreover, he thought the responsibility
attendant on the exercise of such a delicate and significant power should be absolutely known. In other
words, that some one beyond question should be answer-
able to the House and to the country. Thus, when it was
proposed in the Forty-seventh Congress (1881) to substitute for this purpose a board or committee of eleven
members, to be selected by log-rolling processes insep-
arable from caucus action, he failed to find the man upon
whom responsibility for weak, sinister appointments
could be fixed. "The Speaker," he said, "is not only under the constant supervision of public opinion, but under
the supervision of this House, and an appointment out
of accord with the proprieties makes him an object of
suspicion. But for the wrongful acts of eleven men
public displeasure could rarely find a victim."

In Mr. Reed's judgment the Speaker's relation to committees did not end with their appointment. It was his
duty to remain in touch with their deliberations and to
keep advised of the progress of their work, for to bring
about a successful legislative session, wherein due regard is given to the relative importance of matters,
some impartial coördinating power must somewhere
exist, and he thought the Speaker, whose eye is continually over the whole field of possible legislation, the best
qualified to exercise this power. To assist him in the

work of coördination Mr. Reed relied upon a Committee
on Rules, the chief function of which was to open ways
for emergency matters that must have immediate attention, and to bring up promptly for consideration public bills that have necessarily been delayed in committee.
For this purpose he preferred a small committee, in harmony with the Speaker's purposes and capable of being
called into action at once. Such a committee, he said,
could not be autocratic, since its recommendations were
without validity until adopted by the House, and their
adoption was possible only so long as the committee
represented the majority's wishes.

But later-day statesmen, regarding this power too
great to be concentrated in one individual, have modified and divided it until an entirely different conception
of the Speakership and its duties exists at present. The
Speaker has been disarmed. He neither appoints the
committees nor is a member of a committee. His influence over legislation is limited to personality and
membership. What business shall be done in the House,
when it shall be done, and how it shall be done, are matters with which he has no concern other than that it shall
proceed in order under the rules. In a word, he is simply
a moderator, who keeps order and decides points of order, and whose recognition of members, except in one
instance, is wholly beyond his discretion.

The appointment of committees by a caucus-selected
board likewise reversed Reed's idea of efficiency and
fixed responsibility, recalling his prophetic exclamations:
"Think of the Speakership of this House going into commission! Think of the log-rolling in order to secure a

board that will favor various measures!" Nor in his opinion would it commend the present method if the chairman of the appointing board or committee controls the appointments, since that would simply transfer the prestige of the Speaker to the floor leader, thus destroying the alleged reason for emasculating the Speakership.

Equally destructive of the Reed idea is the enlarged and elective Committee on Rules, often hampered by the absence of a quorum. Representing several and sometimes conflicting legislative interests, it is as likely to be divisive as advisory. Nor is it longer an emergency committee, but a full-fledged, independent entity, with a room and a clerk, and engaged in matters of its own, which are entirely divorced from questions pertaining to the leadership of the House.

These drastic changes, still in an experimental stage, have not been gradual. They came abruptly, one after another, preceded by forensic battles as picturesque and sudden as those which aroused the country in the last century, and it has been the aim of the writer to make plain each step in the evolution.

To the Honorable John Dalzell, of Pennsylvania, the writer is deeply indebted for his patient, thorough revision of the pages treating of this evolution. As a member of the House Mr. Dalzell was recognized as a profoundly learned and skillful parliamentarian. For sixteen consecutive years, during the administrations of Speakers Reed, Henderson, and Cannon, he was a potent influence on the Committee on Rules, whose judgment upon questions of parliamentary procedure had the quality of finality. Indeed, the confidence of the House

in the accuracy of his knowledge was so deeply rooted
that when a majority in the Sixty-first Congress forced
a reorganization of that committee, increasing its membership from five to ten without the Speaker and making
its members elective, Mr. Dalzell was not only retained
on the new committee, but was elected its chairman. It
is proper to add that he is in no wise responsible for any
of the views expressed in this book.

The eight volumes of the Honorable Asher C. Hinds,
of Maine, entitled *Precedents of the House of Representatives,* have also been an invaluable aid. His great work
happily combines minuteness of research with wideness
of vision. Nothing seems to have escaped his eye, or
to have blurred his appreciation of the historic value
of the slightest incident. Detached from all partisan
prejudices, he has disclosed a long list of obscure precedents, obsolete rules, and antiquated forms, as well as
the latest rulings and up-to-date changes in parliamentary procedure. Congress should ever be proud that
it possessed a teacher whose constructive work must
always remain its richest heritage.

The character studies of the more prominent public
men mentioned in this history, especially those who
figured during the ten years preceding the Civil War,
are based upon the personal knowledge of various members, notably former Speaker Grow, with whom the
writer served during the Fifty-fifth, Fifty-sixth, and
Fifty-seventh Congresses. Of those who gained prominence in the ten years prior to 1850, information came
largely, through the Honorable William P. Frye, of
Maine, from the Honorable Alexander H. Stephens.

After the latter reëntered the House in the Forty-third Congress (1873), Mr. Frye enjoyed his confidence to an unlimited degree. They served upon the Committee on Rules, spending the summer of 1879 at Atlantic City while preparing the historic revision of the *Code* adopted in 1880.

An attempt to delineate the character of the earliest floor leaders, whose names are fading from men's memories, is most difficult. We have a few pages of their debates, but little of the familiar knowledge of contemporaries and less of tradition. Indeed, were it not for the *Diary* of John Quincy Adams we should be practically ignorant of the personality of some of those who lived only three quarters of a century ago. Even with the aid of this distinguished archivist, who wrote for publication, we are without impartial materials, for there is nothing of restraint in his style or of caution in his words. So strong, in fact, was his individualism and so capricious his humor that it would be rash oftentimes to accept his notes as documentary evidence.

THE AUTHOR.

BUFFALO, NEW YORK.

CONTENTS

HISTORY AND PROCEDURE OF
THE HOUSE OF REPRESENTATIVES

HISTORY AND PROCEDURE OF
THE HOUSE OF REPRESENTATIVES

CHAPTER I

APPORTIONMENT AND QUALIFICATION OF MEMBERS

In providing representation for a National House our
Constitution-makers borrowed nothing from the system
which obtained in the British Commons. That system
could scarcely have been worse. "The notorious bor-
ough of Old Sarum," writes Lord Rosebery, "was an
area of about sixty acres of ploughed land, on which had
once stood the old city of Salisbury, but which no longer
contained a single house or a single resident. The elec-
torate consisted of seven votes, which returned two
members. When an election took place, the returning
officer brought with him a tent, under which the necessary business was transacted." [1] No less an authority
than Sir Courtenay Ilbert, present Clerk of the Commons, says that "a small number of powerful and
wealthy men controlled all the elections, while it has
been estimated that from 1760 to 1832 nearly one half
the members owed their seats to patrons whose interests
they studied and whom they obeyed." [2]

Edmund Burke, who profited by this system, resisted
all changes. "Our representation," he said, "has been
found perfectly adequate to all the purposes for which

[1] *Lord Chatham*, p. 119.
[2] *Parliament, Its History, Constitution, and Practice*, pp. 42, 43.

a representation of the people can be desired or devised."
He thought the variety of franchises in the boroughs,
and the mode in which constituencies were controlled,
represented the various interests of the nation and its
ruling forces. If a candidate, not so fortunate as Burke,
failed to find a patron, or refused to be dependent on
one, he bought a seat, as Hume, Romilly, and other reformers did. Seats were advertised like livings in the
Church, and sold during Burke's time for four hundred
to two thousand pounds each. From 1812 to the passage
of the Reform Act of 1832 the price advanced to five
and six thousand pounds.

It is not surprising that the fathers of the new republic avoided this sordid system. To prevent the nesting
of "rotten " or "pocket" boroughs, they wisely provided
that districts be reapportioned every ten years; [1] that
representatives be chosen every two years; that their
number should not exceed one for every thirty thousand
inhabitants, provided each State have at least one representative; and that every representative must, when
chosen, be an inhabitant of the State whence he was
elected.[2] The method of choosing representatives was
left to legislation by the States and at first was not the
same in all of them. Massachusetts, New York, Virginia, North Carolina, and South Carolina were divided
into districts, each of which chose one representative.
New Hampshire, Connecticut, Pennsylvania, New Jersey, and Georgia elected their representatives on a general ticket.

In 1901 the law making an apportionment of repre-

[1] The Constitution, art. I, sec. 2.   [2] *Ibid.*, art. XIV, sec. 2.

sentatives in Congress among the several States required that "representatives should be elected by districts composed of contiguous and compact territory, and containing as nearly as practicable an equal number of inhabitants." [1] So, too, State law and custom have practically established that a representative must be a resident of the district from which he is elected. Probably the Federal Supreme Court would not so hold, for a State cannot narrow the qualification of a Federal legislator; but thus far, districts have very rarely chosen non-residents, on the theory that members should be completely identified with local interests.

In fixing the membership of each State, the House, when preparing its first apportionment bill, divided the population of the State by thirty thousand, allowing an additional representative for a fraction over one half of the divisor or ratio. President Washington vetoed the measure, because the use of major fractions allotted to the State more than one member for every thirty thousand inhabitants. A second bill, fixing the ratio at thirty-three thousand and ignoring fractions, promptly received executive approval. This disregard of fractions necessarily deprived many States of full representation, and to avoid injustice, apportionment bills presented under the Census of 1800, 1810, 1820, and 1830, very cleverly fixed a small ratio, which retained the existing memberships in States having the least growth. Although these ratios doubled the membership of the House, little injustice was done except to New England, which had good reason to protest. Daniel Webster, in

[1] 31 Stat. L., pp. 733–34.

1832, when a member of the Senate's Census Committee, complained that the disuse of fractions left one hundred and thirty thousand of its people unrepresented, while it gave New York, with forty thousand less population, two members more. Other States, including Pennsylvania, similarly benefited. President Washington, continued the distinguished senator, did not object to remainders. His veto applied to their abuse, which could be avoided by first fixing a definite number of representatives for the whole country as a divisor of its aggregate population, the quotient thus becoming the ratio to determine the membership from each State, one representative being added for each major fraction. On this principle Webster drafted a measure which the Senate accepted as a substitute for the House bill.[1]

This met with ugly opposition in the House. James K. Polk, of Tennessee, chairman of the House Committee, cloaking his opposition under the unconstitutionality of fractions, insisted upon a ratio of forty-seven thousand seven hundred. This accentuated the injustice to New England. "I passed an entirely sleepless night," wrote John Quincy Adams. "The iniquity of the bill and the disreputable means by which so partial and unjust a distribution of the representation had been effected, agitated me so that I could not close my eyes. I was all night meditating in search of some device, if it were possible, to avert the heavy blow from Massachusetts and from New England." But the die was cast. New York, Pennsylvania, and the South benefited, and when the House finally adopted the Committee report,

[1] 20th Cong., 1st Sess., Gales and Seaton's *Register*, pp. 487-90.

Adams "hung his harp upon the willow."[1] In the end the Senate also yielded. This gave Webster the opportunity of charging, in his incomparably impressive manner, that the Senate had lost the chance of securing the relative rights of the States, for the preservation of which it was solely responsible.[2] When the House, in 1840, again adopted a low ratio without fractions, swelling its membership to three hundred and six, the principle discriminated against other sections, and in the heat of a ten days' debate, Polk's artificial and uncandid arguments quickly turned to ashes. Fractions suddenly became constitutional, and Webster's method, dropping the House membership to two hundred and twenty-three, met hearty approval.

The feeling generally obtained that the House membership had increased too rapidly. In the debate of 1832 Webster predicted that by the natural operation of events the old States must part with a considerable portion of their representation, and although the Webster bill reduced the aggregate twenty-seven per cent, many thought the number still too large for a population of less than seventeen millions. It overcrowded the old hall, already rearranged and reseated, and added greatly to the confusion. Accordingly in 1850 the House managed to keep the membership down to two hundred and thirty-four. In 1860 it was increased to two hundred and forty-one.

Then came the present period of selfish combination. Older Commonwealths of slow growth, for the purpose

[1] *Diary*, vol. VIII, pp. 471–72.
[2] 22d Cong., 1st Sess., *Register*, p. 935.

of retaining their existing numbers, joined younger States ambitious for an increase. In twenty years this arrangement swelled the membership forty-eight per cent, a greater increase than had occurred in the preceding seventy years. The champions of reform in 1902 demonstrated that a smaller number would result in economy, in freedom from confusion, in decreased power of committees, larger opportunity for the individual, and less rigid rules. To these reasons were added the admonition of James Bryce, the distinguished English writer, that "when the number of the assembly rises to one hundred and fifty or two hundred, a new element of trouble is introduced in the excitement produced by the sympathy of a multitude, under whose influence men will say and do things which the judgment of a single man, or a small group, would at once condemn." [1]

The admitted benefits of a small body, however, could not compete in parliamentary authority with the combination of decadent and ambitious States, and it added thirty-four members. In 1911 similar methods increased the number to four hundred and thirty-three.[2] The retirement of desks and the use of benches tend to lessen confusion and to give working members better opportunity for transacting business; but the reforms so forcefully voiced in the instructive debate of 1902 are not likely to be realized until thinly populated States learn

[1] *North American Review*, vol. 151, p. 386.

[2] Apportionments resulted as follows: —

Apportionment	1787	1790	1800	1810	1820	1830	1840	1850	1860	1870	1880	1890	1900	1910
Number of members	63	105	141	181	212	240	223	234	241	293	325	357	391	433

that increased representation magnifies rather than minimizes their disproportion with populous States.

Upon the passage of an apportionment bill a State Legislature may reform the congressional districts, but after their redivision Congress may preclude other changes during the continuance of such apportionment.[1] If a State fail or refuse to provide for congressional representation Congress may do so, and for the purpose may determine the extent of each district. But members elected on a general ticket will be seated, although Congress require their election by districts. A State, however, cannot disregard the law of apportionment. When a Commonwealth elected on a general ticket one member more than the apportionment allowed, the House refused to give *prima-facie* effect to the additional credential.[2] In 1879 the clerk declined to enroll a representative-at-large to which the State was not entitled.[3] On one occasion when a State, entitled to two members, elected three on a general ticket, the House excluded the one receiving the fewest votes.[4] But the House rarely refuses to accept regular credentials when challenged simply for the reason that a district exceeds statutory limitations, and in one instance it refused to examine whether or not a county was technically entitled to be included within a district.[5] Such action, however, like decisions in contested election cases, is too often prompted by partisan reasons.

[1] 31st Cong., 2d Sess., House Report no. 3.
[2] 40th Cong., 3d Sess., *Globe*, pp. 8–9.
[3] 46th Cong., 1st Sess., *Record*, p. 4.
[4] 37th Cong., 2d Sess., *Globe*, p. 2.
[5] 44th Cong., 1st Sess., House Report no. 39.

Respecting the qualifications of a representative, the Constitution provides that he shall be twenty-five years old, a citizen of the United States for seven years, and an inhabitant, when elected, of the State in which he is chosen.[1] To these qualifications a State may not add,[2] but the House will refuse to permit a member elect to be sworn, if insane, disloyal, a polygamist, or a criminal. It can also do whatever else may seem wise to the majority, regardless of objections technical or meritorious. Nevertheless, in carrying out the expressed will of the people, the House, except in contested election cases, usually endeavors to act justly. Without refusing admission to a member elect under age, it deferred his enrollment until he could qualify. It held a foreign-born citizen eligible, whom a State court, not expressly authorized by the Federal statutes, had naturalized. In like manner it permitted a member, long a resident of the country, but without naturalization papers, to hold his seat. Actual residence in a State at the time of a member's election is not essential,[3] nor does residence abroad while obtaining an education or serving the Government, constitute disqualification. Credentials need not conform to law if no doubt exists as to an election. For this reason the House overruled a State official, who rejected a county return because of a writing on the seal of the clerk's certificate, and it admitted members elected on a day other than the legal day. Equity rules likewise govern the rights of a Territorial delegate, an

[1] Art. I, sec. 2.

[2] 34th Cong., 1st Sess., House Report no. 194; 48th Cong., 1st Sess., House Report no. 794.

[3] 10th Cong., 1st Sess., *Journal*, pp. 2, 6.

office created by the Continental Congress. It is held broadly that a person elected before a Territory has completed its statehood may become a member of the House whenever the new State is admitted, but any part of the Territory not included in the new State must be reorganized before it is again entitled to representation. The qualifications of a delegate in no wise differ from those of a member, and although the former cannot vote he enjoys all other privileges.

No person holding an office under the United States can become a member of Congress, the term "office" being limited to the power to legislate, to execute law, or to hear and determine judicially. In other words, an officer is one having power to bind the Government. This limitation does not exclude regents and other representatives of public institutions, or Government agents or commissioners authorized simply to investigate and report. Neither is a Government contractor an officer of the United States. A postmaster or other Federal officeholder, if elected to Congress, need not resign before taking his seat, and, if he be a contestant, not until the House declares him entitled to the place.

CHAPTER II

THE ROLL OF MEMBERS ELECT

An important step in the organization of a new House, and one fraught, perhaps, with the most serious consequences, is the compilation of a temporary roll of members elect. This roll is made up by the clerk of the preceding House from certificates of election filed with him, which, on their face, must be regular in form, issued within the time required by law, and specific as to the persons elected. It is used during the election of a Speaker, and members whose names do not appear upon it cannot participate in the proceedings except by the vote of a majority of those enrolled. The maker of this roll, therefore, possesses a power like to that of a national committee at a national political convention, and, if opportunity offers to pad the list, he may, if so disposed, exercise his prerogative by enrolling a sufficient number of his own party to constitute a majority, who can immediately proceed to elect a Speaker and organize the House. Such power is the more drastic since an appeal is limited to the members so enrolled.

By an ordinance passed in 1785 the Continental Congress imposed this responsible duty upon the secretary of the preceding Congress. It also made him the presiding officer until the election of a president. In 1791 the House of Representatives continued this arrangement, but to control the preparation of the roll it provided for the appointment of a committee to examine and report upon all credentials. After a time this admirable procedure fell into disuse. Indeed, so little attention was given to credentials that members took their seats without presenting any evidence of their right to do so, while the clerk, in making up his roll, depended largely upon newspaper reports. Adams says that the names enrolled by the clerk at the opening of the Twenty-fifth Congress were thus gathered, "not one member in ten having a certificate." [1] To avoid "such an exceedingly irregular practice," Adams presented a resolution requiring credentials to be filed with the clerk and limiting the roll to those complying with the rule. Although the House failed to adopt this proposition, its consideration seems to have revived the custom of filing credentials; but it left the clerk of a House which had ceased to be the sole arbiter in determining the membership of a House that is to be.

Distrust of such a procedure very soon manifested itself. Scattered through the record are entertaining examples of oratorical sarcasm, minimizing the old clerk's authority and questioning his honesty. As early as 1820, John Randolph, of Virginia, charged him with an offensive assumption of power because he refused to put a motion.[2] John S. Millson, of the same State, was no less severe. "The clerk," he said, "is not the presiding officer of this House in any sense of the word. He has no more control and exercises no other function than the reading clerk. He is simply a mouthpiece." [3] In 1837, Caleb Cushing, of Massachu-

[1] J. Q. Adams, *Diary*, vol. IX, p. 366 (1837).
[2] 16th Cong., 2d Sess., *Annals*, pp. 437-38.
[3] 36th Cong., 1st Sess., *Globe*, p. 66.

setts, charging deliberately, with much feeling, that the clerk had padded the roll with members of whose election there was no authentic information, insisted that one of their own number should preside.[1]   Henry A. Wise, of Virginia, who, according to Adams, possessed "the tartness, the bitterness, the malignity, and the inconsistencies of John Randolph," [2] was aware, he said, that usage had authorized the clerk of the preceding House to prepare a roll and to officiate at the organization of a new House, but the precedent had no force. "There is no clerk of this House. Neither do the orders of a preceding House have any validity. Nothing can supersede the constitutional right of the House to adopt its own method of organization." [3] Wise was correct in his view, but the majority, preferring a tool to an impartial presiding officer, tabled a resolution that Lewis Williams, of North Carolina, the oldest member in point of service, be appointed chairman to serve until the election of a Speaker.

It might be supposed that such power, vested in a partisan clerk, would sooner or later be used in a close election to determine arbitrarily the political complexion of the House, and in the historic crisis of 1839 this condition appeared in a highly developed form. The old clerk, Hugh A. Garland, whom Cushing had denounced in the preceding Congress, discovered that by omitting the names of all contestants from New Jersey the roll would stand one hundred and eighteen in favor of his

---

[1] 25th Cong., 1st Sess., *Globe*, pp. 1–3.
[2] J. Q. Adams, *Diary*, vol. IX, p. 88.
[3] 25th Cong., 1st Sess., *Globe*, pp. 1–3.

own party, a sufficient number to elect a Speaker.
Accordingly, when New Jersey was reached in the roll
call, Garland cunningly explained that as he had no
authority to settle contests he would complete the call
and then submit the New Jersey matter to the House
for its decision. It was a canny maneuver. The comple-
tion of the roll would constitute a quorum and put the
control absolutely into the hands of his friends, who
could immediately organize the House. John Quincy
Adams saw the trick. "This movement," he wrote, "has
evidently been prepared to exclude the five rightful New
Jersey members from voting for Speaker, and the clerk
has his lesson prepared for him. His own election depends upon their exclusion." [1]

An acrimonious debate followed. To add to the excitement the clerk, in the absence of a declared quorum
and without unanimous consent, refused to put any
question except a motion to adjourn. In other words,
says Adams, "he stops calling the roll before a quorum
is established and refuses to put any question until a
quorum is formed." [2] To solve the difficulty members
voiced various expedients side-tracking the election of
a Speaker until the settlement of the New Jersey contests. One proposed establishing a quorum by calling
the uncontested names; another suggested choosing a
temporary chairman and a committee on elections; a
third insisted upon calling the names of claimants who
bore the Governor's certificates with the broad seal of
the State and allowing only the uncontested members
to vote upon their admission. The clerk refused to put

[1] *Diary*, vol. x, p. 143.   [2] *Ibid*.

any of these propositions. His evident effort to establish a quorum without the admission of the New Jersey members finally became so intolerable that Adams, in an eloquent appeal, deeply stirred the House, urging it to seat the "broad seal" delegation. "But who will put the question?" inquired a colleague. "I will put the question myself," thundered Adams.[1]

The preëminence of Adams was acknowledged. He abounded in wit at once genial and penetrating. His scorn of all pettiness made him disdain jobbery. Even the subtler arts of parliamentary manipulation, except the breaking of a quorum, did not appeal to him. There was much in him also that was sublime. He was a puissant orator. His comprehensive grasp of European statecraft and his capacity for taking broad, high views made his achievements world-wide. To distinguished service and exalted station he united superb qualities of intellect developed by ardent study, which splendidly equipped him for the highest public usefulness, and at this supreme moment in a parliamentary crisis his intrepid spirit marked him out among the feebler men about him. It also inspired them. Even R. Barnwell Rhett, of South Carolina, whom Adams subsequently described as "a painted Administration butterfly," fired by the firmness and patriotism of the appeal, asked the clerk if he would now put the questions. Garland hesitated. He had seen the House aroused in the preceding Congress. He had heard Cushing's ugly charge, the penetrating opinion of Wise, and the spectacular speech of Rhett, whose "enunciation was so rapid, inarticulate, and vo-

[1] 26th Cong., 1st Sess., *Globe*, p. 19.

ciferous that his head hung back as he spoke, with his face turned upward like that of a howling dog." [1] In the midst of such strange, exciting scenes Garland had also observed his friends pull the strings that tabled the resolution superseding him. Could they do so again, he wondered? He scented a political catastrophe, but he could scarcely bring himself to bend. He was unwilling, he said, to put any question except a motion to adjourn, but, if so instructed, he would act as the chairman of a meeting of gentlemen and put questions. To this William Cost Johnson, of Maryland, wittily objected. "We are gentlemen," said he, "but this is evidently not a meeting of gentlemen." Then Rhett moved that John Quincy Adams be made chairman, and, putting the motion himself, declared it carried, while two members rushed the "old man eloquent" to the chair. The adoption of the rules of the last House followed.

The affair greatly exasperated the Administration party. Indeed, the noisy scene excited grave apprehension that Garland, encouraged by the support of his backers, would again attempt to preside. To prevent such a *coup d'état*, Adams took the chair promptly at twelve o'clock each day, and by his firmness and great fairness finally conquered opposition. He did not conceal his desire to admit the New Jersey members, whose exclusion he accepted as a political trick to defeat the election of John Bell, of Tennessee, but after members had voted he compelled obedience to the mandate. Finally, at the end of six days of stormy debate and

[1] J. Q. Adams, *Diary*, vol. IX, p. 386.

bluster the House elected Robert M. T. Hunter, of Virginia, "an amiable, good-hearted, weak-headed young man, prematurely hoisted into a place for which he is not fit." [1] Thus, "in consequence of the adroitness of one party (itself the minority in fact) five duly returned members from one of the States were excluded from their seats, and the power of the House thrown into the hands of the minority for the whole of that Congress. It was a great usurpation, a palpable violation of the Constitution — only acquiesced in because there was no remedy short of revolution." [2] In reward for his partisan roll-making Garland again became clerk. "Had the five New Jersey men voted," says Adams, "a tie vote would have prevented his choice. He stands self-elected by the baseness of his treachery to his trust." [3]

Nevertheless, fair dealing would have cost Garland the confidence of his party as obedience to principle subsequently did John W. Forney. Forney was a gentleman of the world. His open and engaging demeanor made him a charming companion, while his signal excellence as a journalist added to his prestige. He delighted in epigram, was without the slightest taint of snobbery, and led the most congenial souls in Washington. These qualities made him serviceable to his party, and in 1851 and again in 1853 it elected him clerk of the House. Thus, at the historic opening of the Thirty-fourth Congress (1855), Forney inherited the difficult task of organizing

---

[1] *Diary*, vol. x, p. 379.
[2] *National Intelligencer* (Washington), December 17, 1849.
[3] *Diary*, vol. x, p. 172.

a body in which no party had a majority and no member was without a vote, for in preparing the preliminary roll of members elect his conscience could not be silenced by office or honors.

During those exciting sixty days, he wrote years afterward, "My position was most peculiar. I was one of the editors of the Washington *Union*, the organ of President Pierce, and the active advocate of James Buchanan for the Presidential succession, and I was also the personal friend of Andrew H. Reeder, who had just been removed from the governorship of Kansas for refusing to join the conspiracy to force slavery into that Territory. Our relations had not changed, and I had earnestly, but vainly, protested against his sacrifice. He was on the floor contesting the seat of J. W. Whitfield, who had secured the certificate as a delegate from Kansas. The struggle for the Presidency was at fever heat. The South was wrought to the highest pitch of excitement. The bold attitude of the Free-State men in Congress and the country, the extraordinary proceedings in Kansas, and the closeness of parties in the House, added to the other perplexities of my position. The opposition looked upon me with a very natural distrust, and the Democrats relied upon me to exert every influence to forward their designs. Their hatred of my friend Reeder was terrible, and I soon found that my unconcealed confidence in him made me an object of general distrust among the Southern leaders. Cobb and Stephens, of Georgia; Garnett and Faulkner, of Virginia; Rust, of Arkansas; Jones, of Tennessee; Alexander K. Marshall and Burnett, of Kentucky; Barksdale, of Mississippi;

George S. Houston, of Alabama; Keitt and Brooks and Orr, of South Carolina, backed in the Senate by Slidell, Toombs, Iverson, J. M. Mason, Hammond, Butler, Wigfall, Benjamin, Yulee, and C. C. Clay, and in the Cabinet by Jefferson Davis, believed if they lost the House all was imperiled. Every day the same scene was enacted. . . . But members soon saw that I was resolved to act honestly at every hazard." [1]

The dominating politicians, piqued by Forney's evenhanded justice, seriously thought of making James L. Orr, of South Carolina, the presiding officer. In fact, the previous question had been demanded on such a motion when some one moved a recess. Johsua R. Giddings, of Ohio, thought the motion incompetent pending a demand for the previous question, but Forney thought otherwise, and the tired members, worn out with interminable ballotings, points of order, debates, and threats of violence, sustained his ruling. [2] This gave time for sleep, and the motion to promote Orr was not again offered. Forney continued to guide the proceedings until February 3 (1856), when the House, on the one hundred and thirty-third ballot, elected Nathaniel P. Banks, of Massachusetts, for Speaker. [3]

Forney got out of his "thankless" job very well financially, for the House doubled his salary; [4] but the fierce asaults upon his rulings filled him with resent-

---

[1] J. W. Forney, *Anecdotes of Public Men*, p. 110.

[2] 34th Cong., 1st Sess., *Globe*, p. 87.

[3] Banks received 103 votes to 100 for William Aiken, of South Carolina.

[4] Forney was reëlected clerk of the House in 1860, and the Senate, at President Lincoln's solicitation, made him its secretary in 1861.

ment, and he seemed never to tire of exploiting the frailties of his persecutors. Of those named in the above list he thought Davis the sternest in his convictions; Jones the most acrid; Houston the noisiest; Keitt the most quarrelsome; Hammond of the least account; Mason, "with his Dombey diction and pompous pretense," the most dictatorial; Slidell, supercilious and satirical, "a scheming politician of undoubted courage, yet never a statesman," the most implacable in his hostility to all who did not agree with him; Wigfall, thundering his anathemas, the boldest and coarsest; Toombs, a stormy petrel, often grand as a declaimer, always intolerant, dogmatic, extreme, and threatening. Of Orr and Benjamin and Soulé and Howell Cobb he had few words of censure. To him Orr was the best-tempered of the able ultras of the South, and Benjamin the possessor of those rare qualities which characterized Henry Winter Davis, of Maryland, whose incisive sentences and ready wit were admirably reinforced by acute reasoning powers and legal training. "Benjamin's handsome Jewish face, his liquid tones, and easy enunciation contrasted well with his skill as a debater and his accuracy as a student." The one man whom Benjamin most disliked, continues Forney, was "poor Pierre Soulé, the brilliant and superficial Frenchman, whose swarthy complexion, black, flashing eyes, and Frenchified dress and speech made him the chief attraction of the Senate. He was an artificial man — brilliant in repartee, yet subject to fits of melancholy; impetuous, yet reserved; proud, but polite, with a vast fund of knowledge and a deposit of vanity which was never exhausted." Although Forney included Howell Cobb in his list of tormentors, he seemed to remember him without bitterness. He thought of him as a different type from the others. "Like John C. Breckinridge," said this delightful and gossipy writer, "Cobb never persecuted the men of his party who refused to endorse extreme measures; yet he was most resolute in behalf of his State and section." [1]

Forney's successors, profiting by his experience, have found it easier and less precarious to submit all questions to the House. They have even declined to call members to order when not confining their remarks to the subject, thus creating scenes of great confusion and contributing to prolong the period of organization. The speakership contest of 1860, rivaling in threats and bitterness all previous exhibitions of partisan and sectional anger, forced the House to adopt the rule that "pending the election of a Speaker, the clerk shall preserve order and decorum, and decide all questions of order that may arise, subject to an appeal to the House." [2] To add to the clerk's power and prestige an act, passed on the last legislative day of the Thirty-seventh Congress, declared that "before the meeting of each Congress the clerk of the next preceding House shall make a roll of the representatives elect, and place thereon the names of those persons only whose credentials show that they were regularly elected in accordance with the laws of their States respectively, or the laws of the United States." [3]

---

[1] *Anecdotes of Public Men*, p. 41.
[2] Adopted March 9, 1860. Rule III, sec. 1.
[3] 14 Stat. L., p. 396.

Under this law the clerk may decline to enroll a member elect if his credentials are informal, or in excess of the apportionment, or indefinite as to returns; or if they challenge the legality of an election, the citizenship of a claimant, or the sufficiency of his age. During the organization of the House the clerk may also refuse to recognize members whose names are not upon his roll; [1] or to allow interruption while calling the roll; [2] or to permit an amendment of the roll until after the election of a Speaker. [3] In theory the House may on appeal correct clerical usurpations, but since such mistakes are committed for the purpose of putting the clerk's party in power, "he would be a sanguine man, indeed," writes Speaker Reed, "who hoped to see a wrong repudiated which was thus premeditated and profitable." [4]

For this reason the clerk of the preceding House is often an object of suspicion. Forney's case was not an exceptional one. Whenever parties are closely divided his roll tends to discredit his fairness, while his rulings, even if he strictly follows precedent, usually arouse resentment. This was more evident after the statute fixed his status, since it occasionally contributes to an undue assumption of superiority. In 1863, when unseemly haste seemed to characterize the organization of the House, William S. Holman felt the sting of such arrogance. The majority, without waiting to hear the clerk's reasons for omitting certain members from his

[1] 39th Cong., 1st Sess., *Globe*, p. 2.   [2] *Ibid.*
[3] 45th Cong., 1st Sess., *Record*, p. 53.
[4] *North American Review*, vol. 151, p. 113.

roll, moved their admission. As the Indianian raised the
point that it was not in order to instruct the clerk as to
his duties, that official quickly overruled him and put
the motion, the House remaining ignorant of the reason
for his original action.[1] Having made up the roll in 1867,
McPherson, clerk of the last House, declined to entertain any proposition for modifying it.[2] James Brooks,
of New York, rising to a question of order, spoke of
the clerk's omission to call the names of members elect
from Louisiana and Georgia. Thereupon McPherson
declared him out of order, declined to entertain an
appeal, and directed him to take his seat.[3] Prior to the
election of Speaker Randall in 1877, Eugene Hale, of
Maine, rising to a question of the highest privilege, proposed substituting one name for another on the clerk's
roll. Samuel S. Cox, of New York, made the point of
order that "the clerk had absolute control over the roll
of the House," whereupon George M. Adams, of Kentucky, the clerk, sustained the point and declined to
entertain an appeal, declaring it "not competent for
representatives elect, in their unorganized capacity,
either to instruct the clerk how he shall perform a
duty which the law has imposed upon him, or to take
it out of the hands of the clerk and themselves perform the duty which the law has said the clerk shall
perform." [4]

It is clear that the inherent right of the House under
the Constitution to make its rules and elect its officers

---

[1] 38th Cong., 1st Sess., *Globe*, pp. 4–6.
[2] 40th Cong., 1st Sess., *Globe*, pp. 3–4.
[3] 41st Cong., 1st Sess., *Globe*, p. 4.
[4] 45th Cong., 1st Sess., *Record*, p. 53.

cannot be limited by the Act of 1863,[1] but "the law has thus far been acquiesced in," says Speaker Reed, "because of the fear that any other course might lead to chaos." [2] However this may be, it is most fortunate, perhaps, that for many years decisive elections have settled the political status of each new House long in advance of its organization, since it is not pleasant to contemplate what might occur in a House of greatly increased membership should a bold hold-over clerk like Garland, regardless of fair dealing, prepare a roll of members which gave his own party the requisite number to elect a Speaker and thus organize the House.

[1] 42d Cong., 2d Sess., *Globe*, pp. 11, 117; but see, also, 44th Cong., 2d Sess., *Record*, p. 1156.
[2] *North American Review*, vol. 151, p. 113.

CHAPTER III

ORGANIZATION OF THE HOUSE

To the visitor who cares for history no place in the country inspires deeper interest than the Capitol at Washington, surmounted by its famous dome, and no occasion, perhaps, unless it be the inauguration of a President, contributes more pleasure than the organization of the House. Richly dressed ladies garland the galleries; foreign diplomats, glittering with emblems of their order, occupy boxes set apart for their use; and long rows of spectators from all parts of the country, packed and orderly, add a holiday character to the scene. In the House of Commons lady visitors sit behind an iron *grille* as if the wives of Mohammedans, but in the American House they are openly welcomed. On exceptional days they appear in the press gallery, and on rarest occasions have even dared to view the brilliant scene from the rail that guards the hall itself.

On the floor of the great chamber are gathered several hundred eager politicians, — not more intelligent than any equal number of selected professional and business men, or better speakers than are found in any large assembly of clerical or legal representatives; but as "the House" they constitute a body more interesting than any other in the country. The individual is nothing. The presence of a few highly distinguished ones of whom every one knows lends an interest, but they are not the loadstone. It is "the House" that attracts. What is "the House"? An aggregation of vigorous elements, having different objects, antagonistic notions, and selfish interests, centered about indefinite party policies and moved by personal, political, and sometimes patriotic purposes. In appearance it is constantly changing. Often half a dozen members are "the House" — not infrequently nearly half a thousand. From a trifling expense for printing it may pass to the consideration of a policy that divides the nation into halves. At one moment it is calm like a mill-pond — in the next as boisterous as the Niagara rapids. Frequently it can do nothing but adjourn, and often, although helpless, it refuses to adjourn. There is a "feeling of the House" and a "sense of the House." It is a common saying that "the House has more sense than any one in it." It is likewise full of whims. It gets out of sorts and sulks. But it is never unhitched. However dull it may become, some one is on guard, and hidden from sight and from the knowledge of spectators, like the delicate wheels of a watch, are restraining rules and restrictive precedents which safeguard it from the petulance of its moods and the violence of its passion. Moreover, it is always thinking and planning and talking. For days the contending elements may be as wide apart as ice cakes in a swollen river, when suddenly, as if swept by a cold wave, the "mind of the House" is made up, and the country is quieted or disturbed.

To witness the organization of such a body, though simple and void of the spectacular, captivates all classes — their imagination dwelling upon its history, its important functions, its tremendous responsibilities, its incessant activities, and the picturesque scenes, dramatic, pathetic, and comic, which are constantly entering into its life. To many it is a pleasure simply to sit in a place which has echoed the voices of the starry spirits whose brilliant discussions, scintillations of wit, and sober wisdom have made it a center of historic memories. One lives with the great dead, whose names imparted inspiration to one's childhood, or pointed the way to one's future. Within those massive walls men have assembled who led the nation during the years when it slowly raised itself from conscious independence to assume its place as a world power.

More dignity marks an initial session than formerly. The custom of wearing hats was discontinued in 1837. Prior to that, members remained covered, though not always with the highly polished "topper" so familiar in the House of Commons. Until 1871 it was the practice of members to smoke, giving the air a grayish hue. Formerly, too, admiring friends adorned the desks of members with flowers, flooding the hall with a mass of color and incidentally concealing the faces of the beneficiaries. But in 1905, long before the removal of the desks, the custom became obsolete, thus leaving the House ready for business and giving visitors an opportunity of studying the strong and weak features of the men, who, for a brief spell, are to aid in making the country's laws.

But nothing of this gala-day spectacle is new to the veteran of several terms save the faces of new members, and nothing so sad, perhaps, as the absence of old ones. The House grows accustomed to its losses, proud in its conviction that no man is indispensable to it.

Nevertheless, those of long service know that the place is never quite the same after the loss of an able leader. "Now that Mr. Gladstone is no longer with us," plaintively writes a veteran Commoner, "who can fill the House and hold the audience in charmed attention?" Members of the House of Representatives have reason occasionally to feel as lonely. The promotion of Schenck, the defeat of McKinley, the withdrawal of William L. Wilson, of West Virginia, the death of Randall, the resignation of Reed, and the transfer to the Senate of Blaine and Dawes and Hoar and Frye and Hale and Carlisle and Vice-President Sherman — such changes occurring from time to time have made the chamber seem lonesome. These distinguished leaders gave *éclat* to debate. Most of them were expert talkers, trained in a parliamentary school, and their words, like cooling showers in August, often revived a tired House and put new life into the routine. There was about them in the heat of battle a certain chivalry of manner which makes debate the more effective and tends to disparage cheap, torrent-like declamation.   Such speakers become an example to all, and their departure leaves vacancies which only time can fill.   This was especially true of Eppes and Lowndes, of Clay and Evans and Bell, of Blaine and Garfield and Randall and Reed. They occupied so large a place in the thoughts, the lives, and the affections of so many hundreds of their colleagues that their loss combined with many of the dramatic elements of their lives to convert their memory into a sort of legend, so that members who had known them well grew at last to be envied by later comers.

Nevertheless, when the House sheds a veteran leader the spirit of politics is often changed for the better, since younger members, unprejudiced by the past and eager for a new order of things, come to the front. The transition is gradual, but it usually makes for progress. There is little to be feared, however, from longevity in the House, since each biennial election is the curfew of one fourth of its members. Thus the House, like the heathen goddess, devours its own children. But the rapidity with which the process goes on is a bit startling. Of the three hundred and ninety-one members who appeared in March, 1911, at the first session of the Sixty-second Congress, only four belonged to the House in 1891.[1] This represents the havoc usually made every twenty years by death, defeat, and other circumstances. The average length of a member's service is less than six years.

A new House is usually organized on the first Monday in December of each odd year, although the ceremony may occur earlier if the President calls a special session. But whatever the day, the clerk of the preceding House raps for order promptly at twelve o'clock meridian, and while the chaplain prays the members, standing in their places, give reverent attention with bowed heads. Then the clerk calls the roll of members elect. In earlier days this sometimes meant parliamentary confusion, and the conditions that characterized the New Jersey wrangle in 1839 may again cause trouble. During the past half-century, however, decisive results at the polls and

[1] Joseph G. Cannon, Illinois; Sereno E. Payne, New York; Henry H. Bingham, Pennsylvania; John Dalzell, Pennsylvania.

early caucus action have turned the call into a mere formality and the election of a Speaker into a public ceremony. If the roll-call discloses a quorum,[1] candidates for Speaker are immediately placed in nomination. In presenting them the chairmen of the respective party caucuses rise in their places, and, without remarks, announce the names selected. This done, the clerk appoints tellers, representing each party, and proceeds a second time to call the roll, arranged not by States as before, but alphabetically.[2] Each member, without rising, declares his choice *viva voce*. Prior to 1839 the House used the ballot, and subsequent efforts to restore it occasionally found a few supporters. But after the long, fierce contest of 1849 members resented the suggestion, holding that open voting prevented secret bolting. In 1855 a motion to restore it was defeated by two hundred and fourteen to seven.

The number of votes required to elect a Speaker depends upon the will of the House. For many years the rule, accepted without objection, fixed a majority of all the members as the minimum. But in 1809, when Speaker Varnum received a less number, the House, heedless of John Randolph's declaration that "a Speaker should be elected *more majorum*," [3] held a plurality sufficient, a quorum having voted.[4] This precedent,

[1] In the earlier years a quorum rarely responded on the opening day. At the first session of the First Congress, called to meet on March 4, 1789, a majority of the House did not appear until April 1. But railroads long ago eliminated excuse for such delays.

[2] If two members have the same surname, the State of each is added. If two from the same State have like surnames, the first names are called.

[3] 11th Cong., 1st Sess., *Annals*, pp. 54–56.   [4] *Ibid.*

based upon party expediency, found no favor with succeeding Houses until a desire to end the protracted
struggle of 1849 encouraged the adoption of a special
rule providing that if no choice be made in the next three
ballots a plurality should elect. It was argued that a
plurality would be equivalent to a majority since it
required a majority to give effect to a plurality, but
after the selection of Howell Cobb under the resolution
anxiety to preserve the Randolph rule led to the confirmation of his title by a majority vote.[1] In the famous
contest between Banks and Aiken in 1855, a similar
special rule was adopted, and when the third ballot
disclosed a plurality for Banks, a teller, in announcing
the result, said: "According to the resolution adopted
this day Nathaniel P. Banks is declared Speaker of the
House of Representatives for the Thirty-fourth Congress." Immediately a member from Kentucky protested that, the precedent of 1849 not having been followed, Banks had not been chosen Speaker. Upon this
the pent-up emotion of many weeks broke forth in wild
tumult, but when order was partially restored, Aiken,
with a chivalry that did him honor, rebuked the cavil-
lers, declaring Banks fairly and legally chosen. Nevertheless, it was deemed expedient to confirm his title
by a majority vote.[2] An exception to this rule has
occurred only once. In the Forty-sixth Congress, out
of a total membership of 293, Samuel J. Randall received 144 votes, a plurality of 21 over James A. Garfield, but 3 less than a majority. After the announce-

[1] 31st Cong., 1st Sess., *Journal*, pp. 157–63.
[2] 34th Cong., 1st Sess., *Globe*, p. 343.

ment of the choice of Randall, a member, swelling with indignation, asked if it did not require a majority of all to elect, to which the instructed and obedient clerk promptly replied: "It requires a majority of those voting to elect a Speaker as it does to pass a bill, a quorum voting." [1] A similar ruling, had it been permitted in 1839, 1849, 1855, and 1860, would have made other men Speaker than those finally chosen. In the presence of such a continued and chivalric observance of the Randolph rule, its violation in 1879 seemed unpatriotic. Nor would the House have acquiesced had the votes in opposition aggregated a majority. Nevertheless, it served the Pennsylvanian's purpose!

After announcing the election of a Speaker, the clerk appoints a committee to conduct the honored one to the chair. In early Congresses it consisted of one member distinguished for long or other service; but in 1849, after the historic contest between Cobb and Winthrop, during which the rival candidates had observed toward each other conspicuous courtesy, the House increased the committee to three, the appointment of Winthrop as its chairman being received with wild applause. "Mr. Winthrop," says the *Globe*, "approached Mr. Cobb with much good humor, both shaking hands cordially." [2] This gracious custom became hallowed when Aiken, after the savagely partisan contest of 1855, smilingly offered his arm to Banks, and presented him to the House as the "gentlest of gentlemen." [3] In later

---

[1] 46th Cong., 1st Sess., *Record*, p. 5.

[2] 31st Cong., 1st Sess., *Globe*, p. 20.

[3] The vote stood: Banks, 103; Aiken, 100.

years the absence of hotly contested elections may
have robbed this pretty ceremony of much of its sentiment, but men yet living can recall Kerr conducting
Blaine to the chair, and Blaine conducting Kerr; Garfield arm in arm with Randall, and Randall arm in arm
with Keifer; Reed supporting Carlisle, and Carlisle
supporting Reed; Reed escorting Crisp, and Crisp escorting Reed. Such are the vicissitudes of politics.
After Crisp's death and Reed's resignation, James D.
Richardson, of Tennessee, accompanied Henderson,
John Sharp Williams walked by the side of Cannon,
and eight years later James R. Mann, of Illinois, escorted Champ Clark.

Thus escorted, the Speaker elect mounts at once to
the dais. In the English Parliament the ceremony is less
abrupt. Standing with one foot on the topmost step, the
Speaker elect of the Commons bows three times to the
chair, and, looking back, recites a brief formula of thanks.
Then, taking the last step, he seats himself upon the
people's throne, while the sergeant-at-arms lifts the
mace to the table in token that the House is in session.
The Speaker elect of the American House escapes less
easily. He must listen to the words of an introduction,
and recite or read an original address. The enthusiastic
audience, eager to end the monotony of roll-calls, ex-
pects a rousing speech, but as words of self-deprecia-
tion, of commonplace appeal, and hackneyed platitudes
multiply, it begins to wonder how a brilliant talker,
effective in attack and ready in repartee, can be so tame.
The *Record* presents no exception to the rule. Clay
declared himself so sensible of imperfections "that re-

liance upon your generous support alone encourages me
to attempt a discharge of the duties of the Chair." [1]
Even Blaine, bold and dominating as Clay, expressed
great diffidence.[2] After laboriously trying to work out
something new, Reed complained that "the language of
thanks has long ago been exhausted." [3] One wonders
if the English stereotyped formula is not better. Yet
the remarks of Speakers elect are rarely tedious. As
printed in the official proceedings Clay's six speeches
average only twenty-five lines, and Stevenson's and
Cannon's, each four times elected, average seventy
and twenty-seven lines respectively. Of the three-term
Speakers, Macon's average six lines, Colfax's forty,
Blaine's thirty, Randall's twenty, Carlisle's seventy, and
Reed's seventeen. Other Speakers are not more prolix.
Indeed, Crisp's two speeches average only six lines.

When taking the oath the Speaker formerly de-
scended to the floor. It placed him once more on a level
with his associates, and magnified the fact that much
of his power springs from his membership; but for many
years he has remained in his desk. Importance also attaches to the official administering the oath. Very early
in its history the House adopted the English custom of
designating for this duty the member of longest continuous service, known as the "Father of the House." [4]
For four Congresses John Quincy Adams bore this title;
Lewis Williams, of North Carolina, held it for six terms;
and William D. Kelley, of Pennsylvania, sustained it

[1] 12th Cong., 1st Sess., *Annals*, p. 2.
[2] 41st Cong., 1st Sess., *Record*, p. 3.
[3] 55th Cong., 1st Sess., *Record*, p. 4.
[4] For list of "fathers," see Appendix D.

with great credit for sixteen years out of a service of fifteen terms. With questionable taste Speakers Randall and Crisp interrupted the custom by designating William S. Holman, of Indiana, to officiate. Holman had served as many terms as the then "father," but not consecutively.[1] Had later speakers followed this precedent, Joseph G. Cannon must have officiated after the Fifty-fifth Congress, since he represented longer service than Bingham. Indeed, in a parliamentary sense Cannon may be said to have been born before his father.[2]

Having taken the oath of office the Speaker elect becomes the Speaker, and is always and everywhere addressed as "Mr. Speaker." Yet never in his dress and rarely in his manner is there visible change. It is otherwise with the Speaker of the House of Commons. On his reappearance after taking the oath he is attired in Court dress, with knee-breeches, silver-buckled shoes, and a bob-wig. After receiving "His Majesty's Royal allowance and confirmation of the choice made by his faithful Commons," a ceremony performed in the House of Lords, he drops the "bob," puts on a full-bottomed wig, dons a flowing robe, and makes his way back to the chamber of the House, accompanied by the chaplain in full canonicals and the sergeant-at-arms bearing the mace. The cry, "Mr. Speaker," passed along from policeman to messenger, announces his progress. A similar ceremony is daily observed whenever

[1] Holman served from the 36th to and including the 55th Congress, except the 39th, 45th, 46th, and 54th.

[2] Cannon who is still in the House, served continuously from the 43d to and including the 62d Congress, except the 52d, being the longest service in the history of the House.

he enters the House. The Speaker of the House of Representatives, unaccompanied and unannounced, enters the great chamber promptly at twelve o'clock, quickly ascends to the desk, gives one sharp rap with the gavel, proclaims "the House will be in order," and in a softer, lower tone asks the chaplain, already waiting at the clerk's desk, to offer prayer. The Englishman believes that business would proceed much less smoothly without the wig, the robe, and the ceremony, while the American rejoices in the Speaker's ordinary dress and the absence of the spectacular.

The first duty of the Speaker is to administer the oath to members elect, who, as their names are called by States, take position in front of the desk. If one member objects to another being sworn, the Chair may direct him to stand aside until the House decides. In such instances members are usually sworn at once and their cases subsequently referred to a committee for examination. Absent members qualify whenever they appear. Indeed, during their absence the oath may be administered to them by another than the Speaker.[1]

The election of clerk, sergeant-at-arms, doorkeeper, postmaster, and chaplain follows the qualification of members. To save time a resolution containing the five names selected by the majority caucus is adopted. After their election the Speaker administers the oath. Then the sergeant-at-arms, without ceremony and often without being observed by the casual visitor, lifts the historic mace, with its silver globe and massive eagle flashing in the light, to its place on the marble

[1] 49th Cong., 2d Sess., *Record*, pp. 1156–58.

pedestal at the right of the Chair. This symbol of the power of the House as represented by the Speaker, when thus located, indicates that the House is in session and ready for business.[1]

But on this opening day there is little business to transact. Two resolutions are adopted, one instructing the clerk to notify the President and the Senate that the House is ready to proceed to business; the other directing the Speaker to appoint a committee to join one from the Senate to inform the President that Congress is prepared to receive any communication he may be pleased to make. The hour for daily meeting is also fixed, usually at twelve o'clock meridian.

The adoption of the rules of the last House, like the preceding business, is wholly perfunctory. Whatever changes the majority desire are prepared in private, approved in caucus, and presented to the House under a demand for the previous question. This limits debate to twenty minutes on a side, and three or four old members, whose speeches are seldom new and never convincing, exhaust the time. For many years the real interest of the opening day centered in the remarks of William P. Hepburn, of Iowa, a caustic and dangerous adversary in debate, who, while exploiting his objections to the rules, delighted the House with his ready retort and sarcasm. Nevertheless, the code is usually adopted without amendment.[2]

---

[1] The mace represents the Roman *fasces*, the rods, tipped with silver spearheads, being bound transversely with a silver band, from the center of which a silver stem supports a globe of silver, on which perches a massive silver eagle. The height is about three feet.

[2] See chap. IX, p. 170.

The drawing of seats formerly completed the business of the day. The old chamber, now Statuary Hall, afforded fairly good accommodations until the apportionment under the Sixth Census crowded two hundred and forty members into its limited area. After that the desirable seats fell to those who arrived first. This raised the cry that members residing near Washington benefited at the expense of those living at a distance, and several unsuccessful attempts to put all on an equality exaggerated the unfairness of the free-seat system as much as they exploited the benefits of a lottery scheme. Finally the issue became sufficiently acute to attract the attention of Howell Cobb, of Georgia, whose ambition to be Speaker found support in his skill as a parliamentarian, and with arguments that told most readily on the House he engineered the adoption of a plan, which, in spite of its nerve-racking and temper-ruffling results, seemed ever after to defy improvement.[1] Its operation required a box of marbles, each bearing a number corresponding to the number of a member's name on a list alphabetically arranged. When all seats were vacated, except those specially exempted for former Speakers and others of conspicuous or long service, a blindfolded page withdrew a marble, the clerk announced its number, and the member hurried to the most desirable seat unoccupied. This was fair. But as the coveted places rapidly filled, the suspense became more and more intolerable until the unlucky members gladly dropped into any vacant chair, devoutly thankful if they escaped a far-off corner, known

---

[1] 29th Cong., 1st Sess., *Globe*, p. 4.

as "Cherokee Strip," where seeing was difficult and hearing impossible. Nevertheless, the lottery continued as the fairest plan that could be devised until the removal of desks and the substitution of benches in 1913 did away with the necessity for permanent seats. A member entering the chamber may now locate in any unoccupied chair. Although this was practically so under the old arrangement, one who took the seat of another usually vacated it on the appearance of its rightful occupant — not from the feeling of being a trespasser, but because the desk contained books and papers which the latter might wish to consult. Until the erection in 1908 of a building providing rooms for others than chairmen of committees, a member's desk was his office.

CHAPTER IV

THE SPEAKER

THE Speaker is the organ of the House. As its executive head he receives its invitations, represents it at public functions, appoints and removes official reporters, names visitors and trustees of public institutions, issues warrants, executes orders, authenticates proceedings, approves bonds, certifies salary accounts of members, controls committee rooms, corridors, galleries, and the House grounds, regulates admission to the floor and to the press gallery, signs all bills that pass, and notifies the proper state official whenever a vacancy in the House occurs.

As its presiding officer he calls the assembly to order, recognizes members, ascertains the presence of a quorum, presents business as indicated by the rules, preserves order, administers censure by direction of the House, answers parliamentary inquiries, decides questions of order, and, in general, carries out the will of the House. He selects the chairman of the Committee of the Whole, appoints a Speaker *pro tempore* for a day, or, with the approval of the House, for a term not to exceed ten days, and refers or directs the reference of all bills to their respective committees. Until the Sixty-second Congress (1911) he appointed all committees unless otherwise ordered, and for over half a century (1857–1911) was chairman of the Committee on Rules. By the Act of 1816 his salary was fixed at $8

per day. It became $6000 per year in 1856, $8000 in
1866, and $12,000 in 1906.

By custom the Speaker ranks next to the President
and Vice-President. Until 1887 the law designated him
to succeed to the Presidency in the event of the death
or incapacity of the President and Vice-President. Nathaniel Macon regarded the Speaker "as the elect of
the elect of all the people," and disregarding his assignment at a public ceremony, took his place by the side
of the President and Vice-President.[1] At a state dinner
given by the Chief Executive to members of Congress,
the Vice-President sits at the right and the Speaker at
the left of the President. If given to the Supreme Court,
the Chief Justice, as the guest of honor, sits at the
President's right, the Vice-President at his left, and the
Speaker at the right of the Chief Justice. On one
occasion Speaker Cannon declined to attend such a
function unless so seated. "Be as modest as you please,"
said Thomas H. Benton to Speaker Winthrop, who hesitated a moment before taking his seat at a dinner given
by the City of Washington to Congress, "but don't
compromise the House of Representatives." [2] Former
President Adams thought the Speaker should call upon
no one save the President and Vice-President. Several
reasons are presented for this precedent. Speaker
Winthrop based it upon his duty, coequal with that of
the President and Vice-President, to sign all bills. John
Quincy Adams attributed it to the fact that he is "the
representative of the people's representatives." [3] Until

[1] Thomas H. Benton, *Thirty Years' View*, vol. i, p. 118.
[2] M. P. Follett, *The Speaker of the House of Representatives*, p. 297.
[3] *Ibid.*

divested of authority to appoint committees and to head the Committee on Rules, Thomas B. Reed thought the office "had but one superior and no peer," and people generally associated this prestige with its "enormous power," which was surpassed only by that of the President.

The Speaker of the House of Commons is not its prototype. The former declares and interprets the law in a strictly judicial spirit, and his rulings are final. Though he cannot make or alter the law of the House, he may, when precedents and orders are insufficient, adopt such a course as is most consistent with the usages and traditions of the House and the rights and interests of its members. When elected Speaker he renounces party, and merges the lesser office of member into the greater one of Speaker. He is not permitted to advise either party and must not deliver political addresses even to his own constituents. He cannot vote except in case of a tie, a privilege, which, if exercised, is so used that, if possible, it may not involve final action. Indeed, not to maintain strict political neutrality without the House as well as within it is deemed a sufficient breach of the proprieties to deny him a reëlection. When his impartiality is established, however, his tenure of office is not affected by a change of ministry, and, so long as he desires to continue in office, the practice of reëlecting him, whatever party may be in power, has been departed from but once in a century.

The American Speaker, on the other hand, was until recently a political leader. As a presiding officer he interpreted the rules and decided questions of order, subject to appeal, while as head of his party in the House he controlled political legislation along lines representing its established policies.   In other words, the office combined imperfectly the duties of a British Speaker, who is the parliamentary spokesman of the House in its collective capacity, and the legislative functions of a British Prime Minister, who represents a majority of the Commons and endeavors to control legislation by all the adventitious aids known to party machinery. This combination put the American Speaker at a great disadvantage. To shape legislation in the interest of a party and to act impartially as a presiding officer is a difficult rôle, and even when infinite tact and rare skill are exercised, a lurking suspicion exists that political motives influence and govern him. Nevertheless, it has always been held that a Speaker while presiding is in nowise emancipated from the obligation to act impartially, and fairness at such times has largely determined his character as an official worthy of the great trust imposed in him. It may be added that in matters purely political an earnest effort to observe the British ideal has at times marked the conduct of several Speakers, notably of Samuel J. Randall, who, by firm fairness during the passage and enforcement of the Electoral Commission Act in 1877, rose to exalted heights.

In choosing a Speaker the House, unless prevented by a party caucus or outside interference, usually picks its most masterful member. The selection of John White, John W. Jones, and John W. Davis, called "the three Johns" and known as "the three tools," represents the

blighting control of party bosses, while the choice of
Stevenson and Polk was due wholly to the influence
of President Jackson. The chief factor in the election of
Hunter and Pennington was availability, neither being
the first choice of his party. Galusha A. Grow became
Speaker, says Blaine, "because of his activity in the anti-
slavery struggles." [1] After knocking down Lawrence
M. Keitt, of South Carolina, in a fisticuff encounter on
the floor of the House, Grow became a hero,[2] and without a caucus or party nomination he polled a plurality
of votes on the first roll-call. Subsequent changes before
the announcement of the result gave him a majority
over all. As a rule long service, conspicuous ability, and
aptitude for the duties of the chair have governed in
the selection of Speakers, bringing to the high office such
members as Taylor, Clay, Bell, Winthrop, Cobb, Banks,
Colfax, Blaine, Kerr, Randall, Carlisle, Reed, and Cannon.

The selection of a Speaker *pro tempore* who will sustain the elevated character of the high office becomes
important. If the Speaker leaves the chair temporarily,
he may hand the gavel to any member accessible at the
moment. But in selecting a colleague to preside in his
absence, or when custom denies him the privilege, the
Speaker aims to appoint an able parliamentarian, possessing the supreme confidence and respect of the House.
Although the excellent practice long ago became obsolete of choosing eminent members like John Quincy

---

[1] *Twenty Years of Congress,* vol. I, p. 324.
[2] John T. Morse, Jr., *Life of Lincoln,* vol. I, p. 297. See, also, chap.
VII, p. 125.

Adams and Robert C. Winthrop regardless of their political affiliations, the list of appointees includes many
names familiar to the country. A speaker *pro tempore*,
if his appointment is approved by the House, may au-
thenticate papers,[1] sign bills, and appoint committees.[2]
His most important duty, however, is to preside during
the consideration of matters personal to the Speaker, such
as censure, charges of misconduct, a contested seat, or
resolution of thanks. At such times the House is likely
to be testy. Excitement and often resentment are in
evidence, and while free scope must be given to investigation and declamation, exhibitions of malice should
be tactfully restrained. As a rule Speakers court the
fullest inquiry and quickly step aside while the House
probes for the truth. It showed the nobility of Howell
Cobb's character, when charged with mutilating the
House Journal, that he called his distinguished opponent, Robert C. Winthrop, to the chair.[3] In like manner,
Speaker Randall, during an investigation in 1879 which
involved his personal honesty, turned the gavel over to
John G. Carlisle, his great rival.[4] When Carlisle became
Speaker in the Fiftieth Congress, he faced a painful
contest for his seat. A feeling existed that the methods
of his friends would scarcely bear exposure to the gaze
of a fastidious public, and to escape the charge of com-
plicity he absented himself from the Capitol on a plea
of illness during the consideration and settlement of the
case, leaving to the House the selection of a Speaker

---

[1] 48th Cong., 1st Sess., *Journal*, p. 1743.
[2] 28th Cong., 1st Sess., *Globe*, p. 13.
[3] 31st Cong., 1st Sess., *Journal*, p. 1713.
[4] 45th Cong., 3d Sess., *Journal*, pp. 541, 671–74.

pro tempore.[1] Speaker Colfax, after relinquishing the chair to move the expulsion of Alexander Long, of Ohio, adopted a similar course. His action had made an unpleasant impression upon the House. The minority thought it inexcusably rash until his refusal to preside whenever the matter subsequently came up showed that no personal feeling or interest promoted his patriotic action. Speaker Blaine failed to exhibit such tact during the investigation of the Crédit Mobilier scandal. Of those implicated by public rumor Blaine's name stood at the top of the list. He had, in fact, absolutely refused to have anything to do with the disreputable transaction, and when Congress met in December, 1872, he promptly introduced a resolution providing for the investigation of the affairs of the Union Pacific Railroad. The special committee's report came in March, and, although it acquitted the Speaker of any wrongdoing, his colleagues regarded his retention of the chair during its consideration as indelicate. The press likewise censured him.[2]

The early custom of nominating and electing a chairman of the Committee of the Whole proved so unsatisfactory that the House, in the Third Congress, authorized the Speaker to appoint. In selecting members for this very responsible position, he aims to pick skilled parliamentarians whose views accord with his own, unless he wishes to disarm an active opponent by taking him from the floor. "The Speaker called me to the chair,"

---

[1] See chap. xiv, p. 328; 50th Cong., 1st Sess., *Record*, pp. 645–61.

[2] New York *World*, March 5, 1873; 42d Cong., 3d Sess., *Record*, pp. 1867–87.

wrote John Quincy Adams, "so that I could not enter into the debate." This proved a handicap to the distinguished fighter, since "Boon, of Indiana, whose faculty of speech is a yelp, charged me with having slighted the manufacturing interests of the country when I was in power, and Hardin, of Kentucky, let out some of his venom upon New England." [1] In more recent years other members have had reason to complain. Blaine enjoyed calling Samuel S. Cox to the chair, and in moments of facetiousness other Speakers smoothed the way by handing the gavel to flippant talkers. But Cox was never muzzled. Whether in the chair or out of it, his activities and banter did not cease. Reed called him "a whole skirmish line." In one of his funny moments he declared that the Republicans of Maine, in spite of its prohibitory law, drank "a great deal of whiskey clandestinely." To which Reed quickly replied: "When my friend from New York takes it, it does not remain clandestine very long."

Whenever the House is engaged in business other than roll-calls and regular debate, the Speaker is alert and usually on his feet, answering inquiries, putting motions, and announcing results. If deciding points of order, he may stand or sit at his pleasure. At such times controversy with the Chair is never allowed. In enforcing this rule against Roger Q. Mills, of Texas, Speaker Reed, with sharp emphasis, declined to hear him. [2] Even if the Chair refuses an appeal, a member must keep silent. "The Chair desires to state," said

---

[1] *Diary*, vol. ix, pp. 322, 324.
[2] 51st Cong., 1st Sess., *Record*, p. 3976.

Speaker Crisp, "that no member has a right, after the Chair has decided a point of order, to ask upon what ground he bases his decision." [1] During Reed's historic contest to compel Speaker Crisp to count a quorum, the latter declined to entertain an appeal.

"On what ground?" asked Reed.

SPEAKER: "The Chair declines to make any further statement."

REED: "I think I can satisfy the Chair —"

SPEAKER: "The Chair declines to hear the gentleman further."

REED: "The Chair will permit me to explain."

SPEAKER: "The Chair will not."

REED: "The Chair will permit me —"

SPEAKER: "The gentleman from Maine will be seated. The sergeant-at-arms will see that the gentleman takes his seat." [2]

And the former Speaker sat down.

On the other hand, the Chair, under the rule, is restrained from addressing the House either from the desk or floor without its leave. This unwritten rule, derived from the English Commons, does not apply when the House is in Committee of the Whole. Nor does the Chair always respect it at other times. Speaker Clay had a habit of cleverly insinuating his opinions with a captivating smile and a graceful bow, and the House accepted it in the Clay spirit. [3] The tradition, however, has been approved even by others no less distinguished. Speaker Blaine, having left the chair to

---

[1] 53d Cong., 2d Sess., *Record*, p. 4044.   [2] *Ibid.*, p. 4060.
[3] 12th Cong., 1st Sess., *Annals*, p. 1546.

reply to a vicious attack by Benjamin F. Butler, of Massachusetts, declared that "the Speaker should, with consistent fidelity to his own party, be the impartial administrator of the rules of the House, and a constant participation in debate would take from him that appearance of impartiality which it is so important to maintain in the rulings of the Chair." [1] Having thus apologized for the impropriety of his act, he proceeded to punish the offending member. "He came down like a sledgehammer," his wife wrote her son. "Butler was really cowed. Mr. Peters, who sat in front of him, told Mr. Hale that Butler shook so that he (Peters) could feel it where he sat. Butler has brow-beaten witnesses till all the world feared him; but this time he was faced down and pounded and battered and very much surprised. I was surprised, too, to see how little he had to say in reply. He left nearly every point untouched, throwing out a few wild shots. But yesterday he went up to the desk and chatted with Mr. Blaine as if nothing had happened. The whole gallery of reporters were frightfully disgusted, thinking, no doubt, that it was all talk and no tussle." [2] To this presumption Butler's subsequent appointment as chairman of the Judiciary Committee certainly contributed some supporting evidence. Mrs. Blaine's description of the Speaker's effort, however, was not over-colored. Reed once said of him: "His rush was very hard to withstand; he never paused to defend and never ceased to attack."

Samuel J. Randall, like Blaine, left the chair several

---

[1] 42d Cong., 1st Sess., *Record*, p. 125.
[2] Gail Hamilton, *Life of James G. Blaine*, p. 249.

times to address the House without its permission, but
his breach of the proprieties in no wise involved himself. He spoke for the adoption of better rules, helpful
to legislation and for the common good.[1] Of the more
recent Speakers, Crisp and Cannon and Clark addressed
the House, each at least once, without its leave. Cannon's speech simply vindicated him from charges made
by a delegate from Arizona that the Speaker had unduly
prejudiced legislation looking to the admission of that
Territory as a State.[2] But the Crisp episode, growing
out of Reed's effort to compel the counting of a quorum,
climaxed a highly dramatic scene. It was a daring
maneuver. No sooner did Crisp take the floor than the
House was on its feet, and in the midst of an excitement
which filled the air with motions, appeals, and satirical
sallies, the Speaker endeavored to be heard. Very
naturally he received no better treatment than was
accorded other members. Laughter greeted his words,
witticisms interrupted his sentences, and an occasional
sarcasm from Reed intensified the confusion. It demonstrated the wisdom of the tradition that a Speaker
should not participate in debate, and incidentally recalled the fact that Reed, in his famous fight to count
a quorum, never sought the floor.[3]

Speakers, however, are privileged to debate whenever the House is in Committee of the Whole. Henry
Clay reveled in the opportunity, speaking on nine measures in one session. He often arranged that important

[1] 45th Cong., 2d Sess., *Record*, p. 2665; 46th Cong., 1st Sess., *Record*, pp. 336, 1018; 46th Cong., 2d Sess., *Record*, p. 1079.

[2] 59th Cong., 1st Sess., *Record*, p. 8528.

[3] 53d Cong., 2d Sess., *Record*, p. 4056.

matters be taken up in Committee,[1] and once, at least, ventured to resent a motion to close debate before he had spoken.[2] Other Speakers than Clay have frequently asserted their privilege, notably Dayton and Randall, but for a third of a century, if Speaker Cannon's occasional remarks be excepted, the custom has been obsolete. Cannon rarely presumed to debate. It was his custom to give a history of the legislation before the Committee, often dropping into a reminiscent vein to the delight of his hearers. With the possible exception of John Quincy Adams, no one ever entertained the House better. His remarkable memory seemed never to forget an incident in the forty years of his congressional life, while the charm of his manner added immeasurably to his offhand yet finished speeches.

In exercising the privilege of voting Speakers have rarely misused it. The original form of the rule did not allow the Chair to vote "unless the House be equally divided, or unless his vote, if given to the minority, will make the division equal, and in case of such equal division the question shall be lost." [3] Speaker Macon, holding this language to mean whenever a vote would affect the decision of the House, voted to complete a two-thirds majority.[4] Henry Clay went a step further. He held that the Chair, unlike the English Speaker, who renounces the privileges of membership, retained the right as a member to vote upon any pending question, and in 1817 he not only voted to pass the Internal

---

[1] 12th Cong., 2d Sess., *Annals*, p. 677.   [2] *Ibid.*, p. 596.
[3] 1st Cong., 1st Sess., *Annals*, p. 103.
[4] 8th Cong., 1st Sess., *Annals*, p. 775.

Improvement Bill over the President's veto, but, wishing to influence others, demanded that his name be called first.[1] Although no one save Clay ever had the audacity to make such a demand, many members agreed with his view. Nevertheless, the House twice refused to amend the rule,[2] and in 1847 Speaker Winthrop held the Clay precedent "not within the intention of the rule." [3] It is likely Clay himself doubted its propriety, for in 1824, after the House, by a large majority, had voted Lafayette one hundred thousand dollars, the Speaker courteously requested the privilege of having his vote recorded among the "ayes." However, several Speakers, without provoking objection or criticism, followed the Clay precedent, and in 1850 the House amended the rule to read: "He shall not be required to vote except when his vote will be decisive." [4] This gave him the right to vote at any time, a privilege rarely exercised except in Committee of the Whole. Speakers are not more anxious than members to express an opinion on every contested measure, although, when questions of the highest importance to the country are pending, the Chair naturally desires to go upon record. The Speaker's name, however, is not upon the voting-roll, and is not called unless required under the rule or upon his request. It is then called last. He usually responds at once, although a casting vote may be given after the announcement of the result, or when other business has intervened, or even

[1] 14th Cong., 2d Sess., *Annals*, p. 1062.

[2] 23d Cong., 1st Sess., *Journal*, p. 77; 25th Cong., 1st Sess., *Journal*, p. 63.

[3] 30th Cong., 2d Sess., *Journal*, p. 211.   [4] Rule I, sec. 6.

on another day if a correction of the roll makes it necessary.

An important duty of the Speaker is the preservation of order. Authority is given him to suspend all business, to call members by name, to clear the galleries, or even to summon the Capitol police. During the reading of the Mulligan letters in 1876 threats to call the police emphasized the riotous character of the disorder, but threats sufficed. Ordinarily the gavel, or the mace, or a show of good-natured patience is sufficient. In suppressing personalities in debate or preventing expressions offensive to Senators and to the President, the Chair sometimes names a member. This compels the House to excuse or punish.

The Speaker may exclude from the *Congressional Record* words spoken by a member after being called to order, but he has no authority over that publication, or over the House Journal after it is read. Nor is it a part of his duty to rule upon the effect of a proposition or proposed amendment, or to construe the Constitution as affecting legislation, or as relating to the constitutional prerogatives or powers of the House. He may exercise his discretion as to submitting motions offered as privileged questions other than those relating to the privileges of the House and its members, but parliamentary inquiries, which are in the nature of privileged motions, are always heard at once, since answers make clear to the House the effect of its proposed action.

Questions of order that arise in the course of business are likewise decided at the time. In making such decisions the Speaker's power is autocratic. He may decide with or without debate, and announce his ruling with or without reasons. Speaker Clay never gave reasons. "The House will sustain your decisions," he said to Speaker Winthrop, "but there will always be men to cavil and quarrel over your reasons." [1] Nevertheless, Speakers have very generally and properly ignored this advice, for a clear, terse statement not only adds dignity to the Chair and strengthens his position as an impartial judge, but it instructs the House in the parliamentary code governing legislation. Decisions usually follow precedent. In one instance Speaker Cobb did so, though it violated his individual judgment.[2] Other Speakers have made similar admissions.[3] Opportunity to be heard is first given the one raising the point of order, and afterward to those whom the Chair desires to hear. Though a dozen seek recognition he may refuse all, declaring that the Chair is ready to rule. From his decision, however, any member may appeal. "Consequently," said Speaker Reed, "there is not and cannot be any arbitrary control of this body against its will. The Speaker, for the time being and as a matter of convenience arising from the nature of his office, makes a ruling upon the subject which is before the House; but that ruling is always subject to revision by the House itself, and no one can take away that right on the part of the House." [4]

Theoretically this is true. But in practice few mem-

---

[1] Robert C. Winthrop, *Life of Henry Clay*, p. 5.

[2] 31st Cong., 1st Sess., *Journal*, p. 1280.

[3] 26th Cong., 1st Sess., *Globe*, p. 246; 32d Cong., 2d Sess., *Journal*, p. 234.

[4] 51st Cong., 1st Sess., *Record*, pp. 741–49.

bers, especially of a Speaker's party, ever care to offend
by voting to overrule one whose good-will is desired.
All wish to catch his eye, to receive recognition, to
avoid a slight, and to be known as friendly, for, if so
disposed, he can in many ways help or hinder. This
makes members hesitate to displease or irritate him.
Anxiety to succeed inspires every action, and often to
suffer in silence is preferable to insisting upon fair play.
An appeal from the Chair's decision, therefore, although
the boasted parliamentary right of every member, is
seldom indulged by one of his own party or sustained
if taken by the Opposition. Indeed, his party supporters, often at the expense of their better judgment, acquire the habit of falling into line. This subtle power of
the Chair interprets a further remark of Speaker Reed,
that "the conduct of an assembly depends much more
upon the conduct of the chairman than upon all other
conditions combined." [1] In other words, a Speaker who
creates a sentiment that, whatever others may do, he
will treat all with absolute fairness, must incite a similar
spirit on the part of members and thus avoid the confusion that often impedes legislation.

If the duty of deciding questions of order is the most
difficult, administering the Speaker's right of recognition
has been the most embarrassing. Like committee appointments the right of recognition formerly dealt with
the personal ambition of members. In its very nature
recognition is peremptory, absolute in authority, subject to the closest scrutiny, instantaneous in effect, and
to a legislator as necessary to achievement as food is to

[1] Thomas B. Reed, *Parliamentary Rules*, p. 36.

life. Furthermore, to be of service it must be granted at the opportune moment. Thus it becomes a stepladder to a member's success, and the Chair's disposition to ignore him, or to limit his activities, encourages the taunt of partiality.

The rule adopted in 1789 implied that the Chair, when two or more members happen to rise at once, should exercise its judgment.[1] When a member excepted to this interpretation, complaining that the Chair recognized another than the one who first arose, Speaker Boyd replied that "the rules confer authority upon the Chair to name the member entitled to the floor."[2] This did not mean a haphazard recognition, for early in the history of the House unwritten laws governing recognition began to accumulate. Thus, members were entitled to the floor to present questions of privilege, or privileged motions and reports. As a rule chairmen of committees or those authorized to speak for them were preferred to individuals. As early as 1843 Speaker White declared this to be the invariable practice, although another had previously risen and addressed the Chair;[3] and Speaker Randall, in 1880, held that when a member, under instructions from a committee, sought the floor for a motion to suspend the rules, he always recognized him in preference to an individual member.[4] The enforcement of these rules, intended to expedite

---

[1] " When two or more members happen to rise at once, the Speaker shall name the member who is first to speak." (Rule xiv, sec. 2, adopted April, 1789.)

[2] 32d Cong., 2d Sess., *Journal,* p. 405.

[3] 27th Cong., 3d Sess., *Journal,* p. 211.

[4] 46th Cong., 2d Sess., *Record,* p. 925.

important business, has never created complaint. Members recognize the priority of business as quickly as the Chair and gracefully yield. But whenever a Speaker began recognizing members for political or personal reasons, it aroused bitter resentment.

While most Speakers, perhaps, have sought to be fair, many of them adopted methods well calculated to cause irritation. Speaker Cobb, though one of the most amiable of men, arbitrarily refused the floor to advocates of a Homestead Bill,[1] while Linn Boyd, his successor, sought to deprive Thomas H. Benton of time to finish his speech on the repeal of the Missouri Compromise. "I wanted the country to understand," said John Wentworth, of Illinois, "that the oldest man in Congress, who was here when the Missouri Compromise was adopted, was refused a courtesy which had been refused to no other man, and when there was no hope from courtesy, I moved an amendment upon which Benton was recognized. As he concluded in triumph Douglas came to my seat and said, tauntingly: 'The Abolitionists are quite successful under you as their new leader.'"[2] After the Civil War, Speakers used the right of recognition no less arbitrarily. Randall refused the floor to a new member lest something rash might be said.[3] He held that "the right of recognition is with the Chair under the rules and under the practice."[4] It is notorious that Blaine withheld recognition until allowed to censor the proposed measure. The *Nation*

[1] George W. Julian, *Political Recollections*, p. 104.
[2] John Wentworth, *Congressional Experiences*, p. 54.
[3] 46th Cong., 3d Sess., *Record*, p. 2236.
[4] 46th Cong., 2d Sess., *Record*, p. 925.

called it "bargaining with members for recognition." [1]
Carlisle made no secret of refusing recognition to propositions unacceptable to him. For this reason Randall's
pet measure to repeal the tax on tobacco never obtained
a hearing. In like manner Carlisle allowed public buildings, bridges, and other important bills to die for want
of recognition. On one occasion Cannon refused recognition for the consideration of what he thought an extravagant public building bill, although a majority
petitioned for it.

The custom of inquiring, "For what purpose does
the gentleman rise?" before deciding the question of
recognition, belongs to the Reed period. Prior to its
adoption Speakers sometimes inadvertently recognized
members seeking the introduction of undesirable resolutions, but this inquiry disclosed their purpose in advance. In the Fifty-sixth Congress William Sulzer, of
New York, afterward governor of his State, in answer
to the irritating question, explained that he rose to
move the adoption of a resolution expressing sympathy
for the Boers. Speaker Henderson replied that "the
Chair must recognize members upon matters which the
Chair thinks should be considered." [2] This inconsiderate remark strengthened the belief of the country that
the Speaker absolutely controlled legislation. In the
preceding Congress Speaker Reed had exhibited more
tact when Benton McMillin, of Tennessee, a member of
high courage and dogged perseverance, sought the floor.
On being asked the purpose of his rising, McMillin
explained his desire to present for immediate considera-

[1] Vol. XXVI, p. 226.　　　[2] 56th Cong., 1st Sess., *Record*, p. 5227.

tion a resolution favoring Cuban independence. Thereupon the Chair, while fumbling the gavel, looked sharply
at Nelson Dingley, the floor leader, who presently rose
and moved to adjourn. As this motion took precedence
of McMillin's request, the House quickly dissolved,
leaving the Tennessean on his feet indulging in a free
trade of ironical blandishments.[1]

In earlier years when refused recognition a member
had the right of appeal. Speaker Taylor frankly admitted this right. Speaker White did likewise.[2] Hunter
even invited it,[3] and Pennington yielded to the ruling of
his predecessors.[4] Indeed, this was the settled practice
for nearly a century. But in February, 1881, Speaker
Randall, refusing to adopt the precedent, held "the
right of recognition just as absolutely in the Chair as
the judgment of the Supreme Court is absolute in its
interpretation of the law."[5] Two years later Speaker
Keifer made a similar ruling, startling the House with
inexcusable ignorance by declaring that "no appeal of
the kind had ever been entertained."[6] These decisions
put members desiring recognition for measures not privileged wholly at the mercy of the Chair. Although the
Speaker based his power upon the ground of his party
leadership and his right as an individual member to
object to unanimous consent, he did not disarm the
critic who claimed that he should trust to the vigilance

[1] 55th Cong., 1st Sess., *Record,* p. 2449.
[2] 19th Cong., 2d Sess., *Debates,* p. 493.
[3] 26th Cong., 1st Sess., *Globe,* p. 433.
[4] 36th Cong., 2d Sess., *Globe,* p. 496.
[5] 46th Cong., 3d Sess., *Record,* p. 2236.
[6] 47th Cong., 1st Sess., *Record,* pp. 4554-55.

of his floor leader and thus preserve the appearance, at least, of an unprejudiced presiding officer.

For the disposition of resolutions of the Boer and Cuban type, offered largely for political purposes only, the House cared little, while matters of public importance could be reached through privileged motions or on fixed days of the week. But a class of unprivileged public bills, benefiting various districts, deeply concerned the personal welfare of members, and as their consideration depended upon obtaining recognition for unanimous consent or to move a suspension of the rules, scenes of great confusion occurred during the time set apart for such purposes. "We crowd in front of the clerk's desk with bills of which the House knows nothing," wrote a member in Speaker Randall's time, "each seeking for preference and recognition." [1] To avoid these riotous demonstrations the custom of submitting such bills privately to the Speaker gradually became the only avenue to recognition, since he listed and recognized only those measures he approved. This plan worked very well for those whom he favored, but it provoked bitter criticism among the independent spirits of courage whose errands of mendicancy too often proved futile, while it absolutely barred *non grata* members. "Because of this practice," says McCall, "Speakers have probably been denounced more bitterly and have won a larger measure of unpopularity than upon any other single ground." [2]

To these assumptions of power can easily be traced

---

[1] 46th Cong., 2d Sess., *Record*, p. 1053.
[2] Samuel W. McCall, *The Business of Congress*, p. 128.

an increased use of dilatory motions. Inspired by personal resentment, members, invoking all the obstructive methods known to skilled parliamentarians, made the *Record* a valuable publication for disclosing the popularity of such spite work during the administrations of Speaker Randall and his immediate successors. By the time Carlisle reached his third term as Speaker it became so easy to muster a sufficient number of disgruntled members to delay or prevent legislation that the House, in the Fiftieth Congress, although in continuous session longer than any of its predecessors, passed only one measure except such as received unanimous consent.[1]

It is easy to understand how such conditions would not improve the temper of members, and although strong Speakers and large party majorities delayed the adoption of better methods, the House, in the Sixty-first Congress, established, as elsewhere stated,[2] a calendar for unanimous consents,[3] and fixed each Wednesday for a call of committees.[4] These rules at once dispensed with journeys to the Speaker's room. The use of privileged motions, privileged measures, privileged reports, and privileged business on fixed days of the week has also materially limited the Speaker's discretionary recognition, so that when the Chair now asks a member the purpose of his rising, it is to ascertain whether, under the rules, his business entitles him to the floor.

Although the rules specify the subjects of which each committee has jurisdiction, much is left in the reference

[1] Henry Cabot Lodge, *North American Review*, vol. 149, p. 293.
[2] See chap. x, p. 211.
[3] 61st Cong., 2d Sess., Rule XIII, sec. 3.
[4] *Ibid.*, Rule XXIV, sec. 7.

of bills to the Speaker's judgment. Nevertheless, it is in the power of the House to refer bills to any committee. When the Speaker has sent a bill to a particular committee, it is in order under the rules for the chairman of such committee to move a change of reference to some other; and it is likewise in order for the chairman of a committee claiming jursidiction of a bill referred to some other committee to move a change of reference to his committee. Such motions must be put by the Speaker and decided by vote of the House without debate. So it has happened that this control of reference by the House has resulted in securing legislation by the report of a committee that under the rules in the first instance had no jurisdiction of the subject-matter of the bill. This was plainly illustrated on February 26, 1894, when the Oleomargarine Bill, which had been referred to the Committee on Ways and Means, was, on motion of the chairman of the Committee on Agriculture, transferred to the latter committee. As the bill was on its face a tax bill, it belonged to the Committee on Ways and Means, but as it was in point of fact a measure proposing the exercise of the police power under the guise of the taxing power, the House decided to send it to the committee friendly to its enactment.

The alleged inability of members to secure the discharge of a committee from the further consideration of bills which it refused to report caused much complaint. Such measures were usually opposed for party reasons, and the procedure as revised in 1880 made it necessary, in order to carry a motion to discharge, to suspend the rules by a two-thirds vote. This confined the discussion to forty minutes and greatly increased the difficulty of securing favorable action. Under the Reed rules, adopted in 1890, such motions were referred without debate to the Committee on Rules, which brought them directly to the attention of men selected to determine among other things what measures the party in power should support. Although it rarely if ever occurred that any committee declined to report a bill that a majority of the House really desired to consider, the spirit of change which eliminated the Speaker from the Committee on Rules [1] included a rule, adopted in June, 1910, providing that if a bill be not reported by the committee to which it is referred, its author may file a motion of discharge, to be called up in order of its entry on any Monday devoted to the suspension of the rules, and, if seconded by a majority, a debate of twenty minutes shall follow, after which, if the motion again be sustained, the bill shall pass to the "discharge calendar" as if regularly reported. [2] This rule encountered opposition. It was plainly impracticable and as plainly limited the power of the House over its committees; but the fact that the ingenious device, although a doubtful experiment, seemed to give all bills a fair hearing, satisfied the clamor for reform. Thus the Speaker, at the close of the Sixty-first Congress (1911), was practically shorn of his power save the appointment of committees, and the right of recognition for motions to suspend the rules, which latter power he still retains. As anticipated, however, the rule to discharge a committee, even

[1] See chap. x, p. 212.
[2] 51st Cong., 2d Sess., *Record*, pp. 8439–45. Rule xxvii, sec. 4.

after its amendment,[1] has proved impracticable. Within twenty-four hours after its adoption members loaded it with so many motions — some of them being purposely filed to prevent the consideration of a genuine motion — that the House, had it given all its time to their consideration, could not have disposed of them.

[1] The next House amended the rule, allowing a committee to retain a bill fifteen days and limiting each member to two motions at a time. It also limited the chances of reaching the "discharge calendar" by fixing its place below motions to suspend the rules.

CHAPTER V

THE SPEAKER AND COMMITTEE APPOINTMENTS

THE Speaker's greatest power has its source in his authority to appoint committees. At the outset (1789) they were selected by ballot, but this plan having proved unsatisfactory, the House, in January, 1790, adopted a rule that "all committees shall be appointed by the Speaker unless otherwise specially directed by the House." [1] Thus the House, relinquishing even its right of review, gave the Speaker a prerogative which he continued to possess for nearly a century and a quarter.

This power soon made the Speakership a citadel about which factional strife and party warfare continually raged. Instead of being impartial boards as originally intended, committees became actively partisan, being framed to safeguard party policies. As early as 1791 Speaker Trumbull, in appointing a committee to study the slave trade with a view to its limitation and amelioration, selected members either opposed or indifferent to the object of the investigation. [2] For years the election of a Speaker turned on his attitude toward slavery. In 1820, after Speaker Clay's resignation, it required twenty-two ballots to elect John W. Taylor, then known as the anti-slavery candidate. John Quincy Adams,

---

[1] 1st Cong., 1st Sess., *Journal*, p. 140.
[2] 2d Cong., 1st Sess., *Annals*, p. 241.

thundering against the "iniquity" of Speaker-appointed committees, charged that the turbulent and prolonged Speakership struggle in 1839 hinged on saving slavery in the District of Columbia.[1] After the more violent contest in 1849 Joshua R. Giddings expressed the belief that the Speaker, exercising his right to frame committees, exerted more influence over the destinies of the nation than any member of the Government except the President.[2]

If subsequent contests were less violent, they were no less effective. Speakers continued to safeguard party policies by the appointment of partisan committees. Indeed, Speaker Hunter's statement, that "the party upon which it naturally devolved to propose a question ought to have the power to present its proposition in the shape for which it is willing to be responsible," was never disputed.[3] But when personality enters, capriciousness begins, thus creating the impression that Speaker-made committees open a way to reward friends, to cripple the competent, to humiliate the independent, to favor special interests, and to attract wide-reaching support.

It is doubtful if Speakers have, as a rule, been unduly partial in their appointments. Custom based on unwritten law has obliged them to recognize long service, peculiar fitness, party standing, and a fair division among States and important groups of men. Nevertheless, if the sporadic testimony of members be accepted,

---

[1] *Diary*, vol. x, p. 379.
[2] George W. Julian, *Life of Giddings*, p. 215.
[3] 26th Cong., 2d Sess., *Globe*, p. 239.

grounds for complaint have existed ever since Speaker Macon, to gratify President Jefferson, placed John Randolph, then a young man in his second term, at the head of Ways and Means. "Macon," says Adams, the historian, "was a typical, homespun planter, honest and simple, but knowing little of the world beyond the borders of Carolina." [1] This may excuse him for setting a very bad precedent, but with larger knowledge his successors not infrequently followed his example. Diaries, memoirs, and volumes of reminiscences afford abundant evidence of such partiality. John Quincy Adams, the most distinguished complainant, resented the action of one Speaker who put him at the head of a committee which had nothing to do, complained that another desired to injure him because his committee work, if he did his duty, would make him enemies, and charged that a third, offensively subservient to Daniel Webster, refused to give him the chairmanship of Foreign Relations. [2] Giddings had his grievances also. Smarting under Speaker Winthrop's appointments the distinguished Abolitionist refused to support, and probably defeated, him for reëlection in 1849. A few years later Orr's action in dropping him from the Committee on Territories created a storm of indignation, although every one understood it to be for political, not personal, reasons. The Speaker desired to smooth the way for the hotly contested Kansas Bill, and very naturally omitted the ablest opponent of the measure. For the same reason, when framing a special committee of fifteen to

[1] Henry Adams, *History of the United States*, vol. I, p. 267.
[2] *Diary*, vol. X, pp. 214, 541.

investigate the Lecompton Constitution, Orr appointed eight members hostile to the inquiry.[1] In like manner Blaine put Benjamin F. Butler, of Massachusetts, at the head of a committee to investigate the Ku-Klux outrages and selected other members who opposed his radical views. This nettled the bold politician, who charged that the Speaker picked them for their pliability rather than for their ability.[2] The Maine statesman could hobble Butler, but he could not muzzle him.

Blaine's experience throws a flood of light on the difficulties encountered in framing committees. "Your father," wrote a member of the Speaker's family, "left for New York on Wednesday. He had cotton and wool manufacturers to meet in Boston, and, over and above all, pressure to resist or permit. As fast as he gets his committees arranged, just so fast some after consideration comes up which overtopples the whole list like a row of bricks." [3] The construction of committees, having regard for harmony and the effect upon legislation as a whole, requires much patience, rare skill, and a thorough knowledge of the views and fitness of members. There must also be more or less bargaining. It is well known that Speaker Carlisle, before appointing A. H. Buckner, of Missouri, chairman of the Committee on Banking and Currency and Richard P. Bland, of Missouri, chairman of the Committee on Coinage, required personal assurances that the former would not

[1] 35th Cong., 1st Sess., *Globe*, p. 679.
[2] 42d Cong., 1st Sess., *Globe*, p. 124.
[3] Gail Hamilton, *Life of James G. Blaine*, p. 263.

attack the national banking system and the latter would stifle his scheme for the unlimited coinage of silver.[1] In order to secure members of known stability on important committees, subject at times to great pressure, Speaker Cannon, not infrequently preceding appointment with careful inquiry, demoted some and promoted others. The necessity for such vigilance is obvious, since a committee, charged with the passage of desirable legislation at an acute crisis in a party's policy, may need a new head, possessing greater wisdom and rarer tact. But why a Speaker should call on "cotton and wool manufacturers" when arranging his committee lists is not so clear. Possibly these visits were among the occult things creating the oft-reiterated accusation that Blaine, like Randall, had too intimate an acquaintance with "gentlemen of the lobby."

For sins of omission and commission Speakers rarely escape censure. It never comes at the time of offending. Members are too tactful to display pique so long as future favors are needed. But opportunity to express one's displeasure is presented on the closing day of a Congress, when a veteran member, rising in the presence of a full and orderly House, offers the customary resolution of thanks to the Chair. This tribute derives its chief grace from the manner of its bestowal. If the resolution be presented by a member of the Opposition and is adopted unanimously by a rising vote, the compliment is complete; otherwise it becomes a mere formality and is not unlikely to disclose resentment or ill-will. To avoid unpleasant speeches the previ-

[1] New York *Tribune*, December 29, 1883.

ous question is sometimes moved, but this does not cut off a demand for the yeas and nays, which, whether called or not, represents a blight that mars the occasion.

The House has never failed to thank its Speaker, although in 1801 it came perilously near humiliating Speaker Sedgwick. To the end Sedgwick was an implacable Federalist as well as an autocratic Speaker, and on the day of thanks the Opposition not only refused to present or support the resolution, but several of his own party voted against it. In dropping John Randolph from Ways and Means, Speaker Varnum provoked the penalty of a divided vote. Even Henry Clay, the most courteous of colleagues and the most considerate of Speakers, did not please everybody — a success rare in human achievement. But not until Stevenson's day did the word "impartial" become a red rag. When the clerk, reading the stereotyped resolution, reached this expression of fair dealing, wrote John Quincy Adams, "a burst of laughter filled the House." [1] Stevenson acted as a sort of patronage secretary to President Jackson, and when he announced his committees astonishment often deepened into consternation. One member of dauntless courage moved a vote of censure.[2] It was not easy to thank such a Speaker, and after eliminating the irritating word his friends wisely deferred action until the evening session, and then begged its adoption in the absence of a quorum.[3]

---

[1] *Diary*, vol. VIII, p. 532.
[2] 22d Cong., 1st Sess., *Debates*, p. 2580.
[3] 22d Cong., 2d Sess., *Register*, p. 193.

James K. Polk belonged in Stevenson's class. He used the committees to support the President and the right of recognition to weaken his opponents. His appointments aroused the hostility of his party until it finally denied him the privilege of naming a most important committee, charged with the investigation of a sensational defalcation in the New York custom-house. It was said of him that he had followers and enemies, but no friends. To thank him at the close of his last term became serious business. A coterie of distinguished Whigs, the ablest debaters in the House, were ready for a lark, and when the resolution came, Sergeant S. Prentiss, of Mississippi, whose oratory has been compared to Patrick Henry's, precipitated a long parliamentary battle. Of this famous speech little is preserved, but it lingered in the memories of those who heard it as Prentiss's most remarkable outburst. He called the Speaker "the tool of the Executive" and "the despair of his party." As if that were not enough, he recalled oblique recognitions and obsequious appointments, insisting that to speak of such an one as "impartial" was "to declare a lie." These impassioned utterances, so dazzlingly bitter, threw Administration leaders into consternation. Rhett and Mason and Dixon H. Lewis, of Alabama, sat confounded. They were unprepared for such a demonstration, and when, later in the debate, some one moved the previous question, Prentiss threw the House into great laughter by suggesting that the demand was as humiliating as to move it on a resolution of respect to a deceased member. A roll-call showed that the number thanking

Polk fell far short of those who had voted for him,[1] — "an extraordinary opposition," says a careful student of parliamentary precedents, "to a resolution usually considered a mere formal courtesy."[2]

As sincere regard seldom grows in a soil exacerbated by personal slights, it is not surprising, perhaps, that members express their resentment upon these occasions when the Speaker desires a certificate for fair dealing. "I voted against the thanks to Jones," wrote John Quincy Adams. "The testimony to his impartiality was too broad a lie for me to swallow."[3] Thomas B. Reed, unlike Adams, left no written reason for refusing to thank Speaker Crisp at the close of the Fifty-third Congress, but when this great master of parliamentary law kept his seat after all others had risen, the feeling obtained that his action seriously impaired, if it did not actually destroy, the homage of his colleagues.[4] After the Polk episode the word "impartial" proved to be such a handy peg upon which to hang objections that of the eleven Speakers immediately succeeding him seven failed to be honored by its use.[5] Even the grace and

---

[1] 25th Cong., 3d Sess., *Journal*, p. 696.

[2] M. P. Follett, *The Speaker*, p. 87.

[3] *Diary*, vol. xii, p. 179.

[4] Speaker Crisp's remarks on August 29, 1893, gave rise to Reed's action. See 53d Cong., 1st Sess., *Record*, vol. 25, p. 1034.

[5] John White, Kentucky; 27th Cong., 2d Sess., *Globe*, pp. 397–99. Robert C. Winthrop, Massachusetts; 30th Cong., 2d Sess., *Globe*, p. 695. Linn Boyd, Kentucky; 33d Cong., 2d Sess., *Globe*, p. 1175. Nathaniel P. Banks, Massachusetts; 34th Cong., 2d Sess., *Globe*, p. 998. James L. Orr, South Carolina; 35th Cong., 2d Sess., *Globe*, p. 1671. William Pennington, New Jersey; 36th Cong., 2d Sess., *Globe*, p. 1424. Galusha A. Grow, Pennsylvania; 37th Cong., 2d Sess., *Globe*, p. 1544.

fairness which characterized the conduct of Speakers
Winthrop and Banks did not receive the appreciation
conveyed by this term. Howell Cobb profited by it in
1851, but thereafter it remained in eclipse until the
unfailing tact and extraordinary courtesy of Speaker
Colfax, rivaling that of Henry Clay, had mellowed the
House into perennial good nature. Since its revival in
the Thirty-ninth Congress it has lost its place but once,[1]
although to avoid the irritating scenes that embarrassed
the friends of Polk, the passage of the resolution has
occasionally needed the gag of the previous question.
This occurred at the close of James G. Blaine's first
term as Speaker. His appointments, too often representing sinister ends which illuminated if they did not
open the avenue to the White House, had left mixed
sensations on too many minds for his friends to hazard
a discussion of the resolution.[2] Similar tactics to avoid
threatened debate disturbed the close of the Forty-fifth
and Fifty-seventh Congresses. Randall had kept the
unflinching eye of a hawk upon "the timid warblers of
the grove," as he called those who resented the views
of his Committee on Ways and Means, and their readiness to object to the courtesies of the closing day did
not escape the vigilance of his friends.[3] What caused
the trouble with Speaker Henderson is more obscure.
His parliamentary powers remained in the egg, and his
enemies watched and waited. But by ordering the previous question the House lost its opportunity of hearing

[1] It was omitted from the resolution thanking Speaker Keifer.
47th Cong., 2d Sess., *Record*, p. 3769.

[2] 41st Cong., 3d Sess., *Record*, p. 1911.

[3] 45th Cong., 3d Sess., *Record*, p. 2403.

their story. Bourke Cochran, of New York, like Prentiss, would have told it well.[1]

At the close of the Fifty-first Congress, the Opposition secured a roll-call on the resolution thanking Speaker Reed. This new gladiator had slain every kind of dilatory tactics, until broken precedents, like fragments of marble on the Acropolis, indicated the destruction of old and revered forms. But the work of legislation had received an uplift. Nevertheless, one hundred and eighteen members refused to thank him. The result recalled the lines of the poet: —

"When the judgment's weak, the prejudice is strong."

Yet six and eight years later, after Speaker Crisp had approved counting a quorum, many of these members cheerfully and enthusiastically thanked the author of the "Reed Rules." So quickly does prejudice vanish from the House.

But prejudice against the Speaker's authority to appoint committees never wholly disappeared. Personal resentments kept it smouldering, and sometimes

[1] "Mr. Payne, of New York (having finished his remarks). Mr. Speaker, I demand the previous question.

"Mr. Cochran, of New York. Mr. Speaker, I demand the yeas and nays.

[The question of ordering them was taken.]

"The Speaker *pro tempore* (Mr. Cannon). Twenty-one members have arisen. Necessary to call the ayes and noes, forty-two. The yeas and nays are refused. The question now is on agreeing to the resolution.

"Mr. Cochran. I demand the yeas and nays.

[The question was taken.]

"The Speaker *pro tempore*. Seventeen gentlemen have arisen. The ayes and noes are refused. The ayes have it and the resolution is passed." (57th Cong., 2d Sess., *Record*, p. 3071.)

fanned it into a blaze when an ambitious or subservient Speaker became offensive. John Randolph's domination of Speaker Macon provoked a motion in 1806 to restore the ballot system. The House was out of patience with the mischief-maker and it came within two votes of depriving the Speaker of his high prerogative.[1] The next year, after Speaker Varnum had dropped Randolph, a similar motion met with overwhelming defeat, showing that it was the Virginian and not the method that the House desired to abolish.[2] The resolution to choose by lot a select committee to investigate the National Bank betrayed a similar condition in 1832. By his conspicuous partiality and subserviency Speaker Stevenson had become obnoxious, and the vote to deprive him of the right of framing the committee stood, ayes, 100; noes, 100. Modesty did not afflict Stevenson, whose casting vote saved his privilege.[3] This ended the hope of limiting the Speaker's authority until the prolonged and violent struggle of 1849 encouraged the belief that a change in the method of appointments would prevent such passionate contests, and with this in view William A. Sackett, of New York, presented a resolution restoring the ballot system.[4] But the debate, dropping into personalities, developed such an astonishing indifference that the controversy slumbered until the opening of the Forty-seventh Congress (1881).

The sudden transfer of William P. Frye, of Maine, from the House to the Senate advertised a free-for-all

---

[1] The vote stood 42 to 44.   [2] Ayes, 24; noes, 87.
[3] 22d Cong., 1st Sess., *Debates*, p. 2128.
[4] 31st Cong., 1st Sess., *Globe*, pp. 79–85.

race for Speaker, and on the sixteenth ballot, by the grace of a Republican faction then known as the "Stalwarts," J. Warren Keifer won the nomination at a party caucus.[1] Of his six competitors all received desirable chairmanships except Godlove S. Orth, a well-known member from Indiana, who, with two exceptions, was the senior in service of all his party colleagues. Orth did not possess those parliamentary talents which cause jealousy or excite rivalry, but he gave strict attention to business and at his best spoke well. He naturally felt that long experience entitled him to better recognition than he received, and although he had previously approved the Speaker's prerogative of appointing committees, he now voiced his resentment by boldly attacking the system as "a one-man power of far-reaching influence." Then came his specifications. "Not only is the congressional career of every member in the control of the Speaker, but he can so organize a committee as to imperil the country itself."[2] This ringing challenge preceded his presentation of a substitute for a report from the Committee on Rules, the resolution providing for the selection by a *viva-voce* vote of eleven members who should constitute a board to appoint committees. This did not prevent party control, he said. Caucus action could select eleven persons, not necessarily excluding the Speaker, who could be openly

[1] On the final ballot the votes were distributed as follows: J. Warren Keifer, Ohio, 93; Frank Hiscock, New York, 18; Thomas B. Reed, Maine, 11; F. A. Kasson, Iowa, 10; Godlove S. Orth, Ind., 8; M. H. Dunnell, Minn., 3; Julius C. Burrows, Mich., 1. Total, 144. Necessary to a choice, 73.

[2] 47th Cong., 1st Sess., *Record*, pp. 463-64.

elected in the House and to whom party interests might safely be confided. He preferred, however, as his plan indicated, that each party select five, and the majority choose the eleventh, who should act as chairman. Such a commission, he thought, could easily constitute the committees, without exceeding the time usually taken by the Speaker.

Orth knew that many members of both parties regarded with suspicion the tremendous power of such a piece of patronage as committee appointments. For five years Speaker Randall had ignored Democrats who stood for a tariff for revenue only, while the gossip of the cloak-room and of the press indicated that several Republicans, resenting Keifer's method of securing votes in exchange for desirable appointments, were ripe for a change. It encouraged sedition, too, that an old member headed the reform movement. Moreover, the proposed plan was new and simple. Other schemes had required separate elections by ballot, which opened the way for secret combinations; but Orth's proposition enabled each party, by caucus or otherwise, to select its members, and approve or "elect" them by a *viva-voce* vote in the House. Such an arrangement, it was said, could provoke little criticism.

But a topic so sure to excite the spleen of the Speaker and his beneficiaries did not escape the skill of the parliamentarians, who, quickly raising the question of the substitute's germaneness, centered discussion on its parliamentary status. The plan proposed, they said, might be wholly unobjectionable, but it could not be considered under the rules at that time. Nevertheless, Thomas B.

Reed, then chairman of the Judiciary Committee, considered the matter on its merits. He was disposed to treat a grumbler with severity, and in disclosing Orth's motive he declared that "personal grievances exist in all Houses and in all legislative bodies." In ridicule of the plan he suggested that each of the favored eleven would command the chairmanship of a great committee and encounter double the pressure applied to the Speaker. "Think of the log-rolling to secure a board favorable to the measures of selfish men!" he exclaimed. Replying to the intimation that the personnel of a committee could imperil the country, he said: "The Speaker whose committees represent the wishes of the country upon matters of public policy is not only under the constant supervision of public opinion, but under the supervision of this House, and no committee is likely to be constituted or endured which would imperil the country's interests. But for the wrongful acts of eleven men public displeasure could rarely find a victim." [1]

Orth was ignorant even of the language of real controversy, and under Reed's sarcasm he wilted into silence. Nor did others respond. Distinguished Democrats like Abram S. Hewitt, of New York, Roger Q. Mills and David B. Culberson, of Texas, William S. Holman, of Indiana, and William R. Morrison, of Illinois, were ready to vote for a change, but not to speak for it, and so the discussion, which promised much, ended as if its supporters had from the beginning little faith in the issue. The vote was equally disappointing.

[1] 47th Cong., 1st Sess., *Record*, p. 465.

Although it occurred on the point of order, it expressed the sentiment of the House on the Orth proposition, 74 favoring it out of a total of 236. In the long list of those opposed clustered the names of the real leaders in both parties, including John G. Carlisle, Thomas B. Reed, Hilary A. Herbert, Joseph G. Cannon, Samuel J. Randall, and William D. Kelley.[1]

But even this Waterloo did not stifle all protest. Keifer's appointments had stirred up the mud, and William M. Springer, of Illinois, resenting their partisan composition, moved that a minority caucus be authorized to select minority members.[2] Then came the suggestion that the Senate's method of appointments be adopted.[3] These efforts proved futile. Orth offered a resolution that the Committee on Civil Service Reform be instructed to report on the expediency of providing a different system. This the Committee on Rules quickly pigeon-holed.[4] Similar ineffectual attempts, initiated during the administrations of Speakers Carlisle and Crisp,[5] made it plain that so drastic a change needed something more substantial than opposition based on personal grievances, and so the system continued many years longer.

Meantime the country grew more and more into a great industrial nation with "big business" and "soulless corporations," which tended to eliminate the per-

[1] 47th Cong., 1st Sess., *Record*, pp. 463–67 (January 17, 1882). The vote stood, 74 to 162; not voting, 56.

[2] 47th Cong., 1st Sess., *Journal*, p. 338.

[3] *Ibid.*, p. 320.   [4] *Ibid.*, *Record*, p. 358.

[5] 49th Cong., 1st Sess., *Journal*, p. 81; 52d Cong., 1st Sess., *Record*, p. 22.

sonal element between employer and wage-earner. Then began what has been called "government by legislation." Needed reforms in railroad administration and equipment found expression in House bills and reports, until the car-coupler, the locomotive ash-pan, and a score of ingenious devices for minimizing accidents and safeguarding life became prominent in the legislative work of Congress under the broad interpretation of interstate commerce. Hundreds of measures crowded committee files, each proposing a new panacea for every alleged ill or wrong.

Although the opinion obtained in well-informed legislative circles that all measures relating to changing economic conditions were receiving intelligent consideration as rapidly, perhaps, as wisdom justified action, the impression spread that committees should become more responsive to public sentiment. This not only revived the old controversy favorable to some plan of committee selection other than by the Speaker, but turned the appeal into a popular issue. It was not a cry of individual distress. Personal grievances of members were merged in the deeper demand, and the old arguments that had done service for a century found many sympathetic hearers when proclaimed as in the interest of the people. Then came a new House, organized by the Democrats in 1911, which adopted a caucus-approved rule that all standing committees should be elected.[1]

The procedure under this rule differed little from the Orth plan. A caucus of Democrats selected the majority

[1] 62d Cong., 1st Sess., Rule x, sec. 1.

members of the Committee on Ways and Means, who acted as a Board or Committee of Committees in choosing the majority members of other committees. To eliminate Reed's objection that each member of such a body would appoint himself chairman of a great committee, this Board adopted a rule confining its membership to the Ways and Means Committee and limiting the assignment of other members to one important committee. Moreover, in making its assignments the Board in no wise departed from the rules which formerly guided the Speaker. Fitness, experience, and geographical location were recognized as well as the long-established custom of promoting older members and placing at the head of each committee the person entitled by long service to the chairmanship. In like manner it authorized the accepted minority leader to assign places to minority members. Indeed, the administration of the new rule made no perceptible change in the manner of making up committees, which, when finally constructed, were "elected" by receiving the formal approval of a caucus and then of the House. Nevertheless, the work developed grave difficulties. Satisfying several old members and some new ones led to many conferences which disclosed much forboding that did not reach the public; but it is well known that serious embarrassment, if not open revolt, was avoided by materially enlarging the more important committees. It was known, too, that in committee appointments as well as in other matters the chairman of the Board, although exhibiting rare tact, exercised the control usually exerted by the dominating head of a great committee. This tendency to hold the reins became especially marked at the opening session of the Sixty-third Congress, indicating that the Speaker's mantle had fallen upon the shoulders of the masterful chairman of Ways and Means. Indeed, it was as apparent to the country as to the House itself that Oscar W. Underwood, of Alabama, and not Speaker Champ Clark, of Missouri, held the baton of command.

Little doubt exists in the minds of experienced members that several of the recent changes curtailing the Speaker's power are advisable. The pressure of business justifies the elimination of the Chair's discretionary recognition, and no serious harm, if little good, can come from the new and ingenious device which allows members an opportunity to seek the discharge of a committee from the further consideration of a bill. But the withdrawal of the Speaker's right to appoint committees may well be regarded as tentative. Such subtraction of power reduces the Speaker simply to a presiding officer, charged with the preservation of order, the prevention of obstruction, the decision of points of order subject to appeal, and with certain perfunctory administrative duties heretofore enumerated. Nothing of his former authority is left him except his personality.

A great Speaker must have great qualities of mind. He must be just, honest, sympathetic, courageous, and quickly responsive. In other words, his mind must have the quality of being noble. Henry Clay lives unequalled among Speakers because a broad nobility of mind was permeated and controlled by great common sense.

Members felt themselves in contact with a glorious personality and they followed him with enthusiasm. Other Speakers preceding him, notably Sedgwick and Macon, had endeavored to lead, but the former toiled in vain and the latter failed because of his subserviency to John Randolph and the President. On the other hand, Clay, with infinite tact, a fearless nature, and abundant self-confidence, silenced Randolph, opposed Madison, and made the Speakership second only to the Presidency. Whatever the rules did for him, his parliamentary power continued secondary to his personal influence.

What Clay did as Speaker in the first half of the last century, Thomas B. Reed did in its last half. He had the courage to suggest parliamentary remedies and the personal force to apply and establish them. Men recognized him as a preëminently able leader, with Disraeli's gift for the pungent epigram, the vivid repartee, and the rattling attack, and while he lacked the tact and perhaps the wisdom of Clay, evidenced by the disclosure of prejudices and provincial narrowness, he left the Chair a legacy of power which bunglers could easily misuse and make unpopular.

Rules alone never made a desirable Speaker. This is abundantly illustrated by James K. Polk, who preceded Hunter; by "the three Johns," who preceded Robert C. Winthrop; by Linn Boyd, who preceded Banks; by William Pennington, who preceded Grow; and by several others who succeeded in missing the career even of average statesmen. But personality alone cannot carry a Speaker safely through the vicissitudes of a stormy administration. The ablest occupants of the chair, apart from character, experience, and reputation, needed a real authority, derived directly from the rules, to enable them to assimilate different shades of feeling in the party and to keep their forces intact throughout a Congress. The scope of this power resembles that of an English Premier, whose authority to appoint the ministry and to bestow the Crown's ecclesiastical offices tends to increase the number of his followers and to give him a stronger hold upon the House of Commons. Although a Speaker's power has never been so visible as that of an English Premier, it has occasionally contributed surprising strength to national policies and parliamentary reforms. Clay used it with conspicuous advantage during the War of 1812. In 1876 it gave vigor to the administration of Randall, who deemed it politically inadvisable to adopt at that time a tariff policy in harmony with the traditions of his party. Carlisle believed in a tariff for revenue only, and for six years maintained the principle as masterfully as Sir Robert Peel engineered the abolition of the corn duties. Had the organization of the House in the Fifty-first Congress depended upon a Committee of Committees, Speaker Reed could never have marshaled sufficient strength to establish the needed reforms that distinguished his administration.

But the need of a virile Speaker is often even more far-reaching. A congressional election in an "off-year" ordinarily turns upon issues growing out of the Administration's policy, and it is the people's opportunity to approve or disapprove. If they approve, the majority of the House usually continues in harmony with it; if they disapprove, the political status changes and the new Speaker represents the dominating sentiment of the country. This was the intention of the Fathers. Under their political system a new Ministry could not be substituted as in England, but the activities of a repudiated President could be halted. As in the British House, however, it sometimes occurs that a decisive or united majority is not returned, in which event it is necessary, before a Speaker can be elected, to fuse the different factions. This happened in 1854 when the congressional elections exhibited a bitter hostility to the repeal of the Missouri Compromise; but upon the assembling of a new Congress neither party possessed a majority. Anti-Nebraska members, made up of Whigs, Know-nothings, Americans, and Republicans, found it difficult to assimilate, while pro-slavery Americans did not easily unite with the disciples of Calhoun.

It was no secret that the formation of committees prevented a fusion. Giddings demanded a majority of the friends of freedom. Other factions, no less insistent upon their peculiar views, found no common ground, while members of each group pressed their individual claims. It was impossible to select a Committee of Committees, which suggested combinations of cunning leaders. Suspicion likewise tainted the personnel of every tentative committee submitted. Thus, for eight weeks the conflict seemed likely never to end until the fitness of William Aiken, of South Carolina, and Nathaniel P. Banks, of Massachusetts, seemed to measure up to the Clay standard: "Promptitude and impartial-

ity in deciding questions of order; firmness and dignity
in his deportment toward the House; patience, good
temper, and courtesy toward individual members; the
best distribution of the talent of the House in its numerous subdivisions for the despatch of public business;
and the fair exhibition of every subject presented for
consideration." [1] In other words, Clay lifted duty above
party, and the more members studied the character of
Aiken and Banks the more suspicion became disarmed.
Meantime discussion concentrated the public mind on
the slavery question, forcing members into the open
and compelling candidates to define their position.
Finally, when each member had settled the problem for
himself, the House, on the one hundred and twenty-
third ballot, elected Banks by 100 to 103. [2]

It was a stupendous victory. Banks stood for the
triumph of a great moral issue, and under the prerogatives of a full-armed Speaker he could defeat obnoxious
legislation of the Pierce-Douglas type. The country
then for the first time fully appreciated the wisdom of
the Fathers in clothing the office with power.

In December, 1859, at the opening of the Thirty-
sixth Congress, a still greater crisis faced the American
people. The conflict was as long and the vote as close
as in 1855, but in violence it far exceeded that contest,
for in four years disagreements between the North and
the South had grown into strong antagonism. Threats
of disunion which formerly excited laughter now became
too serious to be treated as bravado, while the courtesy

[1] 18th Cong., 1st Sess., *Journal*, p. 8.
[2] 34th Cong., 1st Sess., *Record*, p. 67.

that characterized the preceding struggle gave way to passionate bitterness. According to Senator Grimes, of Iowa, and Senator Hammond, of South Carolina, members on both sides were armed with deadly weapons.[1] Moreover, the tense feeling in the House extended to the country. Even the candidacy of John Sherman for Speaker put his brother, afterward the famous General, then at the head of a military school in Louisiana, under suspicion of being an Abolitionist.[2]

The presence of four parties complicated the situation as it did in 1855. Sherman, the choice of the Republicans, could not secure the support of all the anti-Lecompton members, nor were the Democrats able to unite all the Southern Americans. On the twenty-fifth ballot Sherman came within three votes of election, and three weeks later William N. H. Smith, an American from North Carolina, encountered a similar experience. But neither side was encouraged by the recurrence of such flattering support, and on February 1, eight weeks after the contest began, the Republicans presented William Pennington, of New Jersey, then serving his first and only term in the House. Pennington was colorless. He had said nothing and done nothing which could in any wise involve him in the controversy. Although a man of dignity and poise, who possessed Christian meekness and political integrity, with a desire to be fair and just, his ignorance of parliamentary practice and lack of political management emphasized

[1] William Salter, *Life of James W. Grimes*, p. 121; Lewis Harley, *Life of Francis Lieber*, p. 310.
[2] W. T. Sherman, *Memoirs*, vol. I, p. 148.

his unfitness to direct the House at a time of such excitement. But his ability to organize the House in opposition to President Buchanan, who evinced the servility of Pierce, satisfied his party, while the absence of a public record commended him to anti-Lecompton Democrats and anti-Slavery Americans, who recognized the gravity of the situation. Indeed, all were anxious to get a Speaker without a bloody affray on the floor of the House, and on the fourth ballot of the day and the forty-fourth of the session, Pennington secured the three votes withheld from Sherman, making one hundred and seventeen, the number necessary to elect.[1] Of the three votes thus added, one was that of Henry Winter Davis, the brilliant and caustic orator from Maryland, who aided in the organization of the American party and had declined to vote for Banks in 1855. No one in the North, at least, then thought the Speaker represented too much power save Clement L. Vallandigham, of Ohio, whose sympathies were not hidden under a bushel. "Your Speaker, whatever his natural disposition may be," he declared, "is, by the necessities of his office, a despot." Yet it did not occur to Vallandigham that Speaker Orr, of South Carolina, who enforced rules similar to those used by Pennington, was a "despot."

When the power of appointing committees is vested in the Speaker, responsibility is concentrated and located — not scattered and made impossible of location. Besides, no one is so much interested in the success of his party and of his administration as is

[1] 36th Cong., 1st Sess., *Journal*, pp. 163-64.

the Speaker. To use Reed's expression, "What he does, he does in the open." After four years of testing out a Committee of Committees, the opinion of the most prominent members on both sides of the House, although perhaps not publicly expressed, is, that it is a failure.

CHAPTER VI

OTHER OFFICERS AND THE WHIP

At the beginning of each Congress the House, in addition to a Speaker, chooses a clerk, a sergeant-at-arms, a doorkeeper, a postmaster, and a chaplain, who remain in office until the qualification of their successors. These officers were elected by ballot until the substitution of a *viva-voce* vote in 1839. Since 1865 the custom has obtained of adopting a single resolution containing their names. Although this time-saving method is subject to objection, unanimous consent is rarely if ever withheld.

In 1789, after choosing a Speaker, the House, without preliminary authority, elected a clerk, a title conforming to that in the House of Commons. Beyond certain routine duties, however, the two officers bear slight resemblance. The British clerk is a non-partisan. He is appointed by the Crown on the nomination of the Prime Minister, and holds office for life. He attends sittings only when the Speaker is in the chair, but he certifies all legislation and signifies the Crown's assent. The clerk of the American House, on the other hand, is a partisan, representing the dominant party, and serves only for two years unless reëlected. Moreover, his duties continue in the Speaker's absence. Nevertheless, the office is one of great dignity and responsibility, and has often been held for long periods by men of recognized ability. In 1822 no less a person than John W. Taylor, of New York, who had served one term as Speaker, thought seriously of resigning to accept it. Its permanency probably incited his desire, since New York was then and for many years afterward the most fickle State in the distribution of its popular suffrage. Upon the advice of John Quincy Adams, then Secretary of State, Taylor remained in Congress, serving ten years longer and a second term as Speaker. The incident, however, shows that from the first the high character of the office made it attractive to the ablest men in public life.

The clerk, in the performance of his routine duties, keeps the Journal, refers private bills, assigns bills and committee reports to the various calendars, affixes the seal of the House to writs, warrants, and subpœnas, adjusts the stationery accounts of members, certifies to the Senate the passage of bills and resolutions, contracts for labor and supplies, pays officers and employees of the House, and in the absence of the Speaker certifies the compensation of members. After the final adjournment of a Congress he collects from the several committees all bills, resolutions, and other papers not reported to the House. He must also take certified copies of papers withdrawn from the files by order of the House, and deposit with the Librarian of Congress such bound volumes of original papers as are not needed in his files. At present (1915) he appoints about fifty employees, with salaries aggregating $100,000, and disburses a contingent fund of double or triple that amount. He receives a salary of $6500 and ten cents per hundred words for certified extracts from the Journal.

The clerk's prestige, however, comes from his authority, preceding the assembling of a new Congress, to prepare a roll of members elect. This high prerogative adds a judicial function to his duties. It requires him to examine the credentials of members, and in ascertaining their correctness he may study election returns, investigate contested cases, and institute an inquiry into complaints and alleged irregularities. This opens the door to great temptation, for, as elsewhere stated, he may omit from the list the name of any member, the regularity of whose election he questions. In other words, he can, if so disposed, refuse to recognize a sufficient number of credentials because of technical errors or spurious contests to give his party a majority of those privileged to participate in the election of a Speaker. Although such a betrayal of trust has occurred but once, it is possible whenever a small margin exists between opposing parties. For this reason, if for no other, the life tenure of the British clerk is preferable, since it tends to eliminate partisanship.

The clerk also presides at the election of a Speaker. The British clerk never presumes to do this. Indeed, he may not officially address a member either by his own name or by that of his constituency. At the selection of a Speaker at the beginning of a new Parliament he simply directs the proceeding in a pantomimic manner, dumbly pointing his forefinger at the member who is to submit the resolution indicating the majority's choice. Thereupon the member so signaled announces the name with an appropriate speech, after which the resolution, being seconded with further remarks, is adopted. The Speaker elect, having acknowledged the honor, then takes the arm of his proposer and seconder, and makes his way to the chair. The American clerk, on the other hand, promptly at the noon hour brings the House to order and begins calling the roll. Meantime, he may refuse to answer questions or put a motion except one to adjourn, and since no appeal lies from his decisions while the House is thus unorganized, only those whose names are upon his list can vote for Speaker. Thus for the moment he possesses, perhaps, the most exceptional power of any public official.[1]

The sergeant-at-arms maintains order. He acts under the direction of the Speaker, the chairman of the Committee of the Whole, and, pending the election of a Speaker, under the orders of the clerk. At such times he must bear the mace, the symbol of his office. On a call of the House he is required to detain members present and to return absentees. In conjunction with the sergeant-at-arms of the Senate he appoints the Capitol police, a body of thirty-six men, who possess the power of arrest and may be summoned to the floor of the House. He also appoints an auxiliary force of eleven policemen to care for the House office building. Additional to these duties he executes all processes authorized by the House, prepares the roll of members elect in the absence of the clerk, and pays members their mileage and salaries. In the performance of this latter service he may, under the Act of 1856, deduct a day's

[1] See chap. II, p. 12.

salary for each day's unexcused absence, although with one exception no record exists that he ever did so.[1] For the purpose of maintaining a quorum he once circularized the House, requesting members to certify such absence, and Speaker Crisp ruled that, being a disbursing officer under bond, the sergeant-at-arms could enforce all reasonable regulations before making payments, adding, "and the Chair will not certify the pay of any member unless he first furnishes the information required." [2] Following this announcement Speaker Crisp refused to certify the pay of any member who failed to file a certificate showing the days of his attendance and absence during the preceding month; or to certify pay for absent days unless the result of the member's sickness or of sickness in his family. Many conscientious members at this time suffered abatement of pay, although it was facetiously remarked that an epidemic of sickness existed in the House. Toward the end of the session a resolution authorizing a refund to members who had been docked failed of passage. In the Sixty-third Congress the House instructed the sergeant-at-arms to deduct the pay of members for each day of absence, but prior to adjournment it reconsidered the resolution and ordered a return of the salary. The sergeant-at-arms gives a bond for $50,000, employs eight assistants with salaries aggregating $16,000, and submits a statement of his receipts and disbursements at the close of each regular session. He receives a salary of $6500.

[1] Sec. 40, Act of August 18, 1856.
[2] 53d Cong., 2d Sess., *Journal*, pp. 358–59.

The duties of the doorkeeper are not less varied and exacting. Besides guarding the chamber and keeping unprivileged persons from the floor, he controls the document room containing printed bills, resolutions, and reports for the immediate use of members, and supervises the folding-room where public documents are wrapped and mailed. Janitors, page boys, and messengers, including those on the soldiers' roll, also come under his direction. To his charge is likewise committed the care of rooms and the custody of all property, books, and papers belonging to the House. Admission to the floor, delivery of calling cards to members, and the responsibility of handling thousands of visitors who daily throng the galleries and corridors, also belong among the more serious duties of the doorkeeper. Their acceptable performance, without mistakes and without friction, is evidence of a well-disciplined force of assistants. Quick and courteous recognition of persons entitled to the floor requires tact and vigilance. Among the privileged ones are the President, Vice-President, justices of the Supreme Court, cabinet officers, foreign ministers, governors of States, senators, former members of the House, and those who have received the thanks of Congress. Each is expected upon his appearance at the door to present the Speaker's card, but an experienced officer would blush to stop a privileged stranger the second time. It is the duty of the doorkeeper, also, to introduce messengers from the President and the Senate, and, in the absence of the clerk and sergeant-at-arms, to make up the roll of members elect and preside at the organization of a new House. Upon his pay-roll are carried (1915) 140 employees, whose pay aggregates $160,000. His own salary is $5000.

Originally the doorkeeper had charge of the post-office, established in 1802. So rapidly did the mail increase, however, that in 1814 the House authorized the appointment of a postmaster, who became an elective officer in 1838. At present (1915) he employs twenty-two assistants, with salaries aggregating $30,000. His own salary is $4000.

The four officers named above are required to certify each month to their respective pay-rolls, stating who have performed duty and the reason for the absence of those also paid. The enforcement of this act falls upon the Committee on Accounts, whose approval of the expenses legally chargeable to the contingent fund of the House is conclusive upon all departments of the Government. This committee, subject to the approval of the House, also determines the number of employees and fixes their compensation.

In round numbers the House employs 350 clerks and other employees, exclusive of clerks to members, but instead of selecting them by a civil-service examination and retaining them during good behavior, as with other government appointees, the House, with the exception of its librarians, reporters, and veterans on the soldiers' roll,[1] continues the discredited spoils system. Thus, at every party change ignorance displaces efficiency and experts give way to blunderers. The error of such a

[1] Fourteen messengers on the soldiers' roll, under the control of the doorkeeper, at a salary of $1200 each, are not removable except for cause, with the approval of the House. 23 Stat. L. pp. 164, 393.

system is daily disclosed by comparing the shiftless manner in which the business of the House is often transacted with the intelligent work of James C. Courts, who has fortunately remained clerk of the Committee on Appropriations for upward of thirty-five years. He is an ideal illustration of the great helpfulness of one permitted to survive party changes.

The House librarian and his assistants are appointed by the clerk, with the approval of the Speaker, and cannot be removed except "for cause" approved by the Committee on Rules. The House library, consisting chiefly of volumes of statutes, court and committee reports, journals of the two Houses, and the debates of Congress, is a subdivision of the Library of Congress, the librarian of which is appointed by the President, with the approval of the Senate. The Library of Congress, however, is under the exclusive supervision of the Joint Committee on the Library.

The chaplain opens each day's session with prayer, for which he receives a salary of $1200. It is not stipulated that prayers be short, or that members stand during the service, but brevity and reverence are usually observed. Originally the chaplain was not an official of the House. A concurrent resolution named two clergymen of different denominations, who, interchanging weekly, supplied the Senate and House. The prolonged Speakership contest in 1855 interrupted this custom, the House meantime employing local ministers. Their prayers, it seems, too often evinced something of the partisan spirit that characterized the pending controversy, and in the following Congress (1857) certain

members who claimed that the employment of chap-
lains conflicted with the spirit of the Constitution and
tended to promote a union of Church and State, made
a determined effort to discontinue their use. This
aroused the churches of the country, and at the end of
an acrimonious debate the House, by an overwhelming
majority, adopted the following resolution: "Whereas
the people of the United States, from their earliest
history to the present time, have been led by the hand
of a kind Providence and are indebted for the countless
blessings of the past and the present and dependent for
continued prosperity in the future upon Almighty God;
and whereas the great vital and conservative element
in our system is the belief of our people in the pure
doctrines and divine truths of the Gospel of Jesus
Christ, it eminently becomes the representatives of a
people so highly favored to acknowledge in the most
public manner their reverence for God: Therefore, be
it resolved, that the daily sessions of this body be opened
with prayer, and that the ministers of the Gospel in this
city are hereby requested to attend and alternately
perform this solemn duty." [1] The adoption of this
creed forever crushed objection to the presence of a
chaplain. Nevertheless, his status remained unfixed. It
was objected that neither the Constitution nor the law
recognized such an officer, and not until the payment
of his salary depended upon his taking the ironclad
oath, adopted in 1862, did his official character become
established.

It is creditable to the House that it has always ob-

[1] 35th Cong., 1st Sess., *Globe*, pp. 25, 26.

served Sunday. An adjournment on Saturday carries until Monday, and a recess for three days, authorized by the Constitution, excludes Sunday. A Sunday's session is held only by special order, and although the House may at such times, if it so decides, transact general business, it is usually confined to eulogies of deceased members.

Respect for public opinion has also been shown in a continuous effort to prohibit the sale of liquor within the limits of the Capitol. Until 1837 liquor was sold without question, but under the influence of the Washingtonian movement it was prohibited. The rule, however, proved imperfect, and the traffic, under severe restrictions, continued until 1867, when it was again prohibited. Thereupon the restauranteur surrendered his contract and the restaurant passed under the control of the Committee on Public Buildings and Grounds. Nevertheless, the determination to extirpate the sale of liquor under any conditions, however restrictive, strengthened with the growing temperance sentiment, and in 1903, without debate or a division, the Act of March 3 was passed absolutely prohibiting it.[1]

Reporters of the official proceedings, now six in number, are also officers of the House. They are appointed by the Speaker, receive a salary of $5000 per annum, and may be removed only for cause. The present system of reporting debates was of slow growth. Originally the House made no provision for such work. As the Journal contained all the official proceedings, including the yeas and nays, members did not then see any necessity for

[1] 32d Stat. L., p. 1221.

printing what was said, and accordingly such brief abstracts of the early debates as now exist in the *Annals of Congress* and the *Congressional Debates* were supplied largely by newspaper reporters, who published only what seemed to them important.[1] These reports occasioned much complaint. They were characterized as incorrect and often offensively partisan, with arguments favorable to the newspaper side fully set out, and those adverse maimed, misstated, and confused. Moreover, the dull or inconspicuous member rarely got a line. To secure accuracy and impartiality, therefore, propositions were submitted to place reporters under oath, to make admittance to the floor dependent upon their "decorum and respect to members," and to pay for the publication of correct reports. The House thought it inadvisable to assist financially unofficial publications, but in order to check misreports by fixing responsibility, it authorized (1811) the Speaker to assign press reporters to places on the floor. This led to charges of political favoritism, some being admitted and others excluded. It was noted, however, that the assumption of some authority improved the character of the reports.

A further improvement followed the custom, which began some time before the establishment of the *Congressional Globe* (1833), of paying the publisher for a

[1] The *Annals of Congress*, in 42 volumes, extend from the First Congress through the first session of the Eighteenth, 1789–1824; the *Congressional Debates*, in 29 volumes, from the second session of the Eighteenth Congress to the Twenty-fifth, 1824–39; the *Congressional Globe*, in 108 volumes, from the Twenty-third to the Forty-second Congress, 1833–73; the *Congressional Record*, in 335 volumes, from the Forty-third to the Sixty-third Congress, 1873–1915.

certain amount of space. This arrangement not only increased the number of volumes per session,[1] but whetted the desire to employ a corps of paid stenographers to report everything done and said. Although this ambitious plan to exploit the speech of members was successfully opposed for many years, three *Globe* reporters finally obtained fixed seats in front of the clerk's desk (1851), and four years later were paid by the House. Then came the Government Printing-Office (1860), and the system, begun in 1863, of making annual appropriations to cover the publication of debates. This quickly turned the *Globe* into a daily, freighted with forty columns of proceedings, which doubled the number of volumes formerly published each year. About this time, too (1865), appeared a proposition authorizing the Government Printing-Office to publish the reports and the Speaker to appoint the reporters, making them officers of the House. But it did not become a law until 1872, the statute then recognizing five official reporters, for whose use a room was set apart.

The next year (1873) the *Congressional Record* had its birth. To have every spoken word recorded by their own reporters had long been the dream of parliamentary leaders. It would give the House, they said, absolute control of its proceedings, crystallize its procedure, keep business from drifting, prevent members from duplicating arguments, and hold them responsible for their language. Reporters, too, would more loyally serve the House, their notes would become its property, and their

[1] Twenty-nine volumes of *Debates* were issued in twelve years, against twenty volumes of *Annals* in the preceding twelve years.

hours of work subject to its convenience. To some extent these benefits have been realized. In other respects, however, the *Record* is an imperfect mirror. It was intended to contain a full stenographic report of each day's doings, but bills, even if read in full, are seldom published, and often only the substance of resolutions and other propositions offered by members. So, in revising remarks, language may be added, modified, or left out, although not to affect the import of words spoken by another without his consent. Nor do words appear if spoken by a member after being called to order. On the other hand, "leave to print," first restricted to individual requests and subsequently extended to a "general leave" to continue for several days after debate on a bill is closed, lets in hundreds of speeches never delivered. By unanimous consent leave to extend one's remarks may even be secured in Committee of the Whole. This explains why speeches of half a dozen pages are often interjected into a five-minute debate. Similar surprises often appear when the forty minutes allowed after adopting the previous question is divided among twenty speakers, each given two minutes "with leave to extend their remarks." Thus the *Record* presents not what is really said and done on the floor, but what members and the House please to have printed. Sharp, personal controversies which spice debate and furnish racy reading too often disappear, while thousands of pages are devoted to wearisome remarks never spoken. The custom of granting "leave to print" has contributed to the publication of three times as many volumes of the *Record* in the past forty years as were issued of the *Globe* during the preceding forty years. In other words, the *Record* has become " a cave of the winds," or a mausoleum of oratory, poetry, useful and useless information, and a medley of opinions, good, bad, and quixotic, upon every conceivable subject. Until a topical index is prepared it must practically remain a closed book except to the most intrepid explorers.

The office of "whip" has no official recognition in the House. In the British Commons it is deemed so important to successful party management that the Ministry assigns its duties to the Secretary of the Treasury, with a salary of $10,000, and three junior lords of the Treasury, each with a salary of $5000. As the Treasury Board never meets, its members confine their activities to the passage of government measures. Though the whip is not recognized in the American House, his work has always been performed. Frequently the chairman of a committee, charged with the passage of an important and stoutly contested measure, acts as a whipper-in. John W. Eppes, who headed Foreign Affairs in 1811, rounded up the Administration forces when the House first adopted the previous question. John W. Taylor was a vigorous whip. He knew the sentiment of members, carried a list of absent ones, and kept adherents informed of an approaching vote. In the Twenty-fifth Congress (1837–39) John Bell's vigor in forming combinations and securing their presence at roll-calls angered Cambreleng more than his arguments. For long periods the numerical superiority of the majority party did not demand the services of a whip.

This was especially true in the Jackson régime and during and immediately after the Civil War. But whenever the division of parties approaches equality, volunteers quickly appear to rally and line up opposing forces. When suppressing dilatory motions and securing the adoption of a special order by a majority vote in the Forty-seventh Congress (1881–83), Thomas B. Reed became an ideal whip. In 1875 James Wilson, of Iowa, afterward the distinguished Secretary of Agriculture, became the whip for his party and continued as such for several years. The first whip to be chosen by a party caucus (1899) was James E. Watson, of Indiana. Though a man of dauntless courage, presenting the rare combination of a debater and platform speaker of high order, he won his way more by a gracious manner, easily making friends with everybody. More than this, he was gifted with administrative skill, and though he never seemed to lead or direct, members of his party involuntarily concurred in his suggestions. After him came James A. Tawney, of Minnesota, also the choice of a party caucus. Like Watson, Tawney relied upon brains more than blood, and in rounding up his forces without show or fuss he evinced the poise and calmness that indicated a majority behind him.

But the work never became completely organized until insurgency began to develop in the Sixtieth Congress (1907–09). It was then that Speaker Cannon designated John W. Dwight, of New York, as the whip, assigning him the room formerly occupied by the Speaker and easily accessible to the floor. With the assistance of House employees Dwight organized the work into a system as effective as that of a British whip. He might be seen daily, with whip's book in hand, taking note of the whereabouts of every member, and was able at any moment to report pairs, to give the majority within immediate call, and to indicate the number summonable in twelve or twenty-four hours. If the debate showed signs of closing before the time fixed for members to appear, he not infrequently cautioned disputants to talk until his folks arrived. It became his business, also, to learn the disposition of members toward party measures and to report signs of disaffection. If serious discontent threatened, the intercession of the President was not infrequently invoked. Thus the labor of the whip mobilized the majority party, kept it within call, minimized defeat, and informed leaders of the strength of the Opposition.

CHAPTER VII

FLOOR LEADERS

NEXT to the Speaker in activity, if not in influence, is the floor leader. The head of Ways and Means is the titular leader, and before the division of that committee the multitude of his duties made him the actual leader. But in 1865 the burden of legislation shifted to the chairman of Appropriations, who often becomes the real leader.

The long official list of these leaders presents several names obscure even to the students of history. As elsewhere stated, a few pages of their debates and brief sketches in the *Biographical Congressional Directory* are seldom supplemented in book or newspaper with the familiar knowledge of contemporaries. But their conspicuous place in the House distinguishes them as men of more than ordinary capacity, for in interesting personality and real ability the floor leader is not infrequently the strongest and at the time the best-known man in the House. This was preëminently true of Robert Goodloe Harper, of South Carolina, whom Speaker Dayton appointed in 1797. Intrepid, quick, well-informed, Harper set a high standard. He displayed genius and positive statesmanship, charming the House with the grace and adroitness of his arguments. In the selection of George W. Campbell, of Tennessee, and John W. Eppes, of Virginia, Speaker Varnum enjoyed his greatest triumph. Earnestness of temper gave Eppes an impatient spirit. He was not always understood, sometimes a little envied, but widely beloved. The same may be said of Speaker Winthrop's floor leader, whose name is not readily recalled. Yet in his day the House held Samuel F. Vinton, of Ohio, in higher personal esteem than the Speaker himself. The trying task of leadership under circumstances of peculiar difficulty made "Vinton" a household word throughout the country.

With the possible exception of Henry Clay, no Speaker ever won the confidence or enjoyed the friendship of the House more than William Lowndes, of South Carolina. His genius pointed him out as the triumphant champion of sound legislation, whose achievements, passing into the history of his time, keeps his name familiar, at least to students of parliamentary annals. With a personality far less winning than Lowndes, Thaddeus Stevens, an autocratic floor leader of the most pronounced type, rivaled Speakers in influence and in fame. The eye of the visitor as he entered the House gallery during and immediately after the Civil War first sought a glimpse of this great radical, whom abolitionists admired as much as men of conservative instincts dreaded. At the height of Speaker Blaine's power Schenck and Dawes and Garfield, who dominated the floor, were equally famous. While Randall and Reed were floor leaders no faces were more familiar and no names better known. Cannon's leadership under Reed and Henderson stamped him as a man of preëminent ability and singular energy. He never trusted to his star, or to luck, or to anything save care and preparation; and to this day it remains an unsolved mystery why his party preferred Henderson for Speaker in 1899.

It is said that tact rather than genius is the quality most needed for the work of a floor leader. A distinguished member of Parliament avers that "the essential qualities of a leader are not great powers of intellect. A man of cool head, good temper, firm will, and capacity for appreciating the serviceable qualities of other men, may always make a very successful leader, even though he be wanting altogether in the higher attributes of eloquence and statesmanship." [1] It certainly does not follow that a floor leader is the most effective debater, or the profoundest thinker, or the accepted leader of his party, although he may be and sometimes is all of these. It should imply, however, that in the art of clear, forceful statement, of readily spotting weak points in an opponent's argument, and in dominating power to safeguard the interests of the party temporarily responsible for the legislative record of the House, he is the best equipped for his trade. It is neither necessary nor advisable for him to lead or even to take part in every debate. The wisdom of silence is a great asset. Besides, chairmen and members of other committees are usually quite capable and sufficiently enthusiastic to protect their own measures. But the floor leader must aid the Speaker in straightening out parliamentary tangles, in progressing business, and in exhibiting an irresistible desire to club any captious interference with the plans and purposes of the majority.

[1] Justin McCarthy, *A History of Our Own Times*, vol. I, p. 310.

Their speeches, especially those of the most famous, have rarely exceeded half an hour. Stevens and Randall and Reed, like Disraeli in the Commons, usually presented their stock of good things in fifteen or twenty minutes. It could not be said of them that they "thought of convincing when their hearers thought of dining." Often they lamed an opponent with a single sentence. "The use of cutting sarcasm," confesses Adams, a master of the art, "is seldom politic." Yet a floor leader or the chairman of a great committee, while he must not be venomous, ought to possess the gift of sarcasm or ridicule sufficiently to protect him from pompous mediocrity. It is always well to inspire members with something of the fear that prevents the small boy from pinching a cat's tail.

In selecting a floor leader the Speaker often names his leading party opponent. Thus Winthrop appointed Samuel F. Vinton (1847); Banks designated Lewis D. Campbell (1856); Pennington named John Sherman (1859); and Reed selected McKinley (1889). More often it has seemed wise to promote the ranking member of Ways and Means. This accounted, in part at least, for Clay's appointment of Ezekiel Bacon in 1811; Stevenson's designation of Gulian C. Verplanck in 1822; Polk's selection of Churchill C. Cambreleng in 1835; Orr's advancement of James S. Phelps in 1858; Randall's promotion of Fernando Wood in 1879; Keifer's appointment of William D. Kelley in 1881; Carlisle's disposition of Roger Q. Mills in 1887; and Henderson's selection of Sereno E. Payne in 1899. Nor is it uncommon for Speakers to reward faithful lieutenants. For this reason

Jones selected James J. McKay in 1843; Cobb picked Thomas S. Bayly in 1849; Boyd named George S. Houston in 1851; Kerr and Carlisle selected William H. Morrison in 1875 and in 1883; and Crisp appointed William M. Springer in 1891.

It is noticeable that a floor leader often influences the tone of debate. If one is insolent and overbearing like John Randolph, or moderate and courteous like William Lowndes, his colleagues to a greater or less degree will sympathize with and exhibit such an expression of temper. In other words, the House soon gets accustomed to a condition, and members who engage much in discussion are inclined to evince the spirit of an accepted chief. "When Lord Palmerston was first made leader of the House," writes Bagehot, "his jaunty manner was not at all popular, and some predicted failure. 'No,' said an old member, 'he will soon educate us *down* to his level; the House will soon prefer this Ha! Ha! style to the wit of Canning or the gravity of Peel.' We must own that the prophecy was accomplished, for he degraded us by diminishing a love for principle." [1]

Prior to the floor leadership of Randolph, leaders rarely failed to observe the amenities of debate. Robert Goodloe Harper, of South Carolina (1797), and Roger Griswold, of Connecticut (1800), then in their thirties, set a high tone. In political knowledge, forceful eloquence, and profound legal ability, Griswold ranked among the first men in the nation. And he had spirit. When Matthew Lyon, of Kentucky, spat in his face, Griswold stiffened his arm to strike, but remembering

[1] *The English Constitution*, p. 237.

where he was, he coolly wiped his cheek. But after the House by its vote failed to expel Lyon, he "beat him with great violence," says a contemporary chronicle, "using a strong walking-stick." Of equal mettle, Harper was scarcely inferior in intellectual force. The distinction of his manner matched the accuracy of his scholarship. In the Chase impeachment his argument for the defense is conspicuous for its logic and fine rhetoric.

Following Griswold as floor leader John Randolph leaped into fame. Gifted with ready wit, destructive sarcasm, fluent speech, and a strong, well-modulated voice, he exerted for six years a most remarkable power over the House. Very few members have left so high a reputation for eloquence, and, it may be said with equal truth, so small a basis of statesmanship to support it. He rushed into controversy without fear and without discretion, never betraying a moment's doubt on any conceivable question, and never admitting that two sides existed to any matter of discussion. His natural vanity, inflated by success, became at last irritatingly offensive, while opposition aroused in him a personal malignity which turned debate into such exhibitions of brutality that critics declared him "the image of a great man stamped upon base metal." Many feared him; not a few avoided him; and no one liked him. Yet his influence left its impress upon the manner and the quality of debate. It justified audacity, inspired reckless statements, and encouraged savage personal attacks.

The courtesy of Henry Clay rebuked such conduct. Although the first Speaker to comprehend the influence of a strict application of the rules, and the first to control legislation through committee apppointments, his urbanity, the key to his great power, enabled him to attach and to retain the loyalty of men of startlingly different habits of mind from his own. The occasional encounters of this master of grace and affability with John C. Calhoun, or John W. Taylor, of New York, or Philip P. Barbour, of Virginia, delighted the House and fixed the standard of good manners and good temper. The complaisance of his floor leaders — Cheves, Eppes, Lowndes, Smith, and McLane — was scarcely less marked than his own. Indeed, it is doubtful if one not a Speaker ever acquired a greater personal influence than William Lowndes. He was a Saul in stature, and supplemented commanding ability with an amiable disposition and an irreproachable character. Benton's tribute, though often quoted, will bear to be quoted again: "He was one of those members," said the great Missourian, "rare in all assemblies, who, when he spoke, had a cluster around him, not of friends, but of the House, — members quitting their distant seats and gathering up close about him, and showing by their attention that one would feel it a personal loss to have missed a word he said. It was the attention of affectionate confidence. He imparted to others the harmony of his own feelings, and was the moderator as well as the leader of the House, and was followed by its sentiment in all cases in which inexorable party feeling or some powerful interest did not rule the action of the members, and even then he was courteously and deferentially treated." [1]

[1] *Thirty Years' View*, vol. I, p. 18.

The House always gets on better when the Golden Rule governs. Speaker Cannon's friendship for John S. Williams, of Mississippi, during the latter's long leadership of the minority had a mellowing influence on the whole membership, whereas the disturbed relations between Speaker Crisp and Thomas B. Reed, and later between Speaker Reed and Joseph W. Bailey, of Texas, inclined the friends of each to be somewhat resentful. But for real turbulence, when the House became a bedlam and the center aisle seemed to separate enemies rather than opponents, one must go back to the time of Speakers Stevenson and Polk, when George McDuffie, of South Carolina, Churchill C. Cambreleng, of New York, and John W. Jones, of Virginia, headed Ways and Means. Indeed, to quell riotous disorder provoked by coarse and brutal language, Polk was the first Speaker to snatch the gavel from the hand of a chairman before the Committee of the Whole had formally risen. At this period a degree of personal irritation, rarely if ever equaled in our legislative history, seemed to characterize debate. The moral courage of John Quincy Adams, who fought for the right of petition, undoubtedly contributed to it. It is also true, as Mr. Blaine states, that with very few exceptions the really eminent debaters during those years were in the Senate; [1] otherwise McDuffie, chief of the Hotspurs, could scarcely have justified his title to floor leader. He was a talker; he was *the* talker; he was the genius of talk. More than that he was a magnificent and an unmitigated egotist. Able, bold, impatient, and quick to take offense, he poured

[1] *Twenty Years of Congress*, vol. I, p. 70.

out his noisy denunciations and passionate invectives, often mercilessly personal, until he had exhausted every rhetorical weapon. If an opponent flashed a word in resentment, he promptly indicated a willingness to answer at another place, and although he once balked at a rifle in the hands of Thomas Metcalfe, of Kentucky, he did not lose prestige as a disciple of the code duello. It may be said in extenuation that McDuffie had much to provoke him. His views were resented and his bills rejected, while the tariff acts of 1828, 1830, and 1832, reported by the rival Committee on Manufactures, passed without the acceptance of an amendment proposed by Ways and Means. Yet McDuffie kept the rivalry hot and eager until elected governor of his State, where he was as popular as a later-day music-hall artist.

Cambreleng belonged to a lower type. Although of great authority on financial subjects, he was an ultra of the ranting, declamatory style, without wit or humor, and seemingly fond of being offensive. If interrupted, he bullied and became brutal, sometimes flaming out with a flourish of emphatic malice. If any one doubts the superiority of modern manners, he has only to read the controversies of Cambreleng's day, when "liar, scoundrel, and puppy" was a common combination epithet.[1] Upon resuming his seat, after having replied to a severe personal arraignment of Henry Clay, former Speaker White, without the slightest warning, received a blow in the face. In the fight that followed a pistol was discharged, wounding an officer of the police.[2] John

[1] 26th Cong., 1st Sess., *Globe*, p. 145.
[2] Adams, *Diary*, vol. XII, p. 16.

Bell, the distinguished Speaker and statesman, had a similar experience in Committee of the Whole (1838). The fisticuff became so violent that even the Chair could not quell it. Later in the day both parties apologized and "made their submissions." On February 6, 1845, Edward J. Black, of Georgia, "crossed over from his seat, and, coming within the bar behind Joshua R. Giddings as he was speaking, made a pass at the back of his head with a cane. William H. Hammett, of Mississippi, threw his arms round Black and bore him off as he would a woman from a fire. Black sneaked to his seat and in a tone so low he could not be heard whispered an apology for having trespassed on the order of the House." [1]

"These were not pleasant days," writes Thomas B. Reed. "Men were not nice in their treatment of each other. When Reuben M. Whitney was before a committee of investigation in 1837, Bailie Peyton, of Tennessee, taking offense at one of his answers, threatened him fiercely, and when he rose to claim the committee's protection, Mr. Peyton, with due and appropriate profanity, shouted: 'You shan't say one word while you are in this room; if you do I will put you to death.' The chairman, Henry A. Wise, added: 'Yes; this insolence is insufferable.' As both these gentlemen were armed with deadly weapons, the witness could hardly be blamed for not wanting to testify before the committee again." [2]

It shows how callous the House had become that George Evans, of Maine, could serve for twelve years during the leadership of McDuffie, Cambreleng, and

[1] Adams, *Diary*, vol. XII, p. 162.

[2] *Saturday Evening Post*, December 9, 1899.

Polk without influencing their manners. To find one
so brilliant and highly cultivated in such company is
like discovering, nested amidst floating weeds, a freshly
opened water-lily, sparkling in the sunshine. Probably
no one in his time or in any time had in combination
more oratorical gifts than Evans. His powers of reasoning and of pathos, his elocution and language, his stirring
arguments animated and inspired by deep feeling, his
playful and cutting severity, his mellow voice and gentle manners, made him the most distinguished man in
the House. Blaine says of him: "Of all who have represented New England in Congress, Mr. Evans, as a debater, is entitled to rank next to Mr. Webster." [1]

As the successor of Cambreleng, John W. Jones kept
well up to the level of his time in swaggering. He was
lame and not prepossessing in appearance, but he possessed elements of leadership unknown to the New
Yorker. Of fluent and convincing eloquence, he loved
the platform and delighted in intimate intercourse with
the crowd. He also had the power of saying much in a
few words and appreciated the relative value of speech
and silence. He was indisposed to pluck the peach
before it was ripe. Indeed, instead of forcing issues on
the public or on the House, he preferred to make his
appearance when the air had been warmed, and then
with clever arguments, gracefully expressed in a strong,
well-modulated voice, he held the attention of the House
as if he were its master. Yet his tolerance and the
warmth of his human sympathies were negligible. He
shared his party's general distrust of the liberalists of

[1] *Twenty Years of Congress*, vol. I, p. 72.

his day and never disguised his impatience with the
growing new thought. To him it was a red rag which
made him bellow and paw the dust. At such times he
could outdo Cambreleng.

It was fortunate that the minority in these swaggering days was led by John Bell, of Tennessee, memorable
as the candidate of the Union party for President in
1860. Although incapable of the stirring, brilliant arguments of George Evans, or the quick, piquant replies of
Henry R. Storrs, of New York, Bell was ready for any
fray. He had a way of expressing unmitigated contempt
in a tone that exasperated. With the lance of a *picador*
he kept Cambreleng in a rage. He fought his way by
sheer talent into the front rank of the Opposition. As
a lawyer whose knowledge might fairly be called profound, he rose to celebrity and influence in the prime
of life, entering the House at the age of thirty. His
resources seemed inexhaustible, enabling him on the
shortest notice to marshal facts and arguments, and to
sustain the brunt of debate with the ablest foes. On
occasion he could also pour out an animated, even a
passionate invective, and although once betrayed into
resenting a coarse interruption with a blow of his fist,
he had moderation and discretion. But it never interfered with his physical courage.

The manners of James J. McKay, of North Carolina,
appointed floor leader by his predecessor, Speaker John
W. Jones (1843), were an improvement over those of his
immediate predecessors. McKay was a plain-looking
man, and as careless of dress as John Quincy Adams, of
whom it was derisively said, when President, that he sat

in his shirt-sleeves and wore no slippers; but as a debater of power, of which he was conscious, though with little personal vanity, McKay spoke with astonishing mildness. Even the satirical bitterness of Wise did not disturb him. To strike sparks of light on every subject with no trace of rudeness contrasted so strangely with the dashing, impulsive attacks of McDuffie and the overbearing insolence of Cambreleng, that some thought his moderation covered an insidious spirit under a mask of candor. Perhaps his words were sometimes stealthy, but it remained to his credit that he conducted sharp, forceful debate in a courteous manner.

The civility of McKay's successor, Samuel F. Vinton, of Ohio (1847), made a deeper impression. Backed by twenty years of service, he was in the full flower of his strength and of his fame. Although of slight frame and weak voice, his handsome face, slightly austere, with its prominent forehead and blazing blue eyes, gave assurance of abundant force and will power. After Evans had passed to the Senate, Adams spoke of him as the best and ablest man in the House. Even his veracity was mentioned as a distinguishing merit. Whether this implied that members generally and floor leaders in particular failed to show a preference for the truth, one can only guess. But Vinton had the oratory of conviction. He cared for the substance rather than the graces of speech, and with a well-disciplined temper he rounded out long, heated discussions without the slightest acerbity. With gratifying sympathy he represented a very substantial body of Whigs, and in 1847 the party rewarded his fidelity with a nomination for Speaker. It was practically unanimous. But in opposing the Wilmot Proviso he had disturbed the irreconcilable anti-slavery element, and in the interest of harmony he withdrew in favor of Winthrop, who had sustained the Proviso. It was one of those happenings which occasionally make the game of politics so bewildering. In a day sentiment seemed to change. What had been politically unpopular suddenly became morally popular, and the Whig statesmen who opposed the Proviso quickly felt a loss of power. Winthrop, failing to profit by Vinton's experience, realized the change in 1849 when Howell Cobb defeated his reëlection by two votes. Thus the quick turn of the tide stranded them both — Vinton at the age of fifty-nine and Winthrop at forty-two. Seldom has a political career been so abruptly cut short as that of Mr. Winthrop. Never afterward did he seem to have any particular business in public life. Yet he lived on for over forty years, his intellectual powers unshattered, the foremost citizen of his native Commonwealth.

Speaker Cobb appointed Thomas H. Bayly, of Virginia, floor leader. It was a case of gratitude. Bayly had never served upon Ways and Means, nor disclosed the restless intelligence that pierces a delicately woven web which often conceals an unnecessarily large appropriation; but throughout the long, tedious, fickle contest for Speaker, he watched Cobb's interests, and with good temper and forceful speech gave striking proof of his preference for factional advantage. He was not a far-seeing man. He did not trouble himself about future problems, and in the end he achieved results which a bare majority rather than the country at large welcomed and applauded. These characteristics, dominating his floor leadership, aroused suspicions of inconsiderate conduct, and often left him in a minority. Thus he became a titular, not a real leader, and although he remained in the House until his death in 1856, he dropped out of parliamentary activity at the close of Cobb's two years in the chair.

Speaker Boyd selected George S. Houston, of Alabama. Houston had been a Whig. He supported Winthrop against Cobb, following Toombs and Stephens and Stanly; but in 1851, acting independently of his associates, he shifted his party and took his reward. Although a man of undoubted ability and of a brave, commanding spirit, who had served four years on Ways and Means, ranking next to Vinton, he lacked all the essential qualities of leadership. He had audacity and aggressiveness, but little parliamentary skill and neither patience nor political tact. Besides, his eloquence was massive. He shouted and thundered. John W. Forney, the amiable clerk, called him the noisiest man in the House. One marvels at the boldness of his assertions during the violent controversy over the repeal of the Missouri Compromise. He seemed to talk with a grandiose and oracular vagueness, sometimes baffling and frequently bewildering men of greater knowledge. He left the impression upon many, who watched his restless figure as he stormed and gesticulated, that he discussed subjects of which he evidently knew nothing. Happily for him the clever parliamentary trick of Stephens,[1] releasing the Kansas-Nebraska Bill from

[1] See chap. XIII, p. 268.

Committee of the Whole, saved his leadership from becoming a burlesque. But his influence seriously lowered the tone of debate. Undoubtedly the sudden revival of the slavery issue, fanned into fierce flame by the repeal of a sacred compact, had its influence. It turned good-tempered men into ill-natured ones. Yet Houston's personality itself provoked a rudeness that had largely disappeared after Cambreleng's day. He simply knew nothing of the social temper which in this day insists that the first duty of a gentleman is to apologize for an unjust or offensive expression in debate.

Lewis D. Campbell, of Ohio, succeeded Houston. For a man of marked ability, Campbell proved, perhaps, the most disappointing of floor leaders (1855). His speeches, admirable for freshness and vigor, had given him great prestige. He possessed the happy knack of saying bitter things in an epigrammatic way. In the debate on the repeal of the Missouri Compromise he became the Achilles of the Opposition. He sounded an alarm. He hit the tone and temper of Northern people, voicing their fears and expressing their sentiments. He seemed especially to delight in attacking Houston, whose noisy loquacity presented a shining mark for sarcasm. His colleagues applauded him, talked of him for Speaker, gave him a flattering vote, and after his withdrawal in favor of Banks, the latter made him chairman of Ways and Means. But like Bayly he had neither served on the committee nor studied the art of adjusting duties or paring appropriations, while his erratic views, backed with cynical frankness, soon disclosed weakness as a leader. His bill pleased no one.

Even the Ohio wool-raisers in no wise benefited. He seemed to realize its failure, otherwise his speech in its favor must have found a place in the *Globe*. Indeed, he had a way of talking and not publishing. One looks in vain for his remarks favoring the expulsion of Preston S. Brooks because of his brutal assault upon Senator Sumner (1856). As floor leader he presented the resolution and closed the debate, but he withheld his words from the *Globe*, although he had taken Sumner's hand immediately after the assault, as the blood-stained statesman lay in the cloak-room of the Senate.[1] However, Campbell might have survived these shortcomings, as others have before and since, could he have worked in harmony with his party. But he followed no better than he led, and, although a very able man, his public career ended just as some of his Northern colleagues, destined to become famous, seized the situation with the imaginative courage of creative minds. Only once afterward did he go back to Congress, and then as a supporter of President Johnson.

John Sherman, of Ohio, who became floor leader when Henry Winter Davis refused to make him Speaker (1860), was at once recognized as the steadying power of the combination that finally took control of the House. By temperament he was the least adventurous of statesmen, indifferent to dreams, insensible to idealism, but deeply interested in practical things. He had reverence for a bond, for constitutional precedent, and for international law, with the promptness of a tax collector.

[1] Edward L. Pierce, *Life of Charles Sumner*, vol. III, pp. 478, 490, notes.

He seems, also, to have agreed with the younger Pitt, that the highest virtue of statesmanship is patience, and no man ever exhibited a more abundant supply of it than he during the prolonged and savage Speakership contest at the opening of the Thirty-sixth Congress (1859-61). He was slow to anger, and a cold indifference sometimes made him appear a little flaccid. But once engaged his mind worked with unrivaled power. It may be said that throughout his long, notable career an emergency always found him greater than the need. It brought quickly into play all the resources of a powerful intellect, methodical, clear, masterful, with a passionless detachment of spirit that made him supreme. Yet it was well known to his friends and often revealed to the public that behind a rather frigid exterior he cultivated the sensibilities. While he mobilized the forces of wealth and privilege in the interest of the Union, he exhibited a true instinct for the welfare of all the people, and especially for the amelioration of the down-trodden. It was this sympathy that deprived him of the Speakership.

Only occasionally has an official floor leader represented what Disraeli called "sublime mediocrity." Ezekiel Bacon, of Massachusetts (1811), belonged in this class. Although he could address the House with a fluency not unworthy of Clay himself, he proved neither skillful as a debater nor useful in progressing business. Adams likened him to Joseph Vance, of Ohio, who "rose by his eloquence to Congress and then dropped into his primitive obscurity."[1] With him may

[1] *Diary*, vol. II, p. 388.

be classed Joseph Clay, of Pennsylvania. Gulian C.
Verplanck, of New York (1832), and J. Glancy Jones,
of Pennsylvania (1857), whom Speaker Orr appointed
at the instance of President Buchanan. Like Bacon
these men simply filled a gap, each for a session. It was
during the floor leadership of J. Glancy Jones that the
remarkable scene occurred between Galusha A. Grow,
of Pennsylvania, and Lawrence M. Keitt, of South Carolina.[1] The former had passed to the Democratic side
of the chamber, and while there John A. Quitman, of
Mississippi, asked leave to speak. Grow objected.
Keitt, who stood near, said roughly: "If you are going
to object, return to your own side of the House." Grow
answered: "This is a free hall. Every man has a right
to be where he pleases." Keitt, coming nearer, said:
"I want to know what you mean by such an answer as
that." Grow replied: "I mean just what I said. This
is a free hall and every man has a right to be just where
he pleases." Thereupon Keitt seized Grow by the
throat, exclaiming: "I will let you know that you are
a —— —— black Republican puppy." Grow knocked
up his hand, saying, "No negro driver shall crack his
whip over me." Keitt again grasped him by the throat,
and Grow knocked him down.

"Keitt's fall," says Reed, in writing of this historic
incident, "was the signal for a mad rush to the space
in front of the Speaker, members striking each other,
and a general mêlée ensued, with Washburne, of Illinois,
and Potter, of Wisconsin, most conspicuous. Barksdale,
of Mississippi, rushed at Mr. Covode, who uplifted a

[1] February, 1858.

spittoon; but Barksdale's wig came off and Covode had not the heart to smite his unprotected skull. The Speaker called on the sergeant-at-arms, and the sergeant-at-arms, with his assistants, came with the mace, the insignia of his office, and after several minutes the uproar was quelled. Afterward Mr. Keitt made a most handsome apology, taking the blame on himself." [1]

In the class with J. Glancy Jones belongs William M. Springer, of Illinois, who became floor leader during Speaker Crisp's first term (1891–93). Springer was neither sincere nor intellectually honest. Loquacious, often frivolous, and never impressive, he seemed to be always on his feet and apparently indifferent to the position he assumed. It was in defense of some vagary that he remarked, "I'd rather be right than President." To which Reed flashed the retort, "The gentleman from Illinois will never be either." Reed delighted in pricking him. On one occasion Springer asked unanimous consent to correct a statement. "No correction needed," piped up Reed. "We did n't think it was so when you made it." When Springer accused the Maine statesman of making light of his remarks, Reed replied, "If I 'make light' of his remarks, it is more than he ever makes of them himself." Springer's leadership became so intolerable that Crisp soon transferred its duties to Benton McMillin, of the Committee on Rules. Even the Tennesseean, although exhibiting marked ability and considerable parliamentary aptitude, advocated partisan special orders with proverbial Scottish caution. What his party demanded was a dashing, violent oppo-

[1] *Saturday Evening Post*, December 9, 1899.

sition to Thomas B. Reed, then the minority leader, and in the next Congress (1893) Crisp again shifted the leadership to Joseph H. Outhwaite, of Ohio, with William L. Wilson, of West Virginia, as chairman of Ways and Means. This was a more formidable team, but Reed's rapid-firing gun finally drove Crisp to the shelter of a counted quorum.

William L. Wilson was a scholar, dignified, tolerantly placid, of keen perceptions, and a good speaker, who confined his efforts to shaping a revenue measure (1894). Of his class Millard Fillmore (1841) may be called the prototype. Fillmore was not a ready debater. Though possessing a clear, strong voice, he neither stirred the feelings nor aroused the emotions. Critics said his figures belonged to arithmetic, not to rhetoric. But he had ability, good judgment, and great industry, and although Adams gave McKennan, of Pennsylvania, credit for passing the tariff bill of 1842, it made Fillmore's name familiar in seats of industry and opened his way to the Vice-Presidency.

Other official floor leaders whose names are wedded to the tariff policy of their country are Justin Morrill, of Vermont (1861); Robert C. Schenck, of Ohio (1867); Henry L. Dawes, of Massachusetts (1871); William D. Kelley of Pennsylvania (1881); William McKinley, of Ohio (1889); William L. Wilson, of West Virginia (1894); Nelson Dingley, of Maine (1897); Sereno E. Payne, of New York (1909); and Oscar W. Underwood, of Alabama (1913). Several of these men were noted Speakers, their persuasive arguments, strong and vigorous, often rising into the domain of eloquence. On their feet, as the phrase is, Schenck and Dawes were ideal controversialists; McKinley never fell to the level of rhetorical commonplace; and Payne, like Underwood, though not an orator in the true sense, possessed a clear, thoughtful, and sometimes a stately style of speaking. Nelson Dingley, although slight of figure, with rather a weak voice, whose over-supply of information sometimes made him tedious, was an accomplished parliamentarian and never failed to command close attention. He was such a marvel of industry that Reed declared "he'd rather have a pad and pencil on his knee than a pretty girl."

After the division of Ways and Means in 1865 the actual floor leader, as already stated, was often the chairman of Appropriations. When Schenck and Dawes headed these respective committees (1869–71) it was difficult to indicate the real leader, though Blaine declared Schenck "the unquestioned chief." Like William Lowndes he was admirably fitted for the arduous and difficult duty. Years before, when serving as a Whig (1843–51), Adams said of him: "His manner is cool, firm, unhesitating, with conscious mastery of his subject; his voice clear and strong; his elocution neat and elegant, with a swelling vein of sarcastic humor which makes the hall ring with laughter." [1] Blaine adds that "as a debater he had no equal in the House." [2] It was not so difficult to pick the floor leader when Dawes succeeded Schenck, and Garfield became the head of Appropriations (1871–75). Although both were masters of parliamentary de-

---

[1] *Diary*, vol. xi, p. 479.
[2] *Twenty Years of Congress*, vol. i, p. 499.

bate, Garfield had little of the real fighter in his nature. His forceful speeches, full of the passion and poetry essential to genuine eloquence, deeply stirred the House, but he preferred to leave the rough work of the floor to others.

Under the Speakership of Kerr and Carlisle, William H. Morrison, of Illinois, and Roger Q. Mills, of Texas, headed Ways and Means. Mills talked oftener than Morrison, but in personal force and subtlety of mind he may be paired with Morrison. Their achievements, however, were incommensurate with their efforts, which kept their party expectant and the House distrustful. During these years Samuel J. Randall, chairman of Appropriations, was the acknowledged leader. In fact, it made little difference who topped Ways and Means, the Pennsylvanian was always chief. From the time he entered Congress in 1863 until his death in 1890, his political career was a triumph of character and of intellectual mastery. In many respects his equipment was undistinguished. Unknown in society, indifferent to the currents of modern life, and with limited education, his young manhood reveled in political caucuses and Philadelphia polling-places, with a tendency to govern with his fists as well as his head. But even then the serenity of his manner, the honesty of his aims, and his freedom from artifice combined to give him a unique authority. Reed said of him: "Perhaps there may have been better parliamentarians, men of broader intellect and more learning, but there have been few men with a will more like iron or a courage more unfaltering." [1] Randall

[1] *Saturday Evening Post*, December 9, 1899.

picked lieutenants with great shrewdness. When Speaker (1876–81) he put John D. C. Atkins, of Tennessee, at the head of Appropriations and made Fernando Wood, of New York, chairman of Ways and Means. It was a forceful team. Bold, ready, independent, and sometimes impudent, Atkins threw himself with energy into the task of paring appropriations; but in all the political controversies that gnawed at the vitals of a recently resurrected party, Wood did the heavy work.

Wood was a strenuous, self-asserting character. He had great skill in debate and played a striking part in the politics of his time. But his bitter partisanship gained him a reputation even more unsavory than that of Cambreleng. His personal assaults upon President Lincoln, often revoltingly vulgar, became conspicuous and most offensive. He had a cold, sardonic intellect, and his destructive arguments, imperiously and audaciously mischievous, often drove him into outbursts of denunciation which startled even his party colleagues. He cared nothing for a formally inflicted censure.[1] He accepted it as a matter of course, insisting that his language exactly conveyed what he meant to express. Nobody ever praised his judgment and nothing ever jarred his nerves. His colleagues hinted at "the demonic element," shown by the glare of his eye, which disposed him to attack everything and to blame everybody. Members wondered at Randall's appointment of such an indefatigable and reckless champion; yet those who, like Blaine, had served with him from the beginning, spoke of him as belonging to a manly type, who never

[1] 40th Cong., 2d Sess., *Globe*, p. 542.

allowed political antagonisms to destroy friendly relations.

After Randall retired as Speaker he faced Thomas B. Reed, just then winning his spurs as a fighting leader. Reed never headed Appropriations or Ways and Means, but in his third term, during Keifer's Speakership (1881–83), he began doing the rough-and-tumble work of the floor as the bellicose member of the Committee on Rules, and so quickly did his startlingly revolutionary tactics succeed that in the next Congress, although Keifer was the minority's candidate for Speaker, Reed became its acknowledged leader, and ever after, so long as he served in the House, remained the most conspicuous member of his party. His power as a floor leader was in his directness, his contentiousness, his ability to help men make up their minds, and to justify them in following him. He never scattered. His arguments bore directly on the issue before the House at the moment, and, though he indulged sufficiently in generalities to give force and side-light to his views, he never fell into vagueness. No one yawned while he was on his feet. Perhaps few of his speeches will ever get into school readers or volumes of eloquence, but when spoken with his sonorous, forceful tones and unfeigned earnestness infusing new life into every debate, each one became a masterpiece.

Reed's successor as floor leader was Joseph G. Cannon, of Illinois. For ten years he headed Appropriations, and for many years before had fought in the fiercest of dialectical battles. There were some resemblances between him and Reed. Each was indifferent to studied rhetoric, contemptuous of demagogic appeals to popular emotion, distrustful of theorists, and cautious not to overstate. Both were also slow to anger. But once aroused, their indignation gave an extraordinary impetus to their volition. Reed's intellectual mastery controlled the House. His acknowledged superiority destroyed opposition. Cannon was not so completely trusted. His influence came from his power to absorb the atmosphere of a situation and exhale it with an assured grasp of underlying principles. He never browbeat or intimidated. Sarcasm was not among his weapons. He reasoned and smiled, unbuttoned his vest, unloosed the band of his trousers, and then, with his left arm flying over his head, recalling David and the sling, he let fly a well-aimed stone in the shape of a flashing fact that swiftly pierced the argument of an opponent. Whatever the wave that rolled in, he always rode on its crest. There was something debonair about this Western "Uncle Joe," who, with nothing but his own native wit and dauntless courage, boldly faced any proposition and all comers. As elsewhere stated, Reed usually finished in ten minutes. Cannon talked longer, but his speeches had the quality of finality.

After Mr. Cannon became Speaker (1903–11), James A. Tawney, of Minnesota, followed as chairman of Appropriations and Sereno E. Payne continued at the head of Ways and Means. Meantime, James R. Mann, of Illinois, by the closest and most persistent attention to floor work, gradually won his way to leadership. At first his party sympathies seemed negligible and his activities were resented. His amazing energy and impetus seemed to make him a personal, zealous, and autocratic instrument of the Speaker for killing or retarding certain classes of bills that tapped the Treasury, compelling members benefiting by such legislation to supplement the Chair's recognition with a promise of forbearance on the floor. This was an entirely new departure in parliamentary procedure. Previously resentment or dyspepsia had incited objection. But Mann stationed himself in a front seat, displayed copies of all bills reported, remained throughout each session, and halted every comer. He was not ill-natured or capricious. His adventurous action seemed to be guided by a judicial rather than a whimsical spirit, and when convinced of the propriety of a measure he ceased to intervene. But what won the House was the swiftness of his vision, the accuracy of his knowledge, and the ruthlessness with which his quick questions and ready replies disclosed weakness or mischief. Indeed, so welcome and invaluable did his activities become that upon Cannon's retirement Mann's party selected him as its candidate for Speaker. According to precedent this made him the titular as well as the real leader of the minority, and the thoroughness and far-seeing scope of his preparation to thwart the policy of an overwhelming majority disclosed an initiative and intellectual energy which events did nothing to weaken.

Opposed to Mann appeared Oscar W. Underwood, of Alabama, as floor leader (1911). Perhaps no one ever came into great power with less individual assertiveness. The choice of Champ Clark as Speaker, who had headed the minority on Ways and Means in the preceding

House, left Underwood the ranking member and without
a rival of sufficient strength to contest with him for the
majority leadership. He brought to the place an attractive personality. His gentle simplicity, easy-going manners, and freedom from egotism or personal ambition
seemed to deny the sense of high purpose and firmness
of mind which his presence conveyed. But when he
spoke, whether in the committee room or in the House,
he disclosed a masculine authority. There was nothing
vivid or swift or hot with passionate sympathy. His
quality was intellectual rather than imaginative. Yet,
like other products of modern political study, his sympathies were more popular than his slow, measured
speech, free from artifice or appeal, would indicate.
Before being installed as floor leader he had won envied
prestige as a successful legislator. Although never serving with the majority, or acting as official leader of the
minority, he had had a more than usually valuable experience through service on a variety of committees.
His prominence on Ways and Means opened a path to
distinction, and he traveled it conscientiously, speaking
without anger or sarcasm, and apparently without the
slightest inclination to play the rôle of an idealist, or to
present the visions of a dreamer. He saw real things as
a practical business man with a spacious understanding
and a sound judgment. Of course, his party believed in
him, and his opponents respected him. When he suddenly became floor leader, therefore, the House recognized him as the possessor of intellectual strength, having the tolerance and patience of a statesman, and the
steadying power of high character.

He had, too, an adventitious aid not shared by his predecessors; for, as elsewhere stated, the House, under the rules adopted in the Sixty-second Congress (1911–13), elected the members of the Committee on Ways and Means and endowed them with power to appoint other committees.[1] This prerogative was the Speaker's greatest asset, and when transferred to Ways and Means it gave Underwood, the dominating head of that Committee, a power to control legislation not possessed by former floor leaders.

This power he undoubtedly exercised in making up committees as it had theretofore been exercised by Speakers. Having in mind the recognition due to long service, he also kept in view the triumph of party policies as well as his own success, and so long as harmony existed within his party he was conspicuously its leader. But when, in the preparation of his tariff bill, the President differed with him as to duties on sugar and on wool, the former had his way. So, too, on the non-payment of tolls by coastwise vessels using the Panama Canal, to the support of which he felt himself bound by the explicit declaration of his party platform, the President easily bowled him and the platform over together. In other words, at crucial moments the overshadowing figure of the President obscured that of the floor leader. It is doubtful if a Speaker, possessing the power that formerly belonged to that office, could, under similar conditions, have accomplished more. His failure was not due to the unpopularity of his views, or to the ill-will of his colleagues, for no disaffection existed over com-

[1] See chap. v, p. 81.

mittee appointments or the management of the business of the House, while it was an open secret that at least a majority of his party endorsed its platform both as to revenue and to tolls. It was simply the inability of a floor leader, however strong his personality or potent the influence secured by the rules and practice of the House, to resist successfully a dominating President buttressed by the power of patronage.[1] But it is due to Mr. Underwood to add that his last overthrow occurred after his election to the Senate precluded the possibility of his succeeding himself as chairman of Ways and Means, thus leaving to members the game of securing post-offices unfettered by the chance of losing highly prized committee places in the next House.

[1] For further discussion of this power see chap. XVIII, pp. 381, 382.

CHAPTER VIII

PRIVILEGES, PAY, AND OBSEQUIES OF MEMBERS]

IF a member be indicted for a felony or other crime, prosecution is left to the local tribunal, and in case of conviction he may be expelled from the House; but if the conviction occur before his election, precedents uniformly deny the House jurisdiction of the offense. Thus, when one member resigned to escape expulsion and was subsequently reëlected, the House declined to act, for the reason that his constituents had reëlected him with full knowledge of his sin. "This has been so frequently decided," said Speaker Carlisle, "that it is no longer a matter of dispute." [1] When reëlected at a special election to the same Congress, however, the House declined to admit him. [2]

A member's freedom from arrest applies to writs or other processes in civil suits, and continues only when Congress is in session and while he is traveling to and from his home. The period for such travel is interpreted as a "convenient time," including sufficient opportunity to settle one's private affairs and to deviate from the usual route for rest, convenience, or because of family sickness. [3] Although conceded that a member who remained at home during a portion of the session was

---

[1] 48th Cong., 2d Sess., *Record*, pp. 5750–51.
[2] 41st Cong., 2d Sess., *Globe*, pp. 4669–74.
[3] 24 *Fed. Law Reporter*, p. 387.

neither in actual attendance on the House, nor going to or returning from his home, it was held that he could not be imprisoned under a mesne process in a civil suit, and when the House had knowledge of his confinement the Speaker issued a warrant to the sergeant-at-arms commanding him forthwith to take such member from the custody of sheriff, jailer, or any other person presuming to detain him. This promptly opened the prison door.[1] In like manner a member arrested and imprisoned during vacation obtained his freedom upon the assembling of Congress.

An assault upon a member is usually resented as a breach of privilege. In 1809 the House ignored the fact that the member assaulted was not in attendance, and that the cause of it in no wise related to his official duties.[2] A controversy over an appropriation bill between two members while on their way to the Capitol in an omnibus, which resulted in an assault, was regarded as a breach of privilege. A celebrated case occurred in 1866, when Josiah B. Grinnell, of Iowa, imputed cowardice to Lovell H. Rousseau, of Kentucky, a Federal general in the Civil War. After adjournment Rousseau assaulted Grinnell with a cane in the presence of three members, who admitted their intention to intervene had any one interfered. The House disapproved Grinnell's course as unjustified, but reprimanded Rousseau and censured his friends. Rousseau immediately resigned and was reëlected. The next year President Johnson appointed him a brigadier-general in the army. This

[1] 39th Cong., 2d Sess., *Journal*, pp. 103, 105.
[2] 11th Cong., 2d Sess., *Journal*, pp. 111, 123, 147–48.

smacks of the tension existing between Congress and the Executive in the days of Reconstruction.[1]

A challenge given outside the House was held to be a menace, and therefore a breach of privilege. Speaker Winthrop declared it well understood that if the life or person or liberty of a member was menaced in any way the House could properly act.[2] Indeed, the demand for an explanation of words spoken in debate, if made in a hostile manner, was in theory regarded the highest offense that could be committed against the House. For this privilege the Commons of England made their memorable resistance to the tyranny of Charles I. But in practice the challenge of one member by another provoked little attention. In 1838, when Jonathan Cilley, of Maine, and William J. Graves, of Kentucky, fought with rifles near the boundary line of Maryland and the District of Columbia, resulting in the death of the former, the report of the committee of investigation, recommending the expulsion of Graves, and the censure of Henry A. Wise, of Virginia, and George W. Jones, of Tennessee, who acted as seconds, was laid upon the table by a vote of 103 to 78. This closed the lamentable incident. The evidence showed that James Watson Webb, editor of the New York *Courier and Inquirer*, had stood sponsor for an article charging a member with corruption, and that Cilley, in his remarks moving a committee of inquiry, had reflected upon the character of Webb, who sent him a note by the hand of Graves. Cilley refused either to receive it or to assign any reason

---

[1] 39th Cong., 1st Sess., *Globe*, pp. 3194, 3544, 3818, 4009–17.
[2] 30th Cong., 1st Sess., *Globe*, p. 649.

for declining it other than that he chose to be drawn into no difficulty. This led to Graves's challenge, which Cilley unwisely accepted.

In the debate one member declared the gravamen of the charge rested in the sending of the challenge, and not in the fatal result. Another opposed the severity of the sentence, claiming that dueling had been frequent among members, and generally unnoticed and unpunished by the House. Doubt was even expressed as to its being a breach of privilege, since a rule, proposing to make it so, failed of adoption in 1809. The great majority thought any punishment too severe. "Graves may have been negligent of the privileges of the House," said a member of the committee, "but he did not intentionally offer any indignity to it." [1]

The historic assault of Preston S. Brooks, of South Carolina, upon Senator Sumner, of Massachusetts, three days after the latter's speech (1856), excited an ingenious argument that the attack, being inspired by the publication rather than by the delivery of his remarks, did not come within the Constitution, which limited protection to the delivery of a speech. Nor did the House have jurisdiction of the case, since the assault was not made either upon a member of the House or within it. There was a tendency, too, to plead extenuation on the ground of an excessive "chivalrous" spirit, although Clingman, of North Carolina, defended "the liberty of the cudgel" and justified the act. John H. Savage, of Tennessee, claimed that Brooks "merited the highest commendation," and that Sumner "did not

[1] 25th Cong., 2d Sess., *Globe*, pp. 200–01, 320, 329.

get a lick more than he deserved." Members of the majority, denouncing the assault fearlessly, maintained the power of the House to punish Brooks, but the vote to expel did not reach the required two thirds.

The privilege as to "speech" is not limited to words spoken in debate. It applies to written reports, to resolutions offered, and to the act of voting, if done vocally or by passing between tellers. In other words, a member cannot be questioned or impeached in any court or place outside of the House for whatever he may do or say in relation to the business before it. Speeches may be calumnious to the last degree, or hazardous to the public peace; yet their authors enjoy complete immunity. Even a letter of criticism written to a member, or addressed to the House, constitutes a breach of the privilege, although the Speaker held that a communication from a person assailed in debate, properly asking if the speech was correctly reported, did not come within the rule. But it is otherwise with disrespectful communications, impugning or questioning the motives of members, unless it be an absurd anonymous letter.[1]

These privileges are common to all constitutional governments, and are expected to give lawmakers a sense of entire freedom in denouncing wrongdoing, and in protecting them from arrests instigated by persons masking an unworthy design behind a pretended grievance; but they are not intended to license accusations founded on guesswork, or on the mere vagaries of a morbid imagination, or without any honest effort to get at the facts, and such malicious or reckless talkers may be called to order.

[1] 46th Cong., 2d Sess., *Record*, p. 2501.

It is then for the House to determine whether "the language is justifiable in view of the facts and evidence within the knowledge of the House." [1]

If a member attack through the press another member in his individual and not his representative character, no breach of privilege is involved. So, if a member outside the House charge another member with disreputable conduct before he became a member. It is otherwise if the attack occurs in debate, for words used upon the floor become disorderly and the member could properly be punished therefor. This is upon the ground that the use of any language upon the floor, derogatory to the personal character of a member, is calculated to provoke disturbance and disorder in the proceedings, and bring the body itself into contempt and disgrace. These reasons do not apply to the publication of the same words in a newspaper. [2]

A newspaper charge against a member, to involve a breach of privilege, must present a specific and serious attack, such as being influenced in his action as a representative, or making an unauthorized committee report, or receiving a sum of money for securing a government contract, or an office for a constituent, or abusing the franking privilege, or receiving an excess of mileage, or for entering into a conspiracy to defraud the Government; but not for a mere criticism of his relations with other members, or for being influenced by executive patronage, or for misreporting a speech, or printing remarks that the member denied using, or vaguely charg-

---

[1] 40th Cong., 2d Sess., *Globe*, p. 2945.
[2] 40th Cong., 2d Sess., Journal, pp. 650–53.

ing members generally with corruption. Nevertheless, general charges against members are frequently held to involve a breach of privilege. Although no names are given, newspaper allegations that certain members had entered into a corrupt speculation, or had abused the franking privilege, or had violated the law, without specifying the date of the offense, or had been paid money by an agent of a foreign government, involve a breach of privilege.

On the evidence of members who testified as to acts of bribery, the House held the person so charged guilty of contempt, and, after administering a reprimand, committed him until further orders. To what extent the House may punish for contempt other than its own members, however, depends upon the inquiry. Thus, the Supreme Court held it could punish a contumacious witness who refused to answer questions in an investigation relating to the integrity of its members, although such questions disclosed the affairs of a private citizen; [1] but when it committed one for refusing (1876) to testify to the history and character of a "real-estate pool" in which debtors of the United States had an interest, the court held that if the United States was a creditor of the defendant firm, the only legal redress was in a resort to the courts. "The Constitution," said the court, "expressly empowers the House to punish its own members for disorderly behavior, to compel their attendance upon its sessions, to judge of their election and qualifications, and to impeach officers of the Government, and in performing these functions it has the right to compel the

---

[1] *In re* John Anderson, 6 Wheaton, p. 204.

attendance of witnesses and their answers to proper
questions the same as courts of justice; but no person
can be punished for contumacy as a witness unless his
testimony is required in matters over which it has jurisdiction." [1]

Questions of privilege affect the safety and dignity of
the House collectively as well as the integrity of its
proceedings, and the rights, reputation, and conduct of
members individually in their representative character
only.[2] They relate among other things to the organization of the House; to its power to punish witnesses, members, and other persons for contempt; to the protection
of its records and files; the accuracy of its documents;
the seats of its members; and the right to declare vacant
the office of Speaker. Thus, a charge touching the com-
fort, convenience, health, censure, or the assault of members, or the conduct of an official or employee, or the
violation of the rule relating to admission to the floor, is
presented as a question of privilege, and has precedence
of all other questions except motions to adjourn.[3] But a
question of privilege must not be confused with a privileged question. The latter, which relates merely to the
order of business, gains its precedence by rule, while the
former springs from constitutional prerogatives which
give the House power to protect itself as an organ for
action, and to extend to members freedom to perform
their duties unmenaced and unmolested.

Nevertheless, the powers of the House enumerated in
the Constitution must not be confused with the privileges of the House. The right to legislate for the general

[1] 103 U.S., pp. 170–205.   [2] Rule IX.   [3] *Ibid.*

welfare is among these powers, but the proposals of laws do not become questions of privilege; otherwise, said Speaker Reed, "everything would become a question of privilege and end by making nothing a question of privilege." [1] For this reason subjects relating to the relations of the United States with other nations or peoples do not constitute questions of privilege unless the invasion of some prerogative of the House is alleged. Hence, Speaker Crisp held that a resolution simply recommending the recall of the United States Minister to Hawaii did not involve a question of privilege. "Although the relations of the United States to the Hawaiian Islands have been submitted to Congress the same as a great many other matters of moment," he said, "they do not constitute questions of privilege, but go to a committee, under our rules, to be considered and reported; and even then, unless expressly provided for, they are not what we know as 'privileged questions.'" [2]

An early custom left to the House the decision whether a proposition involved a question of privilege. Subsequently the Speaker determined it. But for many years an appeal from his decision has put the responsibility upon the House. Sometimes a Speaker in giving a preliminary determination goes wrong, but more often veteran members stumble, although guiding precedents are numerous. So distinguished a floor leader as Thaddeus Stevens objected to Henry J. Raymond presenting as a question of privilege the credentials of several claimants from Tennessee. Speaker Colfax declared that all

[1] 55th Cong., 2d Sess., *Record*, p. 3381.
[2] 53d Cong., 2d Sess., *Record*, p. 2425.

decisions held the other way.[1] Quite likely Stevens's dislike of Raymond rather than parliamentary ignorance inspired his objection, for he desired to crush the eminent journalist who had become the defender and patronage dispenser of President Johnson. Thus, on another occasion, Stevens objected to Raymond being furnished a pair, since the gentleman from New York, he said, found no difficulty in pairing with himself. Thereupon an excited supporter of Raymond exclaimed that a member, to escape the shafts of Stevens's bitter sarcasm, must "go it blind." This stirred Robert S. Hale, of New York, who, with an innocent expression, inquired the meaning of the phrase. Instantly Stevens flashed the retort: "It means following Raymond." This double shot was the more felicitous as Hale himself had followed Raymond in his support of Johnson.

A member whose private interests are concerned in any bill may not vote. Whether such an interest be personal is usually left to the decision of the member himself, and, although others may challenge his judgment, it is interesting to note that members have never shown a disposition to confuse direct and remote interests. Thus, when the renewal of the charter of the United States Bank came up in 1830 members who were stockholders promptly refused to vote. For the same reason several avoided voting for the bill extending the time for completing the Northern Pacific Railroad. Others who held stock in the Union and Central Pacific companies were not less modest when Congress legislated upon their payment of interest. Some of these cases affected a class

[1] 39th Cong., 1st Sess., *Globe*, p. 31.

as distinct from individuals, but members raised no opposition.

When the principle was applied to stockholders in national banks, however, the House thought it time to fix a limit governing private interests. Their interest, it was argued, is not distinct from the general interest, and in legislating on the whole question they do not act for themselves any more than do a few pensioned soldiers who vote for a general pension bill. Henry L. Dawes carried the matter a step further. "Shall the right of a member to vote upon a duty on cotton goods be challenged because he happens to be a cotton manufacturer? If so, the cotton-raiser, the sugar-maker, the farmer, and every gentleman in this House may have such a personal interest in a tariff bill that no one can vote for it." "One can go through the whole round of business," added Speaker Blaine, "and find on this floor gentlemen who, in common with many citizens outside of this House, have an interest in questions before the House. But they do not have that interest separate and distinct from a class, and, within the meaning of the rule, distinct from the public interest. The Chair, therefore, has no hesitation in overruling the point of order." [1]

Nor is it difficult to draw the line between proper and improper lobbying. "To lobby," as defined by Webster, "is to address or solicit members of a legislative body in the lobby or elsewhere away from the House, with a view to influence their vote. This is practiced by persons not belonging to the legislature." It is plain that so long as the means employed "to influence" are simply

[1] 43d Cong., 1st Sess., *Record*, pp. 3019, 3020.

to enlighten members respecting legislation before them
without suggesting or raising hope of reward, it is not
only proper, but often desirable. Indeed, the solicitation of constituents personally or by letter sometimes
leads to information of the importance of certain legislation to one's district. Nor is it necessarily improper
for associations to raise funds for defraying the expense
of publishing literature and of sending men to Washington to present reasons for the enactment of legislation
beneficial to them. For many years salaried representatives of labor, remaining at the Capital throughout each
session of Congress, have endeavored to help or to hinder
bills favorable or unfavorable to its interest. Attorneys
of other special interests frequently seek the attention
of members, and no well-informed person regards their
presentation of arguments as improper. They may add
to a member's information if they do not influence his
action, and so long as interviews are limited to arguments no wrong is done. Pending the passage of a tariff
bill lobby visitors are especially numerous and often decidedly annoying. To seek members again and again,
after an argument has been fully presented, although
neither unmoral nor illegal, becomes most wearisome,
and often harmful to the interest represented. In fact,
the giving of dinners had its origin in the desire of
constituents to find a suitable opportunity for presenting their views at times when members have leisure and
inclination to hear. Although such social occasions are
without the zone of impropriety, it is nevertheless true
that the later-day practice of flattering members and
their families by invitations to dinners, to theaters and

late luncheons, and on automobile rides, like the gift of railroad passes in the olden day, is obviously a sinister one. As a rule these attentions go to persons holding prominent committee positions, and it is to their credit that they are disinclined to accept them.

President Wilson's statement of May 27, 1913, provoked by the opposition to the tariff bill of that year, describes a lobby as "insidious" when "newspapers are filled with paid advertisements calculated to mislead the judgment of men"; when "money without limit is being paid to sustain such a lobby"; and when "great bodies of astute men seek to create an artificial opinion and to overcome the interests of the public for their private profit." Very naturally an investigation followed his announcement of the existence of such a lobby. It was admitted that sugar and other interests had raised money to defray the expense of printing literature and to send their representatives to present arguments to Congress explaining why the pending bill would injure them. But no corruption or attempts at corruption appeared. Indeed, the opinion obtained in some circles that the President himself had been the chief influence in seeking to persuade members from the exercise of their conscientious judgment.[1]

The abuse of parliamentary privilege, as well as the unpardonable conduct of some members, has not infrequently been the occasion of bitter and sweeping condemnation. In several instances which can readily be brought to mind the misdeeds of a few have caused the

[1] For further discussion of the President's influence, see chap. XVIII, pp. 381, 382.

whole membership to suffer in the public mind; and yet it is common experience, at least as old as Henry Clay's observation, that the longer one serves in the House the more confidence he gains in the integrity of his associates. Compared to the great number whose lives attest their probity, the faithless ones numerically have been unimportant. In the Forty-first Congress (1870) a member from North Carolina resigned to escape expulsion for selling a cadetship. A few years later (1876) George F. Hoar, of Massachusetts, declared that he had heard the chairman of the Committee on Military Affairs demand the expulsion of four others for similar conduct. Yet for forty years the repetition of such an offense has not been disclosed. This is the more remarkable, since such appointments are highly prized and often sought with indiscreet persistency.

In 1872 the Crédit Mobilier scandal, which involved a dozen prominent members as conspicuous for integrity as for ability, filled the press and the public mind with most distressing suspicions, until it seemed as if wrongdoing, growing out of the Civil War, of inflated values, and of the sudden enfranchisement of millions of slaves, had corrupted the whole House. But after hearing the evidence the committee, composed of men of irreproachable character, reported that with three exceptions [1] the accused members, in becoming purchasers of Crédit Mobilier stock, had indicated no intention of even breaching the proprieties. Of those acquitted one afterwards became President, another

[1] Oakes Ames, of Massachusetts, James Brooks, of New York, and Schuyler Colfax, of Indiana.

Secretary of the Treasury, and several passed to the Senate, while all were returned to public life.

The Act of 1873, known as the "Salary Grab Act," very properly created great popular indignation. Its baseness was in the retroactive clause, giving five thousand dollars bonus to each member of a dead Congress. Although the next House immediately repealed the act, and a majority of the members refused to take the money, or, having taken it, promptly returned it, the public classified its authors and beneficiaries with the Crédit Mobilier corruptionists, whose avarice had outweighed their sworn duty to safeguard the Government's treasury. Nevertheless, in justice to those who preceded and succeeded them, it should be noted that with this exception members have hesitated to meet with additional compensation the ever-increasing expenses in a growing capital city. From 1789 to 1818 their pay amounted to six dollars per day for each day's attendance. In the latter year it was increased to eight. In 1856 it became $3000 per year. Ten years later, when gold held a war premium, it was raised to $5000, and forty years afterwards (1906) to $7500. There are also perquisites. Travel between Washington and a member's home each year by the usual route is twenty cents a mile; stationery to the amount of $120 per year is granted; an office is furnished; and $1500 a year allowed for a clerk. Still more important is the franking privilege, which extends to all letters on congressional business and to all documents prepared by the Government or published in the *Congressional Record*.

So long as this privilege was confined to its original

purpose of correspondence and the dissemination of speeches, it provoked little criticism. But in more recent years, especially since nominations by primary elections have converted it into a vehicle of purely political service, the belief very generally obtains that it ought to be abridged or abolished. By means of it a member, with little or no expense to himself, may circularize his district, asking all voters to indicate such bulletins, documents, and seeds as they may desire. To facilitate answers, franked and addressed envelopes may be enclosed. The supplies are then forwarded under frank. In other words, a member's clerk becomes the head of a campaign bureau, with the hope that franked favors may induce grateful constituents to remember the sender on primary and election days. Moreover, political documents and party appeals, once published in the *Record*, immediately become frankable, and whether printed at government or private expense may be sent out by the ton from any political headquarters. In this way Henry George's work, entitled "Progress and Poverty," — a book of several hundred pages, — became a public document which admiring friends of the great single-taxer freely circulated at the expense of the Government. The burden upon the postal department thus becomes unlimited.

The funeral expenses of members are defrayed from the contingent fund of the House. Originally the mileage allowance limited such payments, but in 1802 it became the custom to pay the entire expense if the funeral was held in Washington. Later, such charges, including those of an attending committee, were paid wherever the death and funeral occurred. At one time these sad rites assumed the nature of scandalous junkets, and although drastic reforms have of late years regulated the expense and moderated their character, the wants of attending committees are not overlooked.

The decease of a member was formerly announced as soon as the House convened, followed by several impromptu eulogies, the adoption of suitable resolutions, and the selection of an attending committee. The House then adjourned for the day and occasionally until after the funeral. As a further mark of respect the member's desk was draped and for thirty days members wore a band of crape on the left arm. Gradually this ceremony became more perfunctory, the announcement, resolutions, and adjournment being purposely delayed until the close of the day's business. Some weeks afterward, usually on Sunday, a dozen or more eulogies are read to a few members, and to the family and friends who occupy seats in the gallery. The custom of wearing crape entirely disappeared in the Forty-eighth Congress (1884), but the draping of seats continued until the removal of the desks in 1913. Upon the death of Michael C. Kerr, the only Speaker who died in office, the chair remained draped until his term would have expired. After the decease of John Quincy Adams the entire hall remained draped for thirty days.

Occasionally the funeral of a member, dying in Washington, is held in the hall of the House. Among those so honored were Jonathan Cilley, of Maine, who fell in a duel (1838); Lewis Williams, of North Carolina, long the "Father of the House" (1842); John Quincy Adams, of Massachusetts, who died in the Speaker's room (1848); William D. Kelley, of Pennsylvania (1890); Nelson Dingley, of Maine (1899); and Sereno E. Payne, of New York (1915). Upon invitation the highest officials at the seat of Government often attend these services, the order of their entrance and the manner of their reception being fixed by rules governing all public functions held in the House. As the Senate and other bodies approach, the Speaker taps with his gavel and members rise. Thereupon the doorkeeper, without addressing the Speaker, announces, "the Vice-President and the Senate of the United States"; "the Chief Justice and the Associate Justices of the Supreme Court of the United States"; "the Ambassadors and the members of the Diplomatic Corps to the United States"; "the President and the members of his Cabinet." Each body occupies the seats assigned it, the House sitting on the left of the Speaker, the Senate on the right, the Supreme Court in front of the Senate, the Diplomatic Corps in front of the House, and the President and Cabinet in front of the Supreme Court. The General of the Army and the Admiral of the Navy, when present, sit at the right of the Diplomatic Corps. At the funeral of John Quincy Adams, the President sat with the Speaker on his right and the Vice-President on his left.

Only in four instances has the House taken action upon the decease of former members except when promoted to the office of President. In 1883 it adopted resolutions of respect upon the death of Alexander H. Stephens. Similar respect was also shown former Speakers Blaine (1893), Reed (1902) and Henderson (1906).

CHAPTER IX

CREATING AND COUNTING A QUORUM

THE Constitution provides that "a majority of the House shall constitute a quorum to do business." [1] The important question is, therefore, what constitutes a majority? Speaker Clay held that it was one more than one half of all possible members. Thus, if an apportionment provided for a total of 400 members, 201 constituted a quorum. This ruling remained unquestioned until the Civil War deprived the House of many members. Thereupon Speaker Grow declared a quorum to be a majority of those chosen. Upon the point that the Chair could have no knowledge of the members chosen except as they appeared and qualified, the Speaker expressly withheld an opinion. The Senate treated Grow's decision as meaning "chosen and living," adding in 1868 the words, "and sworn." This excluded the count of Senators elect from ten Southern States, the existence of whose governments Congress had declared illegal.[2]

In the House Grow's decision seemed inadequate when vacancies interfered with party action, and Speaker Randall, in holding a quorum present, ven-

[1] Art. I, sec. 5.
[2] By the Act of July 19, 1867, Congress declared illegal the reconstructed State Governments in Virginia, North and South Carolina, Georgia, Florida, Alabama, Mississippi, Louisiana, Texas, and Arkansas. (15 Stat. L., p. 4.)

tured the opinion, without deciding the point, that vacancies necessarily lessened the number required to make a quorum.[1] Speaker Carlisle treated this question as an open one.[2] But Speaker Reed, disinclined to walk a trembling plank, sustained Randall's suggestion. "Prior to 1861," he said, "it had always been held that a quorum consisted of a majority of all the possible members. After the rebellion had caused a large number of constituencies to refuse to elect, it was held (July 19, 1861) that a quorum consisted of a majority of 'those chosen.' This language was susceptible of two meanings; first, of members originally chosen, and second, of members chosen then alive. The precedents make it evident that the latter meaning was intended. Such was the decision made by the Senate in 1861, Reverdy Johnson voting in the affirmative; and as late as March 24, 1886, that body, on the death of Senator Miller, of California, had its quorum reduced to thirty-eight. Mr. Randall, in the *Record* of February 25, 1879, intimated that he held the same view." [3]

Several years later the question arose whether members chosen but not sworn should be counted. After reviewing the action of the Senate, which excluded those not sworn, Speaker Cannon held that when "the House is once organized a quorum consists of a majority of those members chosen, sworn, and living, whose membership has not been terminated by resignation or by the action of the House." [4] This decision seemed to cover

[1] 45th Cong., 3d Sess., *Record*, p. 1908.
[2] 49th Cong., 1st Sess., *Record*, p. 4338.
[3] 51st Cong., 2d Sess., *Journal*, p. 370.
[4] 59th Cong., 1st Sess., *Record*, p. 5354.

every possible condition, and although the House, unlike the Senate, has failed to embody it in a rule, it is now the accepted practice, and will undoubtedly be upheld by the United States Supreme Court if the question is ever submitted to it.

When the House elects a President of the United States a quorum consists of one or more members from two thirds of the States. If the House be in Committee of the Whole one hundred make a quorum. This number dates from 1891. Prior to that time the quorum of the Committee was the same as that of the House.

The presence of a quorum is always presumed unless a member declares to the contrary. After such a declaration the Speaker may count the House if, immediately preceding the announcement, a yea and nay vote showed a quorum present. This custom, which began with Speaker Macon,[1] continued without question until Carlisle held that the Chair could count only when the previous question had been ordered. Even if the declaration of "No quorum" came before the reading of the Journal, he held it to be the Chair's duty to cause a roll-call.[2] In 1890 Speaker Reed counted a quorum, whether preceded by a roll-call or not, including in his count all members in sight within or without the bar.

But if a count or roll-call discloses "No quorum," a yea and nay quorum must appear before the House can proceed to business. To secure it the doors are closed and the names of members called. Absentees for whom no excuse is made may, by order of a majority of those

[1] 9th Cong., 2d Sess., *Annals*, p. 655.
[2] 50th Cong., 1st Sess., *Record*, p. 9607.

present, be sent for and arrested wherever found. During the absence of a quorum neither business nor debate may proceed even by unanimous consent. Nor can the point of "No quorum" be withdrawn, or the vote be reconsidered, or a motion for a recess be entertained, although the Speaker may declare the House in recess when an hour arrives previously fixed for such an intermission. In fact, nothing is admissible in the absence of a quorum except motions to adjourn, for a call of the House, and to excuse absentees.

The absence of a quorum began making trouble after John Quincy Adams refused to vote (1832) when within the House. The rules required every member present, unless excused, to give his vote one way or the other. This followed the practice of the House of Commons, and members of the American House cheerfully complied with it. But when the House refused to excuse Adams from voting on a motion to censure William Stanberry, of Ohio, the former declined to answer to his name. In the acrimonious debate the dangerous consequences sure to follow the establishment of such a precedent received full consideration. Nevertheless, Adams, in spite of remonstrances and threats, stood firm, claiming that he acted from conscientious motives.[1] A few years later the disastrous effects so clearly prophesied began to accumulate, Adams himself being an early sinner. "If only five of the thirty-four Whigs had had the firmness to abstain from voting," he wrote, "the majority would have been compelled to adjourn for want of a quorum."[2]

[1] 22d Cong., 1st Sess., *Debates*, p. 3895. [2] *Diary*, vol. x, p. 243.

This practice of blocking public business by sitting silently in one's seat deeply and quickly rooted itself, because the House procedure, then and afterward, required that a final vote must show a quorum present and voting. The House of Commons deemed the presence of a quorum sufficient to establish the validity of any action, and American writers on parliamentary law held likewise. Crocker, one of the ablest, said: "If a quorum does not vote, but is in fact present, the secretary should make entry in the records that on a count of the assembly it was found a quorum was present." [1] It was argued, too, that the framers of the Constitution, by authorizing a smaller number than a quorum to compel the attendance of absent members, evidently considered attendance sufficient; otherwise, if more was needed, they would have provided it. Moreover, the Constitution declares that a majority *of the House*, not a majority *voting*, shall constitute a quorum to do business.

But these reasons availed nothing. Under the practice of the House, the absence of a quorum frequently occurred with two thirds of the members present. The absurdity of such a condition appealed to everybody, for why order the arrest of absentees, if, after their return, their silence destroyed their presence? Yet Speakers found reasons for declining to count a quorum. Colfax thought such a procedure would be revolutionary. When members in the Thirty-eighth Congress resented the lack of such a rule, Speaker Blaine begged "to remind the House that the principle has been the foundation probably for the greatest legislative frauds

[1] *Principles of Procedure*, sec. 114.

ever committed. Where a quorum, in the judgment of the Chair, has been declared present against the result of a roll-call, these proceedings in the different legislatures have brought scandal on their names. There can be no record like the call of the yeas and nays; and from that there is no appeal. The moment you clothe your Speaker with power to go behind your roll-call and assume that there is a quorum in the hall, why, gentlemen, you stand on the very brink of a volcano." [1]

These positive declarations, if they chilled the advocates of reform, did not destroy belief that some way existed to secure a record quorum other than by a roll-call. In 1880 John Randolph Tucker, of Virginia, having the courage of his great namesake, moved an amendment to the rules providing that when a quorum fails to respond, a call of the House should immediately follow, and if those present, voting and not voting, make a majority, the Speaker should declare a quorum present. [2] This suggestion provoked ironical laughter and a speech from James A. Garfield. "Who shall control the Speaker's seeing?" he asked. "How do we know that he may not, for his own purposes, see forty members more than are here? What protection have gentlemen when he says he sees a quorum, if he cannot convert that seeing into a list of names on the call of a yea and nay vote? This would let in the one-man power in a far more dangerous way than has ever occurred before. It would enable him to bring a dying man from his sick bed into this hall, and make his presence, against his will, and, per-

[1] 43d Cong., 2d Sess., *Record,* p. 1734.
[2] 46th Cong., 2d Sess., *Record,* pp. 575-76.

haps, in his delirium, constitute a quorum so that some partisan measure might be carried out over his body." [1]

Garfield did not always speak the last word. He usually led his party in an attack, and afterward left the discussion to others more persistent if not more positive. But in this instance his rhetorical broadside so quickly shattered Tucker's proposition that when Eppa Hunton, of Virginia, whose ability had won him a place on the Electoral Commission in 1877, supported Garfield's view of the matter, Democrats and Republicans, exhibiting their agreement by loud applause, indicated that no reason existed for further argument. But Thomas B. Reed, of Maine, then a young member, just beginning his second term, thought otherwise. At least he secured the floor and added a few crisp sentences that lifted him at once out of the ordinary. "The Constitution idea of a quorum is not the presence of a majority of the members," he said, "but a majority of the members present and participating in the business of the House. It is not the visible presence of members, but their judgments and their votes that the Constitution calls for. This is a privilege [to refuse to vote] of which every minority has availed itself. . . . It is a valuable privilege for the country that the minority shall have the right by this extraordinary mode of proceeding to call the attention of the country to measures which a party, in a moment of madness and of party feeling, is endeavoring to force upon the citizens of the land." [2] This speech had the ring of a new coin. Garfield had reiterated in a wonderful rhetorical picture the old familiar argument of over-counting,

[1] 46th Cong., 2d Sess., *Record*, p. 576.　[2] *Ibid.*, p. 578.

a danger to which Blaine had impressively referred in his nervous, excitable manner. But Reed found a deeper reason. Even if a Speaker counted honestly the principle was wrong. The mere presence of a member was nothing. The Constitution demanded his "judgment and vote." Moreover, he characterized the refusal to vote as highly patriotic, since it tended to alarm the country whenever a party, in a moment of madness, sought to harm the people. Thus did Reed become the determined defender of a "disappearing quorum."

In the mean time this favorite form of obstruction spread over the country, invading state legislatures, municipalities, school boards, and even church assemblies. The silent member thought himself a destructionist as well as an obstructionist. Finally the courts spoke. In New Hampshire it was held that "the exercise of the lawmaking power is not to be stopped by the mere silence and inaction of some of the lawmakers who are present." The court in Indiana, expressing the same view, declared "the rule we have asserted is a very old one." Courts in Maine, Illinois, Tennessee, Ohio, and Kentucky gave similar decisions. The rules of judicatories adopted by the Presbyterian General Assembly declared that "silent members" must be considered as acquiescing with the majority.

Other parliamentary bodies rebelled against such obstruction. In 1883 the Democrats, controlling the New York Senate, wished to remove the commissioner of the capitol, and when Republican senators maintained silence, David B. Hill, then lieutenant-governor and president of the Senate, made a quorum by counting those present who refused to vote. It is peculiarly the duty of the president, he said in substance, to see if a quorum is present. His certificate must evidence that fact. No precise method is prescribed as to how he shall ascertain it, and no law makes the roll-call its only evidence. The presence of senators is a physical fact, known to the president and to the clerk. If they vote, he is bound to make a record of it, and if they are present and refuse to vote, he should make a record of that fact also. If a stranger occupies a senator's seat and responds to his name, it is the duty of the clerk not to record the vote and of the president not to allow it to be recorded. The presence or absence of a response, therefore, is not absolutely conclusive. Whether a senator is present and responds is a question for the observation of the officers of the Senate. If they refuse to vote, they are not absentees, because they are in fact present. No proceeding can be instituted to compel their attendance, because they are not absent, and if really absent, why compel their presence if silence makes them in effect still absent? [1]

This able ruling attracted little attention at the time. Opposition senators called it "a Democratic trick." Several journals thought it a "partisan ruling," one paper suggesting that "at least one of the reform mayors advanced to high office last fall has already proved a failure." [2] But it provoked no discussion of the principle involved. Indeed, it would probably have passed

[1] Delivered March 13, 1883, and read to the House of Representatives on January 30, 1890. See 51st Cong., 1st Sess., *Record*, pp. 952–53.

[2] New York *Times*, March 14, 1883.

unnoticed had not the measure legislated a Republican out of office.

Two years later the Tennessee Assembly, in which two thirds of the members constituted a quorum, followed this precedent. A Republican minority of more than one third refused to vote for a new registration law, and the Speaker, directing the clerk to count those present not voting, declared the bill duly passed.

These precedents had no influence in the National House. In fact, Carlisle's administration tended to encourage the "disappearing quorum." On one occasion, when a few members reduced the proceedings to roll-calls for eight consecutive days, he refused to count the House unless the previous question had been ordered, holding that a yea and nay vote must answer every shout of "No quorum." At times conditions became pitiable. Never was man, in mind and spirit, more heartily and vividly and incessantly alive than Carlisle. Although holding himself under stoical self-control, he liked fighting. Discussion and argument were his delight, and being a confirmed intellectualist he stood rocklike by his intellectual conclusions. This explains his apparent helplessness in the absence of a quorum. He sincerely believed a visible presence insufficient until it became an answering one, and rather than surrender this conclusion, he preferred roll-calls and humiliating delays.

Thomas B. Reed probably reached the intellectual conclusion, which he announced in 1880 and reaffirmed in 1882, as carefully as Carlisle arrived at his; but when he became Speaker, with a majority of less than a dozen

votes, he knew that a quorum could rarely if ever be
marshaled to overcome a filibuster. Under these circumstances it is not strange, perhaps, that he evidenced
the disposition that controlled him in the Forty-seventh
Congress.[1] It is not known just when he made up his
mind to count a quorum. The need of reform during
Carlisle's Speakership affected him deeply, and although
he gave no sign of having modified his views until John
Dalzell, of Pennsylvania, on January 30, 1890, called up
the contested election case of Smith *vs*. Jackson,[2] he had
grown slowly into the conviction that the traditional
procedure had broken under the strain of increased business. Only the fear that his own party might not sustain
him brought embarrassment, and in that event he had
determined to resign, retire from the House, and practice law in New York, entering the office of Elihu Root.[3]

Dalzell's service began in the preceding Congress.
He had already won high distinction at the Pittsburg
bar, and his whole career in the House during twenty-
six years was destined to become one long parliamentary
success. Even at this early date he could hold his own
against any antagonist, and when he made his motion
to take up the Smith-Jackson case, he opened the storm-
iest and most violent scenes in the history of Congress.
Crisp raised the question of consideration, and the roll-
call showed 162 voting, three less than a quorum.[4] Im-

[1] See chap. x, p. 197.
[2] See chap. xvi, p. 326.
[3] Samuel W. McCall, *Life of Thomas B. Reed*, p. 167.
[4] The House consisted, after the death of William D. Kelley, of
Pennsylvania, of 329 members, a quorum being 165. 51st Cong., 1st
Sess., *Record*, p. 922.

mediately came the cry of "No quorum!" Thereupon Speaker Reed directed the clerk to note upon the Journal the names of 41 members whom he reported present and refusing to vote. Upon that record he declared a quorum present and the consideration of the election case in order. In his ruling the Speaker referred to the New York and Tennessee precedents, to the Speaker's practice in the House of Commons, and especially to the real scope of the Constitution compelling the attendance of members. "It is a question," he declared, "simply of the actual presence of a quorum, and the determination of that is entrusted to the presiding officer in almost all instances. There is a provision in the Constitution which declares that the House may establish rules for compelling the attendance of members. If members can be present and refuse to exercise their functions and cannot be counted as a quorum, that provision would seem to be entirely nugatory. Inasmuch as the Constitution provides for their attendance only, that attendance is enough. If more was needed, the Constitution would have provided for more."

To excuse his speech made in 1880, he referred to the Tucker amendment, adding that "the evils which have resulted from the other course were not then as apparent as now, and no such careful study had been given the subject as has been given to it since." Then, as a sort of appendix to his decision, he caused to be read the full text of Lieutenant-Governor Hill's opinion.[1] An appeal from this ruling again showed the absence of a quorum. Thereupon the Speaker, without hurry or hesitation,

[1] 51st Cong., 1st Sess., *Record*, pp. 949-60.

repeated his former action of counting those present who failed to vote. He also declined to entertain further appeal on the ground of its being dilatory, suggesting that the precedent had been fully established.

After this, pandemonium reigned in the House for several hours. Excited members rushed through the aisles, filled the area in front of the clerk's desk, and threateningly ascended the steps toward the Speaker, denouncing him as "tyrant" and "czar." In Blaine's phrase it seemed as if the House "stood on the very brink of a volcano." To those who witnessed the commotion it recalled Macaulay's description of a disturbance in the House of Commons. "I have never seen such unseemly demeanor or heard such scurrilous language in Parliament," wrote the distinguished historian. "Lord Norreys was making all sorts of noises. Lord Maidstone was so ill-mannered that I hope he was drunk. At last, after much grossly indecent conduct, a furious outbreak took place. O'Connell was so rudely interrupted that he used the expression 'beastly bellowings.' Then rose such an uproar as no mob at Covent Garden Theater — no crowd of Chartists in front of a hustings — ever equaled. Men on both sides stood up, shook their fists, and bawled at the top of their voices. O'Connell raged like a mad bull. . . . At last the tumult ended from a physical weariness. It was past one, and the steady bellowers had been howling since six o'clock." [1]

Reed had led the minority for eight years. His knowledge of the House procedure, his acquaintance with Opposition leaders, and his experience in playing the

[1] *Diary*, Thursday, June 11, 1840.

parliamentary game to the limit, thoroughly equipped him for such a contest, and although excitement changed to exasperation and language dropped at times to the level of a brothel, he gave no evidence of disturbance, much less of fear. In one of his impressive appearance, giant-like stature, and deep, penetrating gaze, it was impossible to imagine the existence of such a quality even had a gun been leveled at his head. Nor could one discern in gesture or in accent the slightest sign of resentment. He counted coolly, he listened patiently, and he spoke pleasantly, using the lower tones of his voice, which were of great sweetness. "I deny your right, Mr. Speaker, to count me as present, and I desire to read from the parliamentary law on that subject," shouted a member as he held up the book in his hand. With his customary coolness and drawl, Reed replied: "The Chair is making a statement of fact that the gentleman from Kentucky is here. Does he deny it?" This simple question and the laughter that followed indicated the strength of his position. In fact, he acted as one inspired by the consciousness not only of being right, but of feeling sure that his loudest and most riotous opponent would in time approve and follow the new departure. Nevertheless, when resting for brief intervals in the seclusion of his private room, he relieved himself of a pent-up fury that struck terror to the heart of Amos L. Allen, his amiable college classmate and devoted clerk. After such an exhibition of feeling it seemed unhuman that he could again preside with gentle, calm firmness. But as he began, so he continued to the end, betraying no sign of the unquenchable fire within, except that occasionally, with a powerful, strident voice, reaching the farthest corner of the great chamber, he dropped a sentence of destructive ridicule, which, for the moment at least, stilled the uproar and threw his party supporters into cheers.

Nevertheless, Reed's procedure opened the door to honest criticism. His speech, in 1880, stoutly reaffirmed in 1882, made his present action a parliamentary somersault. Indeed, the House had never witnessed a more picturesque exhibition of such mental gymnastics. The suddenness of his conversion, too, impressed members who had long abhorred the disappearing quorum as an insincere performance, otherwise he must have previously said a word, at least, in discouragement of the practice. If it had reached the dignity of a national scandal in 1890, as he intimated, it certainly merited rebuke in 1889, when it paralyzed business under Speaker Carlisle. Thus his former silence, contrasted with his present activity, credited him with simply playing a necessary partisan game, inspired neither by principle nor patriotism. His adversaries, measuring the effect of this advantage, made merry at his expense, quoting his own words in defense of their noisy demonstrations. Once, when too jubilant, his demand for order brought out loud shouts of derisive laughter.

The scope of his ruling did not relieve his embarrassment. It answered neither the objection of Garfield nor his own potent suggestion that "it is not the visible presence of members, but their judgments and their votes that the Constitution calls for." If this was true in 1880, why did it not apply in 1890? Nor did his decision disclose a thorough study of the subject. He made no reference t) the numerous court decisions touching the silence or inaction of members, or to the decrees of church assemblies. His declaration, too, that the minority denied the right of the majority to rule was evasive, since the only quorum in evidence was created by count and not by votes. It was evident, also, that reliance on the New York precedent had not materially strengthened his position, for Governor Hill's tortuous political course did not commend his methods to the discriminating student.

But the severest strictures clustered about his failure to adopt a code of rules upon the organization of the House. This was the traditional course observed for fifty Congresses, and his procedure under general parliamentary law, without deigning to assign a reason, gave rise to much speculation. It also emphasized the charge of exercising doubtful powers. With a code once adopted, it was said, obedience would become a plain duty and filibusters would be put in the wrong. But the absence of specific rules authorizing his parliamentary changes strengthened the position of the minority, which claimed that the House, being without a constitutional quorum, was doing business simply on the Speaker's declaration, based upon what he thought he saw. Garfield's telling sentences, delivered in 1880, became the minority's keynote. The accidental counting of one or two absent members by a temporary occupant of the chair emphasized the great orator's question, "How do we know that he may not see forty members more than are here?" Against such procedure a portion of the independent press arrayed itself. "To such methods," said the *Nation*, "we advise every kind of opposition short of violence. Members are bound to obstruct by all peaceable means the transaction of business until rules are adopted, and to protest against the Speaker's conduct, persistently and vociferously, whenever the occasion arises." [1]

Nevertheless, throughout the long and exciting daily sessions the Speaker displayed a consciousness that the Constitution contemplated such a procedure, and that the country's business required it. Besides, the open avowal, voiced in his decision, that he had learned by experience to disdain the consistency which conceals conscientious changes in judgment, recalled a former declaration made under similar conditions. "I do not promise members to give them wisdom of adamant," he said. "I do not promise them I shall not change my opinion when I see good reason for doing it. I only promise that I will give them honestly what my opinion is at the time. They must take their chances of its being for eternity." [2] This equaled the high display of judicial equipoise exhibited by Lord Chancellor Hardwicke when he said: "These are the reasons which incline me to alter my opinion, and I am not ashamed of doing it, for I always thought it a much greater reproach to a judge to continue in his error than to retract it." It added to Reed's prestige, moreover, that no one could compete with him in parliamentary authority. Randall died in April, 1890, and Carlisle passed to the Senate in the following month. Although Reed himself had been

[1] February 6, 1890. [2] 49th Cong., 1st Sess., *Record*, p. 210.

in the House but twelve years, so rapidly do changes occur that only twelve of the three hundred and twenty-nine members had preceded his entrance.

Of these twelve veterans none regarded the new procedure when finally established as extremely offensive. It curbed an impulsive minority quick to resent fancied snubs, but by eliminating delay it increased the time for discussion and made the work easier. With a flush of energy, however, opponents of the drastic innovation noisily resisted its withering influence. Charles F. Crisp, of Georgia, with a keen intuition of popular impulses, seized the opportunity to lead his party as the apologist if not the champion of a disappearing quorum. Indeed, he evinced such a bold and steady hostility to the Reed Rules that in the next Congress it opened his way to the Speakership. His election restored the old procedure and his large majority enabled him to avoid the long, dreary interruptions occasioned by a disappearing quorum, which saddened the closing years of Carlisle's service. Even in the Fifty-third Congress the Speaker's party had thirty-eight more than a quorum. But sickness, repair of political fences, and other causes for absence had dissipated this advantage by March, 1894, and when Reed discovered it, he determined to force Crisp to count a quorum. For three years he had sought such an opportunity. Moreover, he was just the man to lead in a contest of that character. It inspired if it did not justify audacity, gave him a chance to use his remarkable power of sarcasm and rhetoric, and made the goal, if he reached it, a monument to his parliamentary skill and courage.

The struggle centered in an effort to stop the approval of the Journal. Until its approval no business could be transacted. Another advantage consisted in the right of one fifth of the members to demand a yea and nay roll-call. By refusing to vote for approval, therefore, the minority could break a quorum, while by creating one on a call of the House the question immediately recurred on the approval of the Journal. This proved an endless chain. The absence of a quorum compelled a call of the House, and as often as this established a quorum, it was broken on a vote to approve. Thus, day after day Reed kept the House in continual roll-calls unless it preferred to adjourn, and adjournment did not avoid approving the Journal.

This condition sorely vexed the Speaker. He had staked everything to avoid a count. Motions were declared dilatory, points of order were decided without giving reasons, and appeals were denied. Threats of arrest, the employment of additional deputy sergeants-at-arms, and appeals to absentees, testified to his efforts to collect a quorum. But nothing availed him. Indeed, Crisp was as helpless as Sir Robert Peel on the night that Disraeli divided his party. No rule could save him, since Reed acted under a provision of the Constitution, and no special order could be secured until a quorum could be marshaled. According to William M. Springer, of Illinois, one of the Speaker's busiest lieutenants, "two days of actual work were not accomplished in a month."[1] In fact, Charles Stewart Parnell never had the House of Commons more at his mercy than Thomas B. Reed

[1] 53d Cong., 2d Sess., *Record*, p. 4666.

had the House of Representatives. Yet, if so disposed, Speaker Crisp, like Speaker Brand of the British House, had power to end the tie-up. But he still hesitated. He sought to find a way of his own invention, and one morning his Committee on Rules proposed the plan of fining all unexcused members ten dollars each whenever they failed to vote on the question of approving the Journal.[1] This was parliamentary if not manly, and it quickly drew a shattering shot from Reed. Fixing his eyes on the Speaker, he declared that "gentlemen ought to be able to do their work without turning this House into a justice of the peace shop, with ten dollars jurisdiction, less than one half we have in the little State of Maine."[2] The prolonged laughter, which ran into shouts of applause, made the silence that followed oppressive, for no one could muster a reply. The next evening the majority held a caucus. All admitted that business could not longer go on under such conditions, and in the absence of some new device it was agreed that the Speaker, before every roll-call, should appoint two tellers, one from each side, who should note those present refusing or failing to vote, and upon their report the Chair should declare a quorum present.[3]

This was the Reed Rule. It differed slightly in method, but it counted a quorum. Reed noted the members present who did not vote and announced a quorum. Crisp appointed two tellers for the purpose and upon their report announced a quorum. In other words, the caucus had surrendered to the minority, and the decision

---

[1] 53d Cong., 2d Sess., *Record*, p. 4501. [2] *Ibid.*, p. 4510.
[3] *Ibid.*, p. 4660 (April 16, 1894).

that followed proved a threnody. Benjamin E. Russell, of Georgia, a new member, declared it ridiculous for his party, with thirty-eight members more than a quorum, to invoke such an exceptional and revolutionary measure.[1] Others expressed similar views. William Jennings Bryan, then serving his second and last term in the House, opposed it because, contrary to the law in many States, it permitted the fraction of a majority to coin a bill into law. This objection appeared in the Constitutional Convention, some preferring that more than a majority ought to be required for a quorum, and in particular cases, if not in all, more than a majority of a quorum for a decision. But the Constitution simply requires that a majority shall constitute a quorum, thus leaving the decision of a question to the majority of that quorum. It sometimes happens that "a minority of a quorum" decides a question. This occurs, of course, only when 'the majority of a quorum, by its silence, allows it.

The speech of Constantine B. Kilgore, of Texas, also attracted attention. Although not in any sense an eloquent speaker, Kilgore was fluent, positive, and rather droll. It did not occur to him that there could be two sides to any matter of discussion. In opposing the Reed Rule he had been ably active, and the vigorous applause which now greeted his recognition, advised the House that his views, if singular even to the verge of being Quixotic, found favor in the galleries as well as on the floor. Rules, he said, should be made not to expedite business, but to hinder hasty and inconsiderate legisla-

[1] 53d Cong., 2d Sess., *Record*, p. 4666.

tion. Important and necessary measures need no aid from rules. It is the pernicious bill in the interest of jobs and schemes of plunder that need despotic methods like the proposed rule, which enables a Speaker and the tellers, if only ninety members vote for a measure, to pass it by counting eighty-nine indifferent men who happen to be walking through the hall or sitting silently in their seats. He believed in bridling the majority and conserving the rights of the minority.[1]

While it is improbable that a majority of the Speaker's supporters held the views expressed by Kilgore, only a few of his party gave the resolution hearty support. The question is, said Springer, of Illinois, whether this House shall have rules that will enable it to do business, and "I shall hail the adoption of the resolution as the dawn of a new and better era in American legislation."[2] Outhwaite, of Ohio, spoke in a similar vein, "rejoicing that the rule will deprive a dozen or two members from obstructing business."[3] The Republicans, massed and silent, watched the surrender with evident enjoyment. Even Reed declined to speak on the general subject, simply remarking that "this scene to-day is a more effective address than I could make. The House is about to adopt the principle for which we contended under circumstances which show its value to the country. I congratulate it upon the wise decision it is about to make."[4]

It remained for Thomas C. Catchings, of Mississippi, who presented the report of the Committee on Rules, to close the debate. Catchings was a man of great courage

---

[1] 53d Cong., 2d Sess., *Record*, p. 4666.   [2] *Ibid.*, p. 4667.
[3] *Ibid.*   [4] *Ibid.*, p. 4666.

and of singularly calm and earnest nature. For nearly ten years he had served with distinction, and, although standing aggressively with his party in every parliamentary contest, he had made no enemies. He formed his opinions deliberately, spoke slowly and well, and in the heat of intense excitement was never inconsiderate or impulsive. Moreover, he recognized that the reforms of one day inspired a mental condition that saw the occasion for further reforms at some future day. But in treating the subject then before the House he did not take the view of the reformer. Nor did he assume the attitude of a pungent critic, or speculate upon the danger of abandoning the old procedure that existed under Carlisle and Randall. He did not even find fault with the absentees who had made possible the crisis so humiliating to their party. With him the adoption of the resolution was simply a parliamentary necessity, and with admirable temper he sketched the situation as every one understood it. For the first time in the history of the House, he said in conclusion, a minority, acting as a unit, had stopped all legislation of whatever kind and nature, and the majority, which has long indulged the courage of despair, must now say whether it will go out of business, or meet such unprecedented opposition with a rule that will silence resentment and defeat conspiracy.[1]

Such a speech at such a time well suited Catchings's temperament, and if it did not greatly please any one except Republicans, it had not exasperated any member of his party. More than that, he had left the impression distinctly that the situation from which there

[1] 53d Cong., 2d Sess., *Record*, p. 4669.

seemed no escape alone induced him to make the con-
cession. The same motive undoubtedly inspired whatever Democratic support the resolution received, the
roll-call showing 213 yeas to 47 nays, with 93 not voting.[1] It was a real triumph for Catchings, who expected
more "noes." To him and to his supporters, however,
the result seemed a Pyrrhic victory, and it was left to
the Republicans alone to applaud the announcement
of the vote. Their derisive laughter and cynical jeers
ruffled the tempers of men who preferred neither to give
nor take quarter, but the first day's rivalry to secure action on delayed legislation quickly allayed resentment.
Indeed, so readily did all parties accept the Reed precedent that the appointment of tellers soon became a formality which the Speaker ignored, and from that day to
this the mere knowledge that a count can be made has
sufficed to enshrine the disappearing quorum among the
memorabilia of Congress.

Meantime, the Supreme Court of the United States,
reviewing the validity of the so-called McKinley Tariff
Act, passed in 1890 with the aid of a counted quorum,
held that as the House Journal showed a quorum present, the bill had received votes enough.[2] In other words,
it matters not how a quorum is obtained so long as the
Journal records one as present and a majority voting
for the bill.

Since the establishment of the Reed rule the House
is rarely without a quorum, unless a session continues

[1] 53d Cong., 2d Sess., *Record*, p. 4671.
[2] United States *vs.* Ballin, 144 U.S., p. 1; opinion by Mr. Justice
Brewer.

beyond the dinner hour or far into the night. At such times, if the business be highly important or the term near its close, the sergeant-at-arms, under instructions to bring in the absentees, carefully searches homes, hotels, boarding-houses, and theaters, and as the shame-faced delinquents appear in evening dress or undress their tired colleagues jeer and deride them. But formal censure is rarely inflicted, although laughable excuses are frequently given. At one time Luke P. Poland, of Vermont, happened to be caught. The Chair addressed him with due solemnity. "Mr. Poland, you have been absent from the session of the House without its leave. What excuse have you to offer?" The distinguished member, in a tone of great gravity and emotion, replied: "I went with my wife to call on the minister, and I stayed a little too long." The Chair thought it a safe answer "for constituents," but "a bit shady" for colleagues. However, the House, rejoicing to get a quorum, gladly excused him.

CHAPTER X

On the day the House elected its first Speaker it appointed James Madison, of Virginia, Elias Boudinot, of New Jersey, Roger Sherman, of Connecticut, and several other distinguished parliamentarians to draft a code of rules. Boudinot had been president of the Continental Congress. He was a far-seeing, benevolent dictator, whose patriotic words acted as a tonic, and his courageous colleagues made him chairman of the committee. His report governed decorum and debate, provided for the introduction and disposition of bills, and outlined the conduct of business in Committee of the Whole. Although it occupied less than a page of the printed proceedings, it included all the principles then used for the government of parliamentary bodies. Decorum was especially emphasized. The Speaker must rise when putting a question or speaking to points of order, and vote whenever a ballot was taken. If he or a member addressed the House, conversation, reading, and "moving about" must cease. Nor could members leave the hall, or pass between a speaker and the Chair; and upon an adjournment all must remain seated until the Speaker had withdrawn. No one could speak twice on the same question without leave, and not then until others who desired had spoken. Only motions for the previous question, or to amend, to commit, or to adjourn, could be received, while no substitute under color of an amendment could be accepted.

The previous question was not materially modified. As used in the House of Commons and in Congress under the Confederation, it ascertained the disposition to entertain the proposition presented. It took the form of a negative — "Shall the main question be not now put?" If decided affirmatively, the debate continued; if negatively, the subject went over.[1] Boudinot recommended the omission of "not," so that if decided in the affirmative, it stopped discussion on the merits of the main question; if in the negative, the matter went over to the next day. He also increased the demand for it from two members to five.

Boudinot's rules hedging the introduction and treatment of bills eliminated at once all undesirable propositions. To him a bill was an inchoate law, and his scrutiny of it resembled the suspicion with which a vidette regards the advance of an unrecognized troop. It could be introduced only by order of the House on the report of a committee, or by giving a day's notice of a motion for leave, which motion could itself be committed. When introduced a committee was appointed to prepare it. Moreover, each bill must be read three times, first for information, and, if then opposed, the question was, " Shall it be rejected?" If not rejected, it was read a second time and committed or engrossed. If committed, it went to a select committee or to the Committee of the Whole. If engrossed, which meant "written in a

[1] *Journal*, Continental Congress, May 26, 1778, and July 8, 1784.

fair round hand," the House appointed a day for its third reading and passage. To avoid favoritism all bills were considered in the order of their introduction unless otherwise specially directed. No bill amended by the Senate could be committed.

The rules governing the Committee of the Whole provided for the election of a chairman, for the consideration of bills by classes, and for the application of the rules so far as applicable. In practice the Committee determined the order of taking up bills, permitted unlimited debate upon each clause, including amendments, left the preamble to be considered last, and rose on finding itself without a quorum, which was the same as in the House. The absence of later-day practices indicates that the need of time-saving regulations had not yet appeared.

The custom of readopting the Boudinot Rules, supplemented by Jefferson's *Parliamentary Practice*, left little to a Committee on Rules. For many years it never made a report. Indeed, so slightingly was it regarded that Speakers, during five Congresses, neglected to appoint such a committee.[1] Whenever it became necessary to expedite business the House, under the persuasive influence of a few members interested, usually adopted a rule intended to fit the case in hand. Thus the rules, accumulating year after year, became intricate, often contradictory, and generally misunderstood. John Randolph, whose caustic censure made the reflections of others seem spiritless, said he knew the rules when he entered the House, but the longer he served

[1] The 15th, 16th, 18th, 19th and 21st Congresses.

the less he understood them. He denounced them (1828) as complicated and "extremely unparliamentary." [1]

Several reasons provoked such criticism. The previous question did not close debate. A motion to lay on the table simply held the matter in reserve for a more convenient season. A motion to reconsider could be made at any time. A majority might change a rule without notice and rescind it on a day's notice. A motion to proceed to the orders of the day, if carried, set aside a pending proposition, "although the rule governing the order of business did not justify such a motion." [2] Moreover, the precedence of motions frequently changed, while the practice of adopting new rules without revising old ones that conflicted increased the tangle. Fortunately, a spirit of courtesy which obtained in the earlier Congresses tended to make the practice less arbitrary and capricious. "Members acted with the utmost deference to the wishes of the House," says Speaker Reed, writing of that period. "They refrained from making speeches, and withdrew motions if the sense of the House seemed manifestly against them. With such deference on the part of each member to the wishes of all, the House was slow to abridge the right of debate and the use of the cloture." [3]

Nevertheless, obstruction very early took its rise in unlimited debate. The purpose of obstruction is to defeat a measure, or to postpone it until certain specified demands are complied with. It is invoked for party

---

[1] 20th Cong., 1st Sess., *Debates*, p. 1002.
[2] 24th Cong., 1st Sess., *Journal*, p. 885.
[3] *North American Review*, vol. 150, p. 389.

advantage or by individuals for selfish purposes. It proceeds on the theory that the effort of a minority to defeat the majority is as legitimate and patriotic as the majority's use of its greater number. Hence, whatever rules the majority construct for the orderly dispatch of business are, if possible, avoided, and when one avenue is closed, the minority seeks another. This constant warfare, waged for a century, resulted in limiting the rights of the minority and intrenching the power of the majority. It developed the previous question, limited the time for debate, made the Speaker a judge of dilatory motions, forced the adoption of a special order by a majority vote, and compelled the establishment of a quorum by counting non-voting members who are present. Indeed, the rules, adopted from time to time, have harnessed the minority until its protests are disregarded and its threats unheeded.

As already stated, obstruction first took the form of long speeches. The previous question under the Boudinot rule did not relieve the embarrassment. Although it cut off debate on the main question, it permitted each member to speak at least once on the expediency of ordering it. This soon became intolerable, and in 1805 the privilege was eliminated. Such a radical change smote the sacred right of debate too severely to be borne with submission, and without leave, or even without asking for permission, William Ely, of Massachusetts, then a new member, continued the debate after the previous question had been demanded. Speaker Varnum promptly called him to order. Scarcely had he announced his decision before Randolph shouted an appeal. In his argument the distinguished Virginian admitted that the word "now" in the formula meant "at this time," but so long as "the present time" continued, he said; it was competent for members to debate it. This quibble, sustained on appeal by the surprising vote of 113 to 14, showed that the House resented the action of the preceding Congress.[1] Thereafter the chamber again resounded with the voices of those who believed that perpetual talking was the best evidence of their fidelity. One year later the question came up again. The Speaker restated his personal opinion as before, but declined to overrule the vote of the preceding session.

It added to the unhappiness that the service of Barent Gardenier, of New York, spanned this period. Gardenier, a robust, dark-featured man, with heavy jaw and closely compressed lips, attained notoriety because of his remarkable capacity to talk indefinitely. John C. Calhoun declared him able to keep the floor for days,[2] and Clay adds that he could talk for twenty-four hours without stopping.[3] Unlike Randolph's long speeches, relieved by caustic wit, vehement outbursts, and ringing invective, Gardenier's monotonous loquacity, often steeped in innuendo, was unbroken by a sparkling sentence. But no way existed of stopping him. George W. Campbell, of Tennessee, the brilliant floor leader, tried it and found Gardenier's courage equal to his verbosity, and although Campbell wounded him, he established a reputation for being as ready with his pistol as

---

[1] 10th Cong., 1st Sess., *Annals*, p. 1183.
[2] Benton's *Thirty Years' View*, vol. II, p. 258.
[3] 14th Cong., 1st Sess., *Annals*, p. 699.

with his tongue.[1] After his recovery Gardenier again
took the floor. It was usually midnight and sometimes
daylight before he ceased speaking.

These obstructive tactics suddenly came to an end
during a controversy growing out of strained relations
with England and France. Regardless of the rights of
neutrals, the British Government had declared all
French ports in a state of blockade, and Napoleon, retal-
iating by his famous Berlin Decree, interdicted all intercourse with the British Islands. Deeply stirred by the
seizure of American ships, President Madison had prohibited all commercial intercourse with England; but
the action of France made it expedient to provide a way
out of the muddle, and for this purpose John W. Eppes,
of Virginia, chairman of Foreign Affairs, hastily reported
a bill. Eppes, like Campbell, was distinguished as one
of the most effective debaters of his day, having rare
skill and discretion, with inexhaustible telling argument.
He possessed, too, a sunny disposition, high principles,
and pleasing manners, making him a popular as well as
an intellectual leader. It added to his prestige that he
had married Jefferson's daughter.

When debate began on his bill, only seven days of the
session remained, and Gardenier held the floor. The
purpose to strangle the measure became more apparent
when Randolph, in the evening of February 27 (1811),
came to Gardenier's relief with a motion to postpone.
Eppes successfully resisted this maneuver and Gardenier continued. At two o'clock in the morning Ran-

---

[1] The duel was fought at Bladensburg on March 2, 1808, Gardenier
being severely wounded.

dolph again moved a postponement, to which Eppes quickly objected. This brought a retort from Randolph, so sharp and disturbing, that Eppes immediately sent him a challenge, and during Randolph's absence to find a second, Matthew Lyon, of Kentucky, to consume the remainder of the night, called for a reading of the bill as amended. To this Willis Alston, of North Carolina, objected. The Speaker having stated the question, Gardenier promptly took the floor.

Nothing remained but to move the previous question. Eppes hesitated to cut off debate, since a cloture rule departed widely from accepted parliamentary codes. The House of Commons avoided it and the Senate refused such drastic methods. It vested combinations with power to forbid expressions of adverse sentiments, and tended to affect the character of the House, making it a registrative rather than a deliberative body. But Madison's supporters thought it time for action. Henry Clay, although then in the Senate, could not stifle his zeal for the Eppes bill, and his advice stiffened the House.[1] He justified the previous question as a constitutional right of the majority as well as on the ground of expediency. "It is nothing more," he said, "than a declaration of the House that it had heard enough and would proceed to decide." [2]

When Gardenier rose to speak, therefore, Thomas Gholson, of Virginia, a bold, bluff, ardent supporter of the Administration, demanded the previous question on Lyon's motion. This was promptly ordered. Then Gar-

[1] Benton's *Thirty Years' View*, vol. II, p. 257.
[2] 14th Cong., 1st Sess., *Annals*, p. 699.

denier, heedless of the result, began talking. Gholson challenged his right. The Speaker recalled the precedent established two years before, and although contrary to his own opinion, he still acquiesced in that action. Gholson appealed and Gardenier again took the floor. Peter B. Porter, of New York, questioned his right to debate an appeal, and when Varnum overruled the point of order, the House reversed the Chair. The question then recurred on Gholson's appeal, and the House by a vote of 66 to 13 again reversed the Speaker, thus establishing the practice that ordering the previous question ended debate.[1] Subsequently Gardenier, having proposed an amendment, offered to debate it, but the House promptly ordered the previous question. Three days later, after members had regained their composure, Gardenier again ignored the precedent, expressing the hope that the spirit of justice would now prevail. The Speaker, however, called him sharply to order, and on appeal the House sustained the Chair.[2]

Other decisive votes exhibited similar vigilance.[3] But very soon the House dropped back into the vice of unlimited debate. Although Gardenier was gone, Randolph remained, often holding the floor for five or six hours.[4] Of Randolph in the last days of his service, Adams says: "His mind is a jumble of sense, wit, and absurdity; his heart a compound of egotism, inflated vanity, and envy; and his speeches are a farrago of commonplace political declamation, mingled with his-

---

[1] 11th Cong., 3d Sess., *Annals*, p. 1092.   [2] *Ibid.*, p. 1106.
[3] 14th Cong., 1st Sess., *Annals*, pp. 696–718.
[4] 16th Cong., 1st Sess., *Annals*, p. 1641.

torical allusions, scraps of Latin, and a continual stream of personal malignity and inflated egotism, mixed in proportion like those of the liquor which he now tipples, about one third brandy and two thirds water." [1] But Randolph was not the only sinner. William Haile, of Mississippi, declared that it took an average orator two or three days to make a speech. [2] To relieve themselves of such eloquence members not infrequently invoked disorderly noises, such as coughing, scraping the feet, and banging desk-covers, often compelling talkers to resume their seats. [3]

During this period the previous question fell into disuse. Calhoun declared that it was ordered only four times in twenty years. [4] Moreover, it had developed into an unwieldy and dangerous weapon. Speaker Clay held that if ordered, pending a motion to postpone a bill with Senate amendments, it brought a vote not on postponement, but on concurring in the amendments. [5] Subsequently he ruled that it cut off pending amendments, bringing a vote on the engrossing of the bill. [6] Speaker Stevenson held in 1830 that if ordered after the Committee of the Whole had reported a bill with an amendment striking out the enacting clause, it cut off the amendment. [7] Its two-edged feature especially startled the House when ordered on a motion to recom-

[1] *Diary*, vol. VII, p. 473; vol. VIII, p. 64.
[2] 20th Cong., 1st Sess., *Debates*, p. 1754.
[3] 16th Cong., 1st Sess., *Annals* p. 2093; 17th Cong., 1st Sess., *Annals*, p. 1301; 22d Cong., 2d Sess., *Debates*, p. 1919.
[4] Benton's *Thirty Years' View*, vol. II, p. 257.
[5] 12th Cong., 1st Sess., *Journal*, p. 533.
[6] 13th Cong., 1st Sess., *Annals*, p. 398.
[7] 21st Cong., 1st Sess., *Journal*, p. 987.

mit the famous tariff bill of 1833 with instructions, the Chair holding that it brought the House to a vote on the bill itself.[1] To those who sought logical ways of advancing legislation such decisions seemed the embodiment of partisan puerility, and in 1840 the House amended the rule, declaring that the previous question "shall put an end to debate and bring the House to a direct vote upon amendments reported by the committee, upon pending amendments, and then upon the main question."[2] This did not lock the partisan door, however, for in 1845, when the previous question was ordered on a motion to recommit a joint resolution admitting Texas, with instructions to report it with a proviso prohibiting slavery, the House overruled the Speaker, holding that it removed the motion to recommit. Nor could the House under the rule, as amended in 1840, control debate on an amendment to an amendment, since the previous question, if ordered, precluded further amendment on whatever sections remained unconsidered. So, if ordered on a motion to postpone a bill, it brought the House to a direct vote both on amendments and the bill. In other words, a motion to postpone a bill when first presented compelled the House either to hear a protracted debate on the subject of postponement, or to order a vote on the bill before it had been debated.[3]

During these years little of the parliamentary burden fell upon the Committee on Rules. It remained a

---

[1] 22d Cong., 2d Sess., *Debates*, p. 1701.
[2] 26th Cong., 1st Sess., *Globe*, p. 121.
[3] 36th Cong., 1st Sess., *Globe*, p. 1209.

select committee, varying from three to five members, whose jurisdiction extended to revising a code that had already been adopted. It was without privilege, and its report found quick burial beneath the propositions of members eager to expedite their own business. Indeed, the first gleam of its power occurred in 1841, when the House authorized it to report "at all times." A month later, after the minority, by means of obstructive tactics, had held an important measure in Committee of the Whole, the Rules Committee made a report permitting a majority to suspend the rules for the purpose of discharging the Committee of the Whole after it had acted without debate upon all amendments. It was a startlingly clever play. To suspend the rules required a two thirds vote, which the Whigs lacked; but a majority could adopt the report. Immediately the Democrats rose in protest. The Rules Committee, they claimed, could not report "in part" except by unanimous consent or by suspending the rules, and its privilege to report "at all times" confined it to the legitimate object for which it was created. The indisposition of Speaker White to recognize fine distinctions, however, found abundant precedent. "I have learned," he said in substance, "that the rules conform to the will of the majority," and he held that "at all times" meant in part or in whole "at any time." On appeal a majority sustained the Chair — 119 to 103.[1]

The result was cataclysmal. It not only gave a majority power to control debate in Committee of the Whole, but made it master of the House. The bewilder-

[1] 27th Cong., 1st Sess., *Debates*, pp. 9, 153; *Journal*, p. 144.

ing excitement which followed opened the way for the adoption of the still more important resolution of limiting speeches to one hour.[1]

Although subsequent Houses curbed the power of the Rules Committee, the Thirty-third Congress permitted it to report at any time with right of present consideration. This high privilege, however, was soon withdrawn. Meantime, the rules were declared to be "cumbersome and useless." In 1853 the cry began that the Speaker, although not then a member of the Committee on Rules, obstructed business. Five years later Israel Washburn, of Maine, a distinguished parliamentarian, admitted his ignorance of the meaning and purpose of some of the rules. "They need to be amended," he declared. "But their observance is most needed. The good nature of members in granting unanimous consent breeds ignorance, and when applied they provoke criticism because a different practice obtains." [2]

In 1860 Washburn reported his famous revision, which included twenty-eight amendments. Although most of these changes corrected contradictory provisions, combined several rules into one, and made others conform to the established practice, drastic modifications were introduced. One destroyed the trick of striking out the enacting clause in Committee of the Whole and then disagreeing to the report in the House.[3] Another provided that the previous question, when negatived, should leave the pending business undis-

---

[1] 27th Cong., 1st Sess., *Journal*, p. 145.
[2] 36th Cong., 1st Sess., *Globe*, pp. 1178, 1209.
[3] See chap. xiii, p. 268.

turbed, and when ordered on a motion to postpone, should act only on such motion; or, if on an amendment or an amendment thereto, that it should not preclude debate on the bill. This gave the House the facility for amendment enjoyed in Committee of the Whole. To avoid a repetition of the riotous scenes preceding the election of Speaker Pennington, the rules of one House were made binding upon its successor unless otherwise ordered. Although parliamentarians generally held this rule invalid whenever seriously questioned, it survived for thirty years.[1]

Washburn did nothing to strengthen the Committee on Rules. The House followed the precedent, established in 1859, of making the Speaker *ex-officio* its chairman; but this conferred no new privilege. When it had once reported, its functions ceased. Indeed its limited privileges compelled Speaker Randall in 1876 to ask that authority be given it during the closing days of the session to report "at any time" upon questions relating to the currency.[2] As late as 1879 the Speaker declared that never, to his recollection, had it divided politically upon any subject.[3]

In the meantime criticism of the rules again became common. Washburn's revision had served its purpose well, but no one, in 1860, could anticipate that business would increase fivefold in twenty years, congesting legislation and limiting the liberty of the individual. Moreover, the House had added forty-four unclassified rules

---

[1] For the discussion and adoption of these changes see 36th Cong., 1st Sess., *Globe*, pp. 1177–1237.

[2] 44th Cong., 1st Sess., *Journal*, p. 1051.

[3] 46th Cong., 1st Sess., *Record*, p. 2329 (June 25, 1879).

and established many new precedents. To remedy this condition it directed the Committee on Rules, consisting of Speaker Randall, Joseph C. S. Blackburn, of Kentucky, Alexander H. Stephens, of Georgia, James A. Garfield, of Ohio, and William P. Frye, of Maine, to "simplify, revise, and codify." Their report became the historic revision of 1880. It "neither surrenders the right of a majority to control business for which it is held responsible," said the committee, "nor invades the powers of a minority to check temporarily, if not permanently, the action of a majority believed to be improper or unconstitutional." [1] What it did was to retain twelve rules entire, drop thirty-two because obsolete or unnecessary, and condense one hundred and twenty-five into thirty-two, making a total of forty-four, each subdivided into clauses, and arranged with logical relation to its subject, thus enabling members to glance at a rule and find its correlative.

This revision centered in an effort to economize time as well as to simplify the practice. It stopped voting after the second call of the roll; it dropped the penalty system of absenteeism without leave; and it authorized the clerk to announce "pairs" instead of members. It abolished the practice of changing a few words in a pending bill to make it germane as an amendment; it caused a motion to reconsider, made during the last six days of a session, to be disposed of at the time; it sent a bill, to which objection was made to its present consideration, to the Committee of the Whole or to the House calendar; it gave preference to revenue and ap-

[1] 46th Cong., 1st Sess., *Record*, p. 198.

propriation bills in Committee of the Whole; it required bills on the private calendar to be taken up and disposed of in order; and it provided that the previous question should bring the House to a direct vote upon a single motion, a series of allowable motions, or upon an amendment or amendments, the effect being to carry the bill to its engrossment and third reading, and then, on a renewal of the motion, to its passage or rejection. To afford "the amplest opportunity to test the sense of the House as to whether or not the bill is in the exact form it desires," it authorized a motion, pending the passage of a bill, to recommit it with or without instructions. Other changes of less note modified the duties of minor officers, extended former members' admission to the floor, safeguarded the filing, disposition, and withdrawal of papers, made the Committee on Rules a standing committee of five members, gave a conference report precedence over all other business, created the House calendar, to which were referred all public bills not carrying an appropriation, and added an hour to the time of the member closing a debate whenever it extended over a day.[1]

The revisers of 1880 were not reformers. They tactfully avoided the abolition of disreputable practices, such as "riders" on appropriation bills and the "disappearing quorum." They simply sought, as their report stated, to foster "order, accuracy, uniformity, and economy of time," and experience has justified their

[1] For report and discussion see 46th Cong., 2d Sess., *Record*, pp. 108–208; 478–91; 551–58; 575–79; 603–14; 658–65; 708–13; 727–35; 954–59; 1195–1208; 1255–67.

recommendations; but by shunning "riders" and the "disappearing quorum" they left the real red-light dis-'rict undisturbed.

Although the Committee on Rules profited little by becoming a standing committee, Speaker Randall added greatly to its prestige, holding that all propositions to change the rules, in order to be agreed to by a majority vote, must be referred to it,[1] and that it might report at any time on matters relating to the rules.[2] This enabled it to intervene and secure immediate consideration of its reports. But it did not prevent a strong, well-disciplined minority, directed by competent leaders, from annoying and often defeating the majority by the use of dilatory motions, such as to adjourn or to adjourn to a day fixed. Indeed, these motions became so obstructive in 1875 that a despairing member asked how they could be avoided. To which Speaker Blaine replied: "The Chair has repeatedly ruled that pending a proposition to change a rule dilatory motions could not be entertained. The right of each House to determine what shall be its rules is an organic right expressly given by the Constitution. The House is incapable by any formal rule of divesting itself of its inherent constitutional power to exercise the functions of determining its own rules. Therefore, the Chair has always announced that upon a proposition to change the rules of the House he would never entertain a dilatory motion."[3]

If Speaker Blaine ever made such a ruling it is not of

[1] 44th Cong., 1st Sess., *Record*, pp. 5262–63.
[2] 46th Cong., 2d Sess., *Record*, p. 768.
[3] 43d Cong., 2d Sess., *Record*, p. 806.

record. Nor did he show the courage of his conviction during the passage of the Civil Rights Bill (1875), since the House, to enable it to do business, suspended the rules and adopted a resolution providing that "whenever a question is pending the Speaker shall not entertain any motion of a dilatory character except one to adjourn and one to fix the time to adjourn." To avoid all question respecting the adoption of this report Speaker Blaine took pains to announce that it had received a two thirds vote.[1] Samuel J. Randall asked if it required a two thirds vote. To which the Speaker artfully replied: "The Chair does not so state." [2]

This was the parliamentary situation on May 29, 1882, when the House sought to consider a contested election case in which Joseph Wheeler, of Alabama, the famous Confederate cavalry chieftain, appeared as contestee. Wheeler had secured a certificate of election based on a majority of 47, while the contestant, also a former Confederate officer, presented alleged proof of having received 600 majority. The minority showed a waspish partiality for Wheeler. Local prejudices seemed to be transferred to Washington, and to prevent consideration of the case, Wheeler's friends muzzled the House with roll-calls. Thereupon Thomas B. Reed, from the Committee on Rules, presented a report allowing the Speaker to entertain only one motion to adjourn or to take a recess pending "the consideration of any question which may arise on a case involving the constitutional right to a seat." [3] This touched the mooted

[1] 43d Cong., 2d Sess., *Record*, pp. 891-92.   [2] *Ibid.*, p. 892.
[3] An amendment to par. 8, Rule xvi.

question, and Samuel J. Randall began to filibuster. After raising the question of consideration, he moved to adjourn. Again defeated, he moved to adjourn to a day certain. Then Reed made the point of order that dilatory motions could not be entertained pending a proposition to change the rules. This peremptory challenge startled the House. It meant a fight, and members quickly gathered to witness the forensic duel.

Randall had led the minority in the time of Thaddeus Stevens. He did not possess the latter's uncurbed acerbity, or the scintillating badinage of Blaine, but he could be pitiless. He had dealt many trenchant blows. His famous retort that the Republican party was an "organized hypocrisy" made Garfield wince. Democrats had coined into familiar quotations his hard hits at Blaine. More fierce and cutting was his accusation that Robert C. Schenck borrowed his tactics from the Whigs. For nearly twenty years his genius had lent great interest to the proceedings, and the House knew that a bout with the rising young member from Maine would add another dramatic film to the *Record*.

Reed had just entered his third term. He was cold and brusque in manner, and seemed in general to have hardly a gleam of the emotional in him. In fact, his friendships and affections were most enduring. Yet in his ordinary bearing there was little to suggest genuine warmth. He had been the solicitor of his city, the attorney-general of his State, and a dominating force in the legislature of Maine. There was peculiar courage, too, in the part he took in the House. He had shown that he could hold his own in retort and in sarcasm against any antagonist. But he had not met Randall. He came into the House during the latter's second term as Speaker, and opportunity to justify an attack had not before been presented. From the chair Randall had studied him. He had heard his sarcastic replies sweep the chamber like grapeshot, and he had learned, from his cross-examination of Samuel J. Tilden, of his habit of going ungloved after results. But Randall probably had little suspicion that the member whom he then faced was a man of as cool judgment, as long a head, and as complete a capacity for the control of a great party as any statesman who had appeared in the House for generations.

Nevertheless, it was a crucial moment for the new leader. Pitted for the first time against the veteran sense-carrier of his party, it put to proof the real stuff in him. He was venturing on new ice. Blaine had pointed the way, but he was to try it. The twinkle in Randall's eye and the quick appearance of his well-worn *Manual*, which opened at the desired section, did not escape Reed's observation as he made his point of order. Nor did he forget that the distinguished Speaker, often to his party's disadvantage, had safeguarded the rights of the minority. But Reed was exactly the man to be audacious, and at the opening of the debate he declared that "whenever it is imposed upon Congress to accomplish a certain work, it is the duty of the Speaker, who represents the House, and who, in his official capacity, is the embodiment of the House, to carry out that rule of law or of the Constitution. It then becomes his duty to see that no factious opposition prevents the House from doing its duty. He must brush away all unlawful combinations to misuse the rules and must hold the House strictly to its work." [1]

To most members Reed's proposition was novel. Cannon had heard Blaine's dictum. So had Holman, of Indiana, Kelley, of Pennsylvania, Kasson, of Iowa, Mills, of Texas, Cox, of New York, and some others. But to the great majority Reed's terse, vigorous sentences, with an occasional metallic note of sarcasm, proclaimed a new doctrine. Their right to suspend the rules was clear. So, too, was their power to adopt a report which changed a rule. But it seemed a great stretch of power for the Speaker, preceding the adoption of such a report, arbitrarily to eliminate motions to adjourn and the like, because the Constitution authorized the House to make its own rules. Indeed, Randall had overruled a similar resolution proposed by Mills,[2] and in replying to Reed the former Speaker calmly but with great earnestness enlarged upon the reasons then given. During the count of the electoral vote in 1877, he said, he had ruled out such motions because the law creating the Electoral Commission specifically required it. But no law supported the proposed action. Blaine had suggested it, but he wisely refrained from enforcing it. Until now no one had seriously thought of it. The House, having already acted in pursuance of its constitutional power, had adopted certain limitations as to changing its rules. It was estopped, therefore, from enlarging these limitations. To permit it would deprive the minority of its

[1] 47th Cong., 1st Sess., *Record*, p. 4306.
[2] 45th Cong., 3d Sess., *Record*, p. 175.

only weapon to stop the wickedness of a lawless majority. On this point he submitted the remarks of Speaker Onslow, of the British House: "As it is always in the power of the majority, by their numbers, to stop any improper measures proposed on the part of their opponents," said the distinguished parliamentarian, "the only weapons by which the minority can defend themselves against similar attempts from those in power are the forms and rules of proceeding which have been accepted as they were found necessary from time to time and are become the law of the House, by a strict adherence to which the weaker party can only be protected from those irregularities and abuses which these forms were intended to check, and which the wantonness of power is but too often apt to suggest to large and successful majorities." [1]

Onslow's statement undoubtedly crystallizes into the fewest words the argument upon which rests the hope of every minority. But the hope of the minority, Reed replied, must not become the despair of the majority. Protection of the minority did not mean the destruction of the majority. The Speaker must protect the rights of each, but first of all he must see that the House performs the duty for which it exists under the Constitution. This was a pat answer, and his party backers roundly applauded. But Blackburn came back double-shotted. If the Speaker can arbitrarily brush away all factious opposition which prevents the House from doing what the Chair regards it to be its duty, he asked, why may he not on the same principle destroy a far

[1] 47th Cong., 1st Sess., *Record*, p. 4308.

worse form of obstruction by counting a quorum? This was a body blow. To make it more incisive, the Kentuckian had Reed's speech in opposition to such action read from the desk. Reed must have known that he was open to this savage thrust, for his argument covered the "disappearing quorum" as well as "dilatory motions"; but he felt little daunted on that score. He was more eager just then to destroy dilatory motions than to be consistent, and without hesitation, but to the discouragement of the friends of orderly procedure, he reaffirmed his former position.[1] However, he fared very well, since the Speaker ruled in his favor and the House sustained it on appeal. His report was then adopted; yeas, 150; nays, 2; not voting, 139; constituting a quorum, 147. It was a great victory, since it enabled the Committee on Rules to have its reports promptly adopted, and from that hour Reed became the real leader of his party. Ever after, so long as he remained in Congress, his voice gave the word of command.

In the next session Reed undertook a more perilous adventure. A House bill with Senate amendments reducing the internal revenue tax had rested upon the Speaker's table for several weeks, since the Republicans, lacking a two thirds majority, could not suspend the rules and send it to conference. It was a party measure. Although several Republicans opposed it, a desire for its passage found generous expression, and the delay created much anxiety. As the closing week of Congress appeared, it turned anxiety into exasperation. Suddenly, without notice, Reed startled the House by pre-

[1] 47th Cong., 1st Sess., *Record*, pp. 4313. See also chap. IX, p. 162.

senting a report from the Committee on Rules providing that it be in order at any time during the remainder of the session to suspend the rules by a majority vote, take the bill from the Speaker's table, declare a disagreement, and ask a conference thereon, the committee on the part of the House to be composed of five members.[1]

Instantly the House was on its feet. It recalled the clever play of the Whigs in 1841 and provoked a scene not less riotous. Cox, of New York, declared that "it outrages every principle of parliamentary procedure. It is a fraud on all that is just and fair in our politics. It is revolutionary." The fiery Blackburn paced the floor, charging coercion. "If common rumor be credited," he said, pointing his finger at Reed, "you dared not trust a count, but have obligated your forces by a written and signed agreement." Even Carlisle, the gentle logician, pronounced it "a monstrous proposition," while Randall, who exercised a control over his long obedient followers somewhat like that of the heart of Bruce in the old Scottish story, declared that, although partisan opposition had sorely tried his patience, he had refused during his service as Speaker to imperil the rights of the minority and perhaps the life of the Republic by violating a practice which all his predecessors save one had observed.

Reed recognized the bizarre character of his innovation. "Unless there was a great emergency," he said, "I should not be in favor of its passage." Men of dominating minds often see "a great emergency" when

[1] 43d Cong., 2d Sess., *Record*, p. 892.

opposition confronts them. His success in the preceding session probably aided his vision. But he was no dreamer. As a master debater he might carelessly precipitate a hot discussion, but he was too shrewd to stake his growing prestige on this latest adventure without due warrant, and so he spent several days in overcoming scruples and obtaining pledges. His precaution, however, scarcely justified his final action, for the disappearance of thirty-two members of his own party left him without a quorum. Even the next morning when he appeared with a file of recruits, failure stared him in the face until several Nationalists, suddenly seized with a desire to go upon record in opposition, swelled the total vote to a quorum.[1] After such a harassing experience it is not surprising, perhaps, that Reed concluded, whenever opportunity offered, to strike the "disappearing quorum" a shattering blow.

The Committee on Rules, after the adoption of this procedure, began to fill the public eye. Like Pandora's box it seemed to conceal surprising possibilities. Speaker Carlisle stimulated the country's curiosity by appointing to its membership (1883) the chairmen of Ways and Means and of Appropriations. This combine gave him watchful floor managers, who held the purse-strings and distributed favors. Nevertheless, Carlisle did not yield readily to the elimination of dilatory motions or the adoption of special orders by a majority vote. Like Randall he believed the minority possessed

[1] The House numbered 293 members, divided as follows: Republicans, 152; Democrats, 130; Nationalists, 9; Readjusters, 2; necessary for a quorum, 147. First vote, yeas, 120; nays, 20; not voting, 151. Second vote, yeas, 129; nays, 22; not voting, 142.

rights which, if destroyed, might imperil free government, and although the Rules Committee reported during the Forty-eighth Congress three special orders which a majority adopted, the procedure grew slowly in favor. In the Forty-ninth Congress, however, Carlisle not only used it more freely, but added greatly to the Rules Committee's prestige by extending its jurisdiction to the order of business. After the gift of this high privilege, the House, accustomed to parliamentary surprises, stood aghast when the Committee, in a single special order, adopted by a majority, fixed the order of business for sixteen legislative days.[1] Had Reed prophesied in 1883 that Carlisle, within five years, would make such a wholesale use of this "monstrous proposition," members would have regarded him a senile sorcerer.

Yet Carlisle's administration during the Fiftieth Congress came perilously near being a failure. His name belongs in the short list of great Speakers. His opinions read like the decisions of an eminent judge. His impartiality and the sweetness of his manner prompted the minority members to present him a loving-cup as an evidence of their affection. But dilatory motions, the disappearing quorum, and his refusal to ascertain the presence of a quorum by counting the House made him the slave of filibusters. As elsewhere stated, their subtle arts prostituted every legitimate motion and kept the assembly in continuous roll-calls.

When Reed succeeded Carlisle (1889), he determined to destroy this evil. Others had revised; he proposed to

[1] 51st Cong., 1st Sess., *Record*, p. 8349.

reform. The code-makers of 1880 boasted that they did not disturb the rights of the minority; Reed declared that a minority should not disturb the rights of the majority. The former minimized the result without abolishing the cause; the latter laid the axe to the root. To enable him the better to succeed, the House, for the first time in its history, refused to adopt rules at its organization, thus substituting the general parliamentary law. During this period the Speaker counted a quorum.[1] Afterward came the Reed Rules. Of the ten modifications, most of them excited little or no opposition. Indeed, members generally approved the readjustment of the order of business, the reduction of the quorum in Committee of the Whole to one hundred, and the relief of the morning hour by filing bills and reports with the clerk.[2] What made these rules famous were additions, not modifications. Having heretofore suppressed dilatory motions, adopted special orders by a majority vote, and counted a quorum, Reed now reduced the practice to written rules.[3]

Charles F. Crisp, of Georgia, led the opposition to their adoption. He appreciated the difficulty of changing fixed habits. He knew that members, attached to old forms and parliamentary ways, would protest against the Reed innovations, and in drawing the rays of prejudice into one focus and kindling them into a flame of resentment, he exhibited such real leadership that his party picked him to succeed Reed (1891). Once in the Chair he naturally dropped the rules he

---

[1] See chap. IX, p. 166.   [2] See chap. XI, p. 220.
[3] Rule XI, sec. 56; XV, secs. 2 and 3; XVI, sec. 10.

had condemned. But to avoid the unfortunate experience of Carlisle he crushed the filibuster by authorizing the Committee on Rules to meet at any time, to report without notice, and to dispose of its report without the intervention of any motion except one to adjourn.[1] In other words, what Reed left to the Speaker, Crisp gave to his committee. One magnified the Chair, the other exalted Rules. Reed met the filibuster face to face; Crisp waited the action of his lieutenants. In refusing at the outset to count a quorum, Crisp relied upon an excessive majority. But his helplessness in the Fifty-third Congress forced the adoption of a rule authorizing the Speaker, before a roll-call, to appoint one teller from each party, upon whose report the Chair announced a quorum.[2] This, also, was Reed's method. Under him, the clerk kept tally; under Crisp, the tellers. In other words, Crisp laid aside Reed's garments and got into others of like pattern. Subsequent Houses, however, have preferred Reed's clothes. Nevertheless, the fear, so often and fiercely expressed, that the gift of such power might sacrifice safety to dispatch, has never wholly vanished. By removing restraints which emasculated the minority, the Reed Rules dropped the bars to all sorts of theoretical panaceas, until the cry is heard of too much legislation and that the House has ceased to be a deliberative body.

How thoroughly the Reed Rules cripple the filibuster was demonstrated when John Sharp Williams, of Mississippi, boldly proposed (1908) blocking all legisla-

---

[1] 53d Cong., 1st Sess., *Journal*, p. 91.
[2] 53d Cong., 1st Sess., *Record*, p. 4660. See also chap. IX, p. 174.

tion until the House should pass certain specified bills. Other minority leaders had tried their hand. James D. Richardson, of Tennessee, sat patiently through two Congresses, but failed to score. Joseph W. Bailey, of Texas, did no better. No one questioned Bailey's preeminent ability. In the higher qualifications of a debater, as in those gifts of lucid exposition, of which he was a master, he had few equals in the House. Even in his errors there was something dashing and captivating; and although his language occasionally betrayed distrust, he left the impression that his strength was sufficient. Perhaps his chief fault was that he was too strong for those around him. Yet whenever he tried to buck the Reed Rules, he discovered the House was harnessed.

Williams did not expect to breach them. He sought to create a campaign issue, and he hoped, by maintaining an all-summer's deadlock, to arouse national attention and interest. Conditions seemed propitious. He had a minority of more than one third, a body of sympathetic lieutenants, and a troop of followers who kept their places with a quiet determination to forego sleep and society. Besides, he had at his side John J. Fitzgerald, of New York, a most skilled parliamentarian. Although sometimes unamiable and unconciliatory, the House liked Williams. He was quite incapable of bluster or violence. His broad sense of humor carried with it a sense of proportion; his mellow voice, tinged with a peculiarly pleasing Southern accent, filled the large chamber; his language seldom gave offense; and when off duty his good nature bubbled over. The circle of his warmest friends included the Speaker. It was "Joe" and "John." Observers noted, too, that in partisan encounters, when the eye sparkled, retorts rankled, and the firm mouth-muscles moved slowly, an occasional smile dissipated the thought that superheated zeal had buried friendship.

Williams relied upon roll-calls. The Chair might declare motions dilatory, but under the Constitution one fifth of the members could demand the yeas and nays upon every division. Reed invoked this constitutional privilege when he forced Speaker Crisp to count a quorum, and in order to obtain the greatest number of divisions, Williams waylaid general appropriation bills on their return from the Senate freighted with amendments. Under the usual procedure of the House these offered unlimited demands for roll-calls, ten or twelve of which exhaust an ordinary legislative day. Moreover, they make a most tedious day. After voting a member may retire to the cloak-room, but not to other work. He simply exists until another roll-call. Before the adoption of the Reed Rules from two to eight days were often thus employed. When Williams disclosed his purpose, however, the Committee on Rules exploited its resourcefulness. It enabled the question to be put: "Will the House disagree with the Senate amendments *en bloc* and request a conference?" This required only one division or roll-call. It declared the motion for a recess privileged. This made the legislative day continuous, thus obviating the daily approval of the Journal. It conferred authority upon the Speaker to declare the House in Committee of the Whole, and upon the chairman of the Committee of the Whole the right to declare it in recess. It also made every day a "suspension day," and provided for the suspension of the rules by a majority vote. In other words, the House temporarily substituted a new procedure of clever parliamentary devices, which gave the Speaker the initiative and left little opportunity for roll-calls. Indeed, instead of delaying business Williams practically expedited it.

Although the House approved the dispatch of business under the Reed Rules, the increasing domination of the Committee on Rules made trouble. In presenting special orders it not infrequently, when it seemed quite unnecessary, moved the previous question, thus limiting debate to forty minutes. Members complained of being neither consulted nor informed. An apparent tendency to avoid the consideration of unprivileged bills on the House and Union calendars, by interposing special orders, also occasioned complaint. It necessitated bartering with the Speaker for recognition to secure unanimous consent, a proceeding always embarrassing and often humiliating. More subtle, yet no less disturbing, was the feeling, created by the tyranny of alleged party necessity, that one must support whatever the Rules Committee brought forward or become irregular. In fact, nothing better illustrates the extraordinary power that the desire to be regular wields in the House than the dumb fidelity with which the great majority of members yield to this shibboleth. Yet members who voluntarily fall into line often resent it. It seems to reduce them to pawns, while knights play the game.

Before Speaker Carlisle retired, propositions appeared

to enlarge the Rules Committee and make it more representative.[1] Other resolutions during Crisp's administration suggested seven, nine, and fifteen members, while the more radical proposed that its membership include all the chairmen of other standing committees. One member thought each State should be represented upon it.[2] But these propositions fell by the wayside. Finally, in the Sixty-first Congress, several members of the majority party, known as "Insurgents," charged that the House had degenerated into an assembly serving no other purpose than to register the arbitrary edicts of a too powerful Committee on Rules. They were profoundly in earnest. Indeed, it seemed certain that their union with the minority would result in an enlargement of the Committee with the Speaker left out, and to avoid the trap, Republicans made allies of several Democrats by adopting amendments providing (1) that on Wednesdays the call of committees should not be interrupted unless by a two thirds vote of those present; (2) that on the passage of a bill, after the previous question is ordered and a motion to recommit is in order, the Speaker shall recognize for such motion a member who is in good faith opposed to the bill; and (3) that a calendar for unanimous consents be created.[3] These provisions ended trafficking with the Speaker, satisfied the minority, and opened a way for unprivileged bills. In fact, the reforms proved so beneficial that all parties exhibited a disposition to be satisfied, and the

[1] 50th Cong., 1st Sess., *Record*, p. 124.
[2] 53d Cong., 1st Sess., *Record*, pp. 73, 1042, 1077, 1084.
[3] 61st Cong., 1st Sess., *Record*, pp. 23–32.

Republican division might possibly have been healed had legislative leaders acknowledged that diversity of opinion within a party must be quickly recognized, and that unity of action depends largely upon conciliatory tactics.

In this instance, however, apparent if not studied inattention fanned the smouldering embers, until, at last, after weeks of watching, the Insurgents caught the Republicans without a majority. Quickly combining with the Democrats they forced the election of a new Committee on Rules composed of ten members without the Speaker.[1] A parliamentary genius never planned a more successful *coup d'état*. It rivaled Reed's discovery of Speaker Crisp's helplessness.[2] In the language of Disraeli, descriptive of Sir Robert Peel's master-stroke, the Insurgents caught the Republicans bathing and walked away with their clothes. It was a savage revenge. It not only deeply humiliated a proud party that had controlled the House continuously for fourteen consecutive years, but it implied a censure of all who had hitherto failed to voice such a change. Yet, in reorganizing the new Committee on Rules under the elective system, all the old members except the Speaker were not only retained, but John Dalzell, of Pennsylvania, who had served continuously as a potent influence on the committee under Speakers Reed, Henderson, and Cannon, was elected chairman. It added to the compliment that the Insurgents themselves voted for him.

[1] 61st Cong., 2d Sess., *Record*, p. 3305.
[2] Chap. IX, p. 172.

CHAPTER XI

THE ORDER OF BUSINESS

IT frequently happens that a new member, seeking unanimous consent, is suddenly stopped by a loud, sharp cry of "Regular order!" If he insists that recognition entitles him to the floor, the Speaker blandly replies that the demand for the regular order, being equivalent to an objection, deprives him of that right. Thereupon he scowls at the discourteous objector, inwardly resolves to be avenged, and helplessly sits down, inquiring of his seat mate what the "regular order" is. "Anything that is in order," he is told. "But what is in order?" he insists. His informant does not know. Only the Speaker and a few watchful parliamentarians keep run of it. It may be a question of privilege, or a conference report, or a bill on which the previous question was ordered the day before, or a special order, or a privileged bill, or any one of half a dozen other matters. If it be none of these, it is the regular "order of business," which changes from Congress to Congress as new conditions make new rules necessary.

The House always opens the proceedings with prayer, followed by the reading and approval of the Journal. Originally no further need existed for an "order of business." Members presented petitions, made long speeches, and submitted committee reports whenever the Speaker granted recognition. But precedent gradually established an order. Thus the custom of presenting petitions in the first or "morning hour" became so deeply rooted that in 1809 Speaker Varnum ruled a resolution out of order when offered in that time. As early as 1794 the business left unfinished at the preceding adjournment had preference. In 1810 the consideration of private bills, which personally concern the political welfare of members, became the regular order for each Friday.

In 1811 the rules provided this order of business: (1) Prayer; (2) reading and approval of the Journal; (3) presentation of petitions; (4) reports from committees; (5) unfinished business; and (6) consideration of reports assigned to a future day, known as "orders of the day." The rapid increase of routine legislation, however, kept parliamentarians busy inventing new devices for the advancement of important measures. The practice of mortgaging the future with "orders of the day" became so unwieldy that the House cut off debate respecting the priority of such business and gave precedence to "special orders of the day." Subsequently it limited (1822) petitions and reports to a "morning hour" of sixty minutes, required a two thirds vote to suspend the rules, gave up Saturdays as well as Fridays to the consideration of private bills, and fixed a definite time for disposing of business "on the Speaker's table" — a parliamentary term indicating the temporary abode of certain messages from the President, communications from heads of departments, bills with Senate amendments, conference reports, and other matters which await the Speaker's presentation to the House.

Meantime petitions became a real menace to the dispatch of business. As the country prospered the demands of the Revolutionary soldier multiplied. "Thirty years ago," wrote Adams, "Uriah Tracy used to say that the old soldiers never died. Had Uriah lived to this time [1834] he would have seen them multiply. As petitioners they are more numerous at every session of Congress, and of late, as some of them have died, their widows have begun to petition; and this day there came a petition from the son of a deceased pensioner praying that the pension may be continued to him." [1] In its early practice the House read all petitions presented, and whenever it failed to act tradition and sentiment raised the cry that the constitutional right of petition was impaired. To add to the confusion the postponement of "orders of the day" became so common that Henry R. Storrs, of New York, facetiously complained that "we continue to make orders of the day for to-morrow while to-morrow never comes." [2] To relieve the embarrassment the House restricted petitions to each Monday, and gave "the morning hour" to reports, resolutions, and motions; but the advent of John Quincy Adams and his numerous petitions praying for the abolition of slavery in the District of Columbia fomented increasing trouble and much bitterness. Adams declared it a "fundamental principle that the House had no right to take away or abridge the constitutional right of petition." Nevertheless, the House, under the famous order known as "Rule 21," continued to consign such petitions to the table without reading.

[1] *Diary*, vol. IX, p. 124.   [2] 21st Cong., 1st Sess., *Debates*, p. 720.

Finally, at the suggestion of Adams himself, it provided (1844) that every petition be handed to the clerk to list and file, if not excluded under the rule.

This arrangement was supplemented from time to time by other parliamentary devices for saving time and expediting business. The simplest of these took the form of unanimous consents. A higher privilege, first conferred on the Committee on Enrolled Bills, granted the right to report at any time, a royal gift jealously guarded, but which is now the prerogative of seventeen committees. The special order appeared in 1832. It was superior to the privilege of reporting at any time because it modified rules governing adjournments, the previous question, and other motions, but its adoption by a two thirds vote, if objection be made, limited its usefulness until Reed forced its passage (1883) by a majority vote. About the time the special order appeared, the question of privilege, especially when involving the rights of members, assumed importance, and although not then so fully developed as in later years, it took precedence over other business. Revenue and appropriation bills became intermittently privileged after 1837, and in 1850 the Speaker held conference reports in order at any time. Setting apart certain days of the week for the consideration of specified legislation also rooted itself early in the House procedure. As already stated, the practice of confining private business to Fridays began in 1810. In 1847 the House limited motions to suspend the rules to each Monday, and in 1870 assigned District of Columbia matters to the third Friday of each month. Subsequent changes confined suspension of the rules to the first and third Mondays (1880) and District legislation to the second (1885) and fourth (1890) Mondays. In 1909 Wednesday of each week was given up to bills on the House and Union calendars.

But the flood of routine work kept rising. No sooner had petitions been relegated to the files without action by the House (1844) than members clamored for more time for the introduction of bills. At first bills were not numerous. The modern habit of using them to advertise a member's activity did not then obsess the legislative mind. To the House a bill was an inchoate law, to be treated with much deliberation, and its reference to the Committee of the Whole generally proved fatal. "It is to-morrow and to-morrow and to-morrow," wrote Adams, "for bills thus referred must be taken up in the order of their commitment and many are never reached." [1] This complaint sounded the sentiment of a House bound to its ideals. But when the fact developed that a bill introduced, though not passed, benefited the member, since it evidenced a disposition to serve his constituents, the House (1860) set apart each alternate Monday for their introduction and ordered them referred without debate. This radical change, encouraging members to present bills on all possible subjects, created such a Monday rush that it increased their number nearly twenty-fold in twenty years, and nullified all notices of intention and requests for leave.[2]

[1] *Diary*, vol. IX, p. 113.

[2] Bills introduced in each Congress between 1860 and 1870 increased from 400 to 4000; 1870 to 1880, from 4000 to 7000; 1880 to 1890, from 7000 to 10,000; 1890 to 1900, from 10,000 to 17,000. During the second session of the 62d Congress over 26,000 were introduced.

Indeed, so quickly did the House, in its desire to save time, forget its own rules that in 1879, when a member insisted upon one day's notice, Speaker Randall overruled the point of order, declaring that in many years of service he had never before heard the question raised.[1]

A more aggravating clog to the dispatch of business grew out of the practice of referring all committee reports involving private or public money bills to the Committee of the Whole House or to the Committee of the Whole House on the State of the Union, and of considering public bills not carrying appropriations whenever reported. This unfortunate arrangement, which often delayed important measures, led to the creation of a private calendar (1839) for reports on private bills, and of a Union calendar (1845) for reports on public bills carrying appropriations. The relief proved more apparent than real, however, since other public bills which continued to be considered when reported, often blocked the way by provoking prolonged debate, not infrequently for obstructive purposes, and to abate the abuse the House (1880) created a House calendar to which such reports were referred without debate. Ten years later Speaker Reed forced the rule providing that all bills and reports be filed with the clerk and referred to their proper calendars. To avoid mistakes members were privileged to move the correction of improper references immediately after the approval of the Journal. Thus, during the first century of its existence the House gradually eliminated from its floor work the presentation

[1] 46th Cong., 1st Sess., *Record*, p. 425.

of petitions, the introduction of bills, and the submission of reports — a burden which had taxed its patience, consumed its time, and impeded its business.

Meantime, the pressure of legislation compelled other and frequent changes in the order of business. To reach "unfinished business" and "the Speaker's table" earlier in the day, the "morning hour" for the consideration of bills was dropped below them. This made it impossible to move bills on the House calendar, which became known as a "legislative graveyard," and to make it accessible Speaker Carlisle (1885) established a second "morning hour" to follow the first, with the provision that a bill should be displaced if not disposed of in two successive hours. It resulted, of course, in disaster, since the opponents of a bill had only to prolong debate to displace it. To remedy this clever parliamentary trick, business on "the Speaker's table" was again dropped below the "morning hour." Immediately requests multiplied for unanimous consents to secure the reference of Senate bills on "the Speaker's table," so that the additional time intended for consideration of bills was practically lost by these time-wasting motions. Thus, in getting out of one trouble, the Speaker plunged the House into another. Carlisle had a velvet glove; he needed an iron hand.

It is interesting to note the course of "unfinished business" in the patchwork changes of half a century. Originally it preceded "orders of the day," and to save its high privilege the House consolidated it with "the Speaker's table." But a future adjustment (1852) dropped it below "the morning hour," so that its business was rarely reached except by unanimous consent. Israel Washburn, of Maine, the most enlightened parliamentarian of his day, pronounced this arrangement "intolerable," and in the revision of 1860 he separated it from "the Speaker's table," placing it immediately after the approval of the Journal. This sacrificed "the morning hour," and to quiet the growing discontent Speaker Randall (1880) restored the latter to its original place. When Carlisle created (1885) a second "morning hour," as stated above, he preferred it to "unfinished business," which again made the latter inaccessible.

In 1890 Speaker Reed made an end of such tinkering. He had observed the futility of trying to put four pints into a quart by rearranging the mixture, and in formulating the Reed Rules the great reformer of parliamentary methods applied his genius to a solution of this difficult problem. It could not be done in a week or a month, and while he worked the House waited somewhat impatiently. But during this interval of suspense, cross-purposes, and innuendoes, a better system was perfected, original in its conception, satisfactory in its practice, and destined to survive new conditions arising from increased business and a larger membership. As elsewhere stated, he first provided that all bills, resolutions, and committee reports be filed with the clerk; that the Speaker refer all public bills to their respective committees; and that members bè allowed to correct such references immediately after the approval of the Journal — a privilege which rarely engages the attention of the House. With a full understanding of its impor-tance he also authorized the Speaker to dispose of business "on the Speaker's table" without action by the House, except on House bills with Senate amendments, which usually go to conference without debate. This wiped out that trouble-breeder. In like manner he minimized "unfinished business" by limiting its jurisdiction to business transacted by the House in its general legislative time as distinguished from business transacted in special periods. That is to say, if a bill, taken up under the "order of business" by a motion to go into Committee of the Whole House on the State of the Union, is left unfinished at an adjournment, it comes up again only when "unfinished business" in the "order of business" is again reached, while business left unfinished in the "morning hour" or on a fixed day of the week goes over until the succeeding morning hour or fixed day. This ingenious device needed no pedestal to advertise it as a master-stroke.

Reed was not less happy in his "morning hour for the call of committees," which followed "unfinished business," for by making the length of the hour indefinite he enabled the House to consider all measures called up, or, if so disposed at the end of sixty minutes, to pass from bills on the House calendar into Committee of the Whole House on the State of the Union for the consideration of bills on the Union calendar. The elasticity of this arrangement, making it responsive to the mood of the House, gave a majority perfect freedom to keep at work as long as it desired, undisturbed by obstructive tactics. Indeed, the right to pass from one calendar to another and from the House to the Committee of the Whole became the brightest star in Reed's "order of business," which has operated with entire satisfaction and without material change for the past quarter of a century.[1]

To one unskilled in parliamentary procedure based on the House rules, the application of these expedients is confusing, for the "order of business" may be interrupted by questions of privilege, privileged bills, conference reports, special orders, measures vetoed by the President, and bills coming from a prior day with the previous question. Hence, when the cry of "Regular order" is heard, it is not easy to determine quickly what is in order. But the Chair, like a train-dispatcher, is presumed to know what has the right of way. Indeed, the running of trains on a single-track railroad may be likened to the passage of measures through the House. The freight gives way to a local passenger train, which sidetracks for an express, which in turn sidetracks for the limited, while all usually keep out of the way of a relief train. Meantime, when a train having the right of way passes, the delayed ones begin to move until again obliged to sidetrack. In like manner the "order of business" gives way to business fixed for Mondays, Wednesdays, and Fridays, which in turn may be sidetracked for privileged bills, conference reports, and special or-

[1] The following is Speaker Reed's "order of business" adopted in 1890: (1) Prayer by the chaplain; (2) reading and approval of the Journal; (3) correction of reference of public bills; (4) disposal of business on the Speaker's table; (5) unfinished business; (6) the morning hour for the consideration of bills called up by committees; (7) motions to go into Committee of the Whole House on the State of the Union; (8) orders of the day. (Rule XXIV, sec. 1.) Although mentioned in the order of business, "orders of the day" became obsolete many years before.

ders, while a question of privilege generally takes precedence of all other business.

Nevertheless, the House is not a slave to its own orders. Although certain committees have the right to report at any time, which carries the privilege of immediate consideration, any member may demand, before debate begins, that the question of consideration be first put. This cannot be required upon a bill brought up by unanimous consent or by a special order providing for its immediate consideration, for the House has already consented. But it may be raised against any other business, although it possesses the high privilege of a conference report or the right of a member to his seat. A refusal to consider, however, simply postpones the measure to another day. Hence, when conference reports or privileged bills or special orders to be carried out on a future day are presented, the House, if it prefers to proceed with other business, declines their consideration. This was the practice as early as 1808, Speaker Varnum declaring the question not debatable. John Randolph spoke of it tartly as "an engine of oppression in the hands of a majority," but Henry Clay thought the right of one or two members to compel a deliberative body to consider a proposition which it is disinclined to take up "can be maintained only by reversing the rule that a plurality is to govern, and would, as to that particular subject, make the mover and his second superior to the whole body." [1] After twice refusing to abandon the practice, the House denied its use unless demanded by some member or deemed necessary by the Speaker.[2]

[1] 12th Cong., 1st Sess., *Annals*, p. 1472 (footnote).
[2] 15th Cong., 1st Sess., *Annals*, p. 445.

The revision of the rules in 1880 limited it to the demand of a member only.[1]

Under the present (1915) rules of the House two Mondays of each month are assigned to the consideration of business relating to the District of Columbia and alternately two other Mondays to the consideration of motions for unanimous consent, for suspension of the rules, and for motions to discharge committees. On Wednesday of each week (known as "Calendar Wednesday") no business is in order except bills already reported and on the House or Union calendar, unless such business be dispensed with by a two thirds vote. The necessity for such vote cannot be avoided even in favor of an appropriation bill; nor can it be avoided by a report from the Committee on Rules. So zealously have the prerogatives of this day been observed that it has come to be spoken of as "Holy Wednesday." On Friday of each week business on the private calendar has the preference. On Tuesdays, Thursdays, and Saturdays the regular order is the consideration of bills reported by committees and of bills on the House and Union calendars. This order of business is liable to be interfered with by the interjection of privileged matters, such as revenue or appropriation bills, conference reports, and the like, or by a report from the Committee on Rules. Prior to the adoption of the unanimous consent rule, recognitions were in order at the will of the Speaker. Consideration of business by unanimous consent can now be had only when the unanimous consent calendar is in order.

[1] Rule XVI, sec. 3.

Business in which the House is engaged in its general legislative time as distinguished from the special periods set aside for classes of business, remaining unfinished at adjournment, is in order the next day; while unfinished classified business is in order to be resumed whenever the class of business to which it belongs is in order under the rules.

CHAPTER XII

COMMITTEES AND THEIR WORK

COMMITTEES report or reject whatever is properly referred to them under the rules of the House. Originally the select committee was the only organ for collecting information, for sifting evidence, or for considering bills and other legislative matters. At present, however, it is used for purposes of ceremony, or to consider special matters about which the House wishes to institute inquiries. It consists of three or more members, is often endowed with power to send for persons and papers, and upon making a final report it ceases to exist, unless new matter is referred to it in open House.

A joint select committee, composed of senators and House members, is usually created by a simple resolution, has a fixed or limited jurisdiction, and expires with the session, although it may be continued by a vote of the two bodies. The Speaker appoints the House members, but the first-named senator acts as chairman. Unlike a conference committee it votes *per capita*, and a quorum is a majority of the whole number. It may be instructed by both Houses acting concurrently, or by either House acting independently, and it may report to both or either according to its instructions. Thus the historic Joint Select Committee on the Conduct of the Civil War, being directed by the Senate in 1862 to investigate the treatment of dead soldiers at Manassas, reported only to the Senate. The advantages of this committee were especially disclosed during the Civil War, in the evolution of the Reconstruction policy, and in the settlement of the electoral count of 1857, growing out of Wisconsin's failure to cast its vote on the day prescribed by law.

A joint standing committee is ordinarily created by statute. Its procedure resembles that of the joint select committee and its use is confined to regulating intercourse between the two bodies. This committee is continuous, although its powers, during the recess after the expiration of a Congress, reside with the Senate portion. At present there are four such committees, namely, Printing, Enrolled Bills, the Congressional Library, and the Disposition of Useless Executive Papers.

A conference committee is practically two distinct committees. The number of senators may exceed the House members, or *vice versa*, but the difference is immaterial, since each acts by its own majority. It is created whenever the two Houses disagree upon any pending legislation, and expires upon the accomplishment or failure of its purpose. In the earlier practice the Speaker, ignoring majority and minority divisions, appointed members specially fitted to exploit the attitude of the House, and if one set failed another was named. But under the modern practice members are selected from the committee or subcommittee which reports the bill, — usually the chairman and next member in rank, with the ranking minority member, — who continue to act to the end. Indeed, so uniform is this custom that it created much comment and some feeling when Speaker Cannon, in appointing managers for the tariff bill of 1909, preferred a member of the committee over one of his colleagues who outranked him.

In the early history of the House the select committee, as already stated, was used exclusively for the consideration of bills, resolutions, and other legislative matters. As business increased and kindred subjects became scattered, however, a tendency to concentrate inaugurated a system of standing committees. It rooted itself slowly. There was an evident distrust of the centralizing influence of permanent bodies. Besides, it took important business from the many and gave it to a few, one standing committee of three or five members often taking the place of half a dozen select committees. But long before the middle of the last century, the standing committee, supplanting its rival, had become the most important organ of the House. It is "the eye, the ear, the hand, and very often the brain of the House," says Thomas B. Reed. "Freed from the very great inconvenience of numbers, it can study a question, obtain full information, and put the proposed legislation into shape for final action." [1]

The membership of a standing committee is fixed by rule, varying from five to twenty-two, depending largely upon the membership of the House. For a century the average did not exceed eight. In the present Congress (1915) it is fourteen. Majority and minority representation often varies with each Congress. The proportion is not infrequently nine to seven, or ten to eight, or eleven to nine. If the minority party be numerically small it is

[1] *Parliamentary Rules,* p. 59.

sometimes fixed at two thirds to one third. Such disproportion, even if technically justified, is unfortunate, for it is likely to minimize, if it does not absolutely destroy, the wholesome influence of a vigilant opposition.

In selecting a standing committee custom favors the retention of its oldest members, thus creating a corps of legislative experts, who quickly detect the weak spots in a bill or the duplication of some provision previously reported or rejected. The member first named formerly became chairman. If he resigned the committee elected a successor, but if he died the Speaker appointed. Under the present rule (1915) a committee elects its chairman, and if a vacancy occurs by death or resignation the House elects. Whatever the form of selection, however, seniority usually governs. Thus, it requires many years of faithful service before one becomes the chairman of a great committee, while the chances are that when the goal is reached the home district changes its representative or the majority passes to the opposite party. For this reason less than seventy-five chairmen out of fourteen hundred have served to exceed two terms each, the great majority being limited to one term. Nevertheless, the record shows notable service, fourteen chairmen having served four terms each, six for five terms, two for six terms, and one for ten terms.[1]

In collecting information a committee usually hears cabinet officials and other experts. Although its hearings are not town meetings "where anybody is at liberty to attend and express his views,"[2] it listens to any one

[1] Thomas Newton, of Virginia.
[2] A. Lawrence Lowell, *The Government of England*, vol. i, p. 268.

who possesses the knowledge it seeks. Such hearings are open. Other sessions are executive and closed, the rules forbidding a disclosure of the proceedings upon the floor of the House except as to matters formally reported. Yet information is never stifled. The press usually obtains it whenever the committee door opens. As elsewhere stated, only a majority of a quorum can authorize a report. Strictly speaking, a minority report is unknown to the House procedure, but the minority attains the same object by submitting its views, which are printed with the report. If a bill is unreported for fifteen days any member of the House may file with the clerk a motion in writing to discharge the committee from its further consideration. This motion is then placed on a calendar of such motions and must await a time for its consideration under the rules.

The right to report at any time distinguishes the more important standing committees. This very high privilege, which carries with it the right of present consideration, is sparingly bestowed. It was early extended to the Committees on Enrolled Bills and Elections, because their reports involved bills already passed and seats of members still in doubt. Afterward the Committee on Printing was similarly favored. But the House, seeming to distrust the gift of such an extraordinary right, withheld it for three quarters of a century from the great Committee on Ways and Means, except for brief periods in 1850 and 1851. Subsequently the several appropriation committees received the privilege, and in 1885 the House extended it to Public Lands. Five years later Territories, Invalid Pensions, and Rules were likewise favored, although usage had long accorded it to the last. But the right is still jealously guarded. Even the Judiciary Committee, which Daniel Webster headed and upon which every lawyer deems it a great honor to serve, remains unprivileged. In exercising this high prerogative committees may not include matters not specified in the rule or construe it too broadly. Thus, the words "raising revenue," for illustration, do not cover bills providing for a tariff commission, or the phrase "printing for Congress" include work done for executive departments. It is likewise held that the insertion of unprivileged matter, unless essential to the accomplishment of what is privileged, destroys all privilege.

The creation of standing committees may be said to mark with historic accuracy the growth of the Republic. In the first decade the House established only four of this class.[1] But the new century, with its important innovations, wrought a great change in the legislative mind. Ways and Means demanded men of experience as well as of capacity, and in 1802 the House promoted it from a select to a standing committee. The Louisiana Purchase in 1803 made necessary a Committee on Public Lands, while a growing capital and a more rapidly growing mail service required (1808) Committees on the District of Columbia and on Post-Offices and Post-Roads.

Very soon the need of additional courts and legislation "touching judicial proceedings" demanded a Committee on the Judiciary (1813). The War of 1812 made

[1] The Committees on Elections, Claims, Enrolled Bills, and Commerce and Manufactures.

Pensions and War Claims permament and a Committee on Public Expenditure necessary. Near the close of Madison's Administration (1816), the House, in response to the clamor for "a house-cleaning," established six committees to supervise the expenditures of the executive departments. On motion of Lewis Williams, of North Carolina, the veteran farmer-member, a Committee on Agriculture had its birth in 1820. Two years later the affairs of the army and navy, which had engrossed the attention of numerous select committees, were committed to standing committees on Military Affairs and Naval Affairs. In the same year a Committee on Foreign Affairs took charge of the relations of the United States with foreign nations. The rush of settlers into the great West necessitated the creation of Committees on Indian Affairs and on Territories (1825). An elaborate system of internal improvements justified the establishment in 1831 of a Committee on Roads and Canals. Then came Committees on Public Buildings and Grounds (1837), Patents (1837), Printing (1846), and Coinage, Weights, and Measures (1864).

The close of the Civil War marked a new era in their creation. A Committee on Education, which had formerly provoked angry opposition, found admittance in 1867 to the sisterhood of standing committees, while industries, internal improvements, and social affairs received recognition. From 1865 to 1893 the creation of eleven committees exploited rivers and harbors, labor, mining, irrigation, ventilation, immigration, reform in the civil service, and the liquor traffic. After the Spanish-American War came the establishment of Committees on Insular Affairs and Industrial Arts. Several of these committees seemed to exist for no other purpose than to furnish rooms for their chairmen — a highly prized perquisite in the absence of an office building. But after its erection (1909) the House dropped the Committees on Ventilation and Acoustics, Militia, Manufactures, Private Land Claims, Pacific Railroads, and Levee Improvements, leaving a total of fifty-five.

But if making and dropping committees caused little complaint their division encountered great opposition. The separation of Manufactures and Commerce precipitated a contest between free trade and protection. The purpose of the former was to foster infant industries, but none of the twenty-two revenue bills reported by Ways and Means between 1794 and 1816 benefited the manufacturer. For this reason the advocates of protection began an active propaganda to separate Commerce from Manufactures for the purpose of having all tariff matters referred to the latter, and to the surprise of free-traders the House, in 1819, made the division. Thereupon Speaker Clay packed the Committee on Manufactures with the friends of protection. Thus it became the great rival of Ways and Means, reporting the historic revenue bill of 1824, the famous Woolens Bill of 1827, the so-called "Tariff of Abominations" in 1828, the Mallory Bill of 1830, and the Adams Bill of 1832. But after Clay's compromise measure of 1833 its influence began to wane, and although it reported on wool duties as late as 1864, it had years before lost its place among forceful committees.

The division of Ways and Means also revealed the indisposition of committees to surrender any of their prerogatives. This great Committee inherited its absolute control of receipts and expenses from its prototype in the British Commons, and no one possessed the temerity to suggest divorcing such closely related subjects until increasing and varied needs multiplied supply bills. At the outset a single annual appropriation bill met all wants. But in 1823 a separate bill for fortifications appeared. Then came bills for pensions (1826), rivers and harbors (1828), post-offices and post-roads (1844), deficiencies (1844), consular and diplomatic service (1856), and finally, in 1857, for legislative, executive, and judicial expenses. Moreover, the habit of burdening Ways and Means with whatever pertained to the finances swelled its jurisdiction until it not only included revenue measures and appropriation bills, but the control of the war debt, the supervision of banking and currency, and the direction of coinage, weights, and measures. It seemed like an Atlas bearing upon its shoulders all the business of the House. Other committees might authorize, but Ways and Means alone could appropriate. Experienced members of Military and Naval Affairs recommended in vain, if Ways and Means thought their recommendations extravagant or unnecessary. So continuously did revenue and appropriation bills occupy the floor that the chairman became in fact as well as officially the "floor leader," ranking in influence next to the Speaker. He arranged the order of business, indicated hours for adjournment, and fixed the time for closing the long sessions.

Members marveled that one committee of seven or nine

men should desire to do so much of the real work of the House. It seemed possible to divide it, since raising and spending revenue were quite distinct; but whenever the suggestion of separating such kindred subjects became serious, it was pronounced destructive of intelligent legislation. Even after the Civil War had increased expenses tenfold, and revenue-raising harassed the most astute financiers, the plea that one committee should control both receipts and expenditures continued to dominate the House. Finally, in 1865, when the inability of members longer to endure the physical and mental strain became apparent, the jurisdiction of Ways and Means over appropriations, banking and currency, and Pacific Railroads was transferred to three committees having corresponding names. In submitting the resolution, Samuel S. Cox, then of Ohio, declared that "powerfully as the Ways and Means Committee is constituted, even their powers of endurance, physical and mental, are not adequate to the great duty imposed by the emergencies of this historic time." Thaddeus Stevens, the distinguished chairman, expressed indifference. He had an innate passion to dominate and a capacity almost equal to his passion, but to head the new committee satisfied his ambition. Justin S. Morrill, of Vermont, one of the kindliest of men, represented the revenue side. If Stevens was more powerful in debate, no one rivalled Morrill in practical wisdom or prudence. He had drawn the great tariff bill of 1861, bearing his name, on which every protective tariff has since been modeled, and although he rarely replied to those who differed from him, he never yielded his conclusions. So, while admitting that the

Committee on Ways and Means might be "over-worked," since "it labored day and night, week days and Sundays," he thought it "indispensable" that one committee "should raise and spend the revenue" in order "to make both ends meet." But the House had settled the question in advance, and the adoption of the resolution without division made Morrill chairman of Ways and Means and Stevens chairman of Appropriations.

Twelve years later the great contest began for a division of the Committee on Appropriations. At the time of the Committee's creation Robert C. Schenck, of Ohio, touched a popular chord when he observed that committees having jurisdiction of kindred subjects should control the several appropriation bills. This sentiment sourced in jealousy. The Committee on Commerce, which had for years at irregular intervals formulated river and harbor items, never ceased to resent their revision by the Committee on Ways and Means and later by the new Committee on Appropriations. It seemed inexcusable that one committee, without additional information, should possess power to modify the carefully studied work of another. Nevertheless, the restraint of precedent proved sufficient until the control of the House, for the first time in sixteen years, passed to the Democrats. This brought John H. Reagan, of Texas, to the front.

Reagan had left the House in 1861 to become Post-master-General of the Southern Confederacy, and upon his reappearance in the Forty-fourth Congress (1875) Speaker Kerr assigned him to the Commiteee on Commerce. He was a likable man. Although obstinate, with a disposition to dominate, he was not unamiable. Moreover, he was energetic, astute, and a forceful debater — clear in statement and terse in expression. His speeches had no brilliant passages, no hint of elevated thought, no single sentence which any one would care to repeat or remember after the emergency had passed. But what he said exactly served his purpose. He knew his time, his opportunity, and his men. He knew, too, what was necessary besides debate to get a bill through, and when he reported the river and harbor allowances in 1877, instead of referring them under the rule to the Committee on Appropriations, he moved to suspend the rules and pass the bill. This would avoid the dreaded pruning-knife of a disinterested arbiter, and more than two thirds of the House came to the support of his *coup d'état*.[1] A year later he successfully invoked similar methods.[2]

The revisers of the rules in 1880 did not approve Reagan's tactics. They invaded the system of control, opened the door to extravagance, and made other committees envious. Accordingly the revisers recommended restoring the authority of the Committee on Appropriations to revise river and harbor allowances. A sharp discussion followed. Joseph C. S. Blackburn, of Kentucky, a fluent speaker and ready debater, argued that the maintenance of a just relation between receipts and expenses, and a fair division of the former among the various departments, required that all appropriations

---

[1] 45th Cong., 1st Sess., *Record*, pp. 2359–60.
[2] 45th Cong., 2d Sess., *Record*, p. 2713.

be reported by one committee. James A. Garfield, a co-reviser, came promptly to Blackburn's aid. Perhaps, at times, when the great orator had not reached the bottom of a subject himself, his statesmanship was of the willow and not of the oak. But he had gone to the root of this question through observation and experience, and his remarks pierced the core of the matter. There never was a time, he said, when a committee, having a special subject in charge, did not resist a cut in its appropriations. For this reason committees entrusted with legislation should not report appropriations. On the other hand, he added, the Committee on Appropriations becomes a fair, impartial arbiter, because it bears no special relation to any department, but having a survey of the whole field it reduces all appropriations to an economical basis and within the limits of the public revenue.

To this Reagan vigorously dissented. He insisted that the Committee on Commerce, to which the river and harbor bill rightfully belonged, could appropriate as economically as the Committee on Appropriations, and he moved that it be privileged to report directly to the House for its consideration and disposition. It was a bold move. It defied Speaker Randall, challenged the floor leader, and attacked the most powerful committee of the House. But the selfish influences that supported him in the preceding Congress again rallied to his assistance.[1] Indeed, so determined was the House to unfetter itself that it granted similar privileges to the Committee on Agriculture.[2]

[1] 46th Cong., 2d Sess., *Record*, pp. 1260–62.   [2] *Ibid.*, p. 684.

This action fanned the flame of jealousy. If Commerce and Agriculture can report appropriations, asked the then "Progressive," why not distribute other appropriation bills to the Committees on Foreign, Military, Naval, and Indian Affairs? Coupled with this feeling was one of increasing discontent growing out of the so-called "Holman amendment," adopted in 1875, which permitted an appropriation bill to change existing law, "provided it be germane to the subject-matter and retrenches expenses." [1] Prior to its adoption such a proposed change would be ruled out on a point of order; but under the rule as amended the Committee on Appropriations had authority to decrease a salary, abolish an office, or recast all legislation concerning the public service not only as to the amount to be appropriated, but as to the size and condition of that service. Thus it invaded, if it did not practically absorb, the jurisdiction of other committees controlling kindred subjects. Moreover, in its desire to economize the Committee occasionally manifested a disposition to use the amendment arbitrarily. As both parties had refused to repeal it, however, the resentment aroused against the Committee proved insufficient to provoke a rebellion until William R. Morrison, of Illinois, took advantage of it with the hope of weakening the power of Samuel J. Randall, its chairman.

Morrison was a radical tariff reformer. More than that, he was a bold, forceful organizer. He had served as speaker in the Illinois legislature, had led a regiment against Fort Donelson where he was severely wounded,

[1] 44th Cong., 1st Sess., Rule cxx, now Rule xxi.

and after the war had entered the Forty-third Congress (1873). Alert, cool-headed, and resourceful, he believed every means lawful to a patriot, and when the Democrats carried the House in 1874 he played a conspicuous part in the selection of Speaker Kerr, who made him chairman of Ways and Means. Then he discovered that Samuel J. Randall measured Democratic interests and policies by the Pennsylvania standard, and with the temerity of a dashing soldier he struck with his lance's point the shield of the formidable Templar. Older members heard with astonishment, and after encountering Randall's terse, withering sentences, which he could summon to his aid with all the force of scornful invective, Morrison knew he had been soundly whipped. Moreover, at the opening of the Forty-fifth Congress (1877) Randall, then Speaker, transferred him from the head of Ways and Means to the chairmanship of Public Lands. Although this savage blow left a deep wound, Morrison discreetly nursed his resentment. He recognized that Randall, a born leader of men, without a peer in his party, was the master, about whom clustered strong, dominating men. Fernando Wood, of New York, topped Ways and Means; John D. C. Atkins, of Tennessee, succeeded William S. Holman on Appropriations; A. H. Buckner, of Missouri, relieved Samuel S. Cox on Banking and Currency; John H. Reagan headed Interstate Commerce; and Alexander H. Stephens, of Georgia, and Milton Sayler, of Ohio, sat with the Speaker on Rules, while with rare tact Randall minimized discontent by the retention of a score of Kerr's original chairmen.

But Morrison's courage was not broken. He went on just as if nothing had happened, and when the Democrats, after an interregnum of two years, returned to power in the Forty-eighth Congress (1883), he boldly took advantage of the reaction against the "Pennsylvania standard," picked Carlisle for Speaker, organized a tariff-for-revenue campaign, and carried the caucus by a majority of twenty-four over the combined vote of Randall and Samuel S. Cox, of New York.[1] This again made him chairman of Ways and Means, and, by courtesy, Randall headed Appropriations. Subsequently, Morrison reported a bill making a horizontal tariff reduction of twenty per cent, which gave him the euphonious title of "Horizontal Bill." For the moment it looked as if the Illinoisan had more than self-confidence behind him. But after getting into Committee of the Whole he found Randall, McGregor-like, at the head of the table, with forty Democrats beside him. These held the balance of power, and when they joined the Republicans in striking out the enacting clause, "Horizontal Bill" stigmatized them as "Randall and his forty thieves." [2] This humiliating defeat became historic. Members shook their heads, said they knew how it would be, and prophesied that it ended the career of the audacious leader. But they were quite mistaken. Although he knew absolutely nothing about the tariff, he kept a cool head, and, with his one hundred and fifty low-tariff followers, made a brilliantly successful attack on Randall.

[1] The vote stood: Carlisle, 106; Randall, 52; Cox, 30.
[2] The vote stood 156 to 151 in Committee of the Whole and 159 to 155 in the House.

Ordinarily a chairman who gets in the way is promptly put out of the way. Morrison had personal knowledge of Randall's method, and at the opening of the Forty-ninth Congress (1885) he urged Carlisle to administer a dose of the same medicine. This would break the Pennsylvanian at once, since Morrison believed his success lay in his ability as chairman of Appropriations to compel members desiring legislation to go to him. But Carlisle refused. He knew that the Speaker who transferred or demoted Randall would probably destroy himself, and so the resourceful Morrison, almost brutally implacable in his pursuit, determined to take advantage of the sentiment favorable to the creation of five additional appropriation committees. To make success certain he first fixed the Committee on Rules. Randall had long been on the committee, and to resist that masterful mind he had Reed, of Maine, appointed with himself. Hiscock, of New York, became the other minority member. Within a week Morrison, Reed, and Hiscock presented a majority report providing among other things that each of the five Committees on Foreign, Military, Naval, and Indian Affairs, and on Post-Offices and Post-Roads, should report a general appropriation bill with privileges similar to those allowed Appropriations. This would leave Randall with only six bills.[1]

The veteran member on Rules, quickly scenting a combination of Reed Republicans and Morrison Demo-

---

[1] Legislative, Executive and Judicial; the Sundry Civil; the Pension; Fortifications and Coast Defenses; the District of Columbia; and General Deficiency.

crats, presented a formidable and an exhaustive minority statement, insisting that the maintenance of a sane, systematic economy was possible only so long as one committee, no more interested in one department or branch of the Government than another, had authority to make or supervise all appropriations. To strengthen his position Randall reprinted the arguments made in 1865 and 1880, declaring that the enormous increase in river and harbor appropriations since 1878 justified those prophetic utterances. This increase had attracted wide attention. It threatened to embarrass the Treasury, and gave conservative legislators deep concern. Finally, in 1884, it provoked a Presidential veto, and many members who voted to override it fell by the wayside in the succeeding campaign. Thus, it became a vital illustration of the extravagance that might occur in the five committees named in the report if the House deprived the Committee on Appropriations of its existing authority.

In the debate Morrison and his supporters claimed that six committees, each one possessing perfect knowledge of a single department, could appropriate more wisely and economically than one committee, laden with the detail of six departments, since for want of time, if for no other reason, it could neither study nor know their real needs. There was some acrimony. Garfield had admitted in 1879 that the Holman amendment "has so overloaded the Committee as to render it quite impossible for its members to devote sufficient attention to the details of legislation proper." [1]   This confession of so

[1] *North American Review*, 1879.

distinguished an advocate of the Committee's sole right to appropriate furnished abundant authority to its critics, who opened a battery of argument upon the character of its investigations, pronouncing them superficial, often perfunctory, and never thorough. A patriotic note also implied that too strict attention to economy, based on parsimonious mathematical calculations, had sacrificed the Republic's best interests, since its honor could not always be measured in dollars and cents. Indeed, it was broadly intimated that the Committee, in obedience to a penurious habit, had not interpreted its duty by a high regard for the country. Thus, a sentiment pervaded the debate that rigid economy never inspired a patriotic view of the public welfare. Conversely, freedom from restraint and an open treasury led to national glory.

In his replies Randall did not indulge in repartee or sarcasm. When such devices would serve his purpose he could fling them almost with the ease of Thaddeus Stevens, his distinguished predecessor on Appropriations. But the temper of the House and the condition of the debate induced discretion, and he answered with good nature. The Committee on Appropriations, he said, was divided into half a dozen subcommittees, each of which had as much time to study the real needs of a department as an independent committee of twelve or fifteen members, while the systematic revision of its work absolutely assured to each department just treatment and to the Government's revenue adequate protection. To remove such restraint meant entrance "upon a path of extravagance you cannot foresee the length of or the depth of until we find the Treasury of the country bankrupt."

Among Randall's able supporters in his own party, Hilary A. Herbert, of Alabama, destined to sit in President Cleveland's Cabinet, ranked with the foremost. He had a graceful and gracious bearing. He never declaimed or ranted, but with a singularly expressive combination of force and ease he used no word that did not bear upon the point he would enforce. He thought a continued and intimate interest in the affairs of one department would become too personal and tend to undue liberality. James H. Blount, of Georgia, a man of gifts, skillful and forceful in debate, boldly charged that a desire for greater influence on the floor and in the social life of Washington, which came to those who held the purse-strings, inspired much of the activity for the proposed change. But Herbert's opposition, though he agreed with Blount, was broader than a rebuke to its selfish advocates. He believed the proposition as wrong in principle as it would be destructive in practice, and in a single prophetic sentence, pronounced slowly and most impressively, he declared: "Scatter appropriations and you will scatter the people's money." William S. Holman, known as the "watch-dog of the Treasury," estimated the cost of such a "scatter" at $29,000,000 annually. Five years before (1880) Garfield had fixed it at $20,000,000. At such a rate of increase the veteran watch-dog saw a bankrupt Treasury as plainly as Randall did.

Of the few Republicans who opposed the Morrison scheme two or three became illustrious. William Mc-

Kinley, of Ohio, spoke with great freedom in opposition to the views of Thomas B. Reed. The latter's distrust of the future President, destined to grow into bitter dislike, had not yet appeared, for McKinley rarely got in his way. He was not a debater. Even when officially the floor leader in the Fifty-first Congress (1889), he left the unpremeditated rough-and-tumble work of floor management to Joseph G. Cannon. He preferred preparation, and when ready, with the priceless advantage of a musical voice aided by the orator's gift, he gave importance to any subject. His persuasive, well-matured arguments, dexterously interposed to break the effect of some telling speech, or delivered with the distinct purpose of convincing the House, quickly created enthusiasm on one side without arousing resentment or anger on the other. This was the result in the pending controversy. He understood the animus of Morrison as well as the cause of the Committee's unpopularity, and his purpose to prevent the one and cure the other was not ambiguous. While admitting that the Committee exercised tyrannical power, he declared the repeal of the Holman amendment sufficient, since it and not the Committee's possession of the appropriation bills created the trouble. "I do not sympathize with the sentiment so prevalent among my party friends," he said slowly, bringing a silence which made a whisper audible, "that it is a good policy to enact rules which everybody admits will lead to extravagance." This declaration fell with shattering effect. "Oh, no. Nobody admits it!" exclaimed Morrison. "It is admitted all over the House. The distinguished leader from Pennsylvania admits it," retorted the speaker. "Oh, he would admit it, of course," interrupted Reed. To this McKinley calmly replied: "When the gentleman from Pennsylvania, who for twenty years has occupied a conspicuous place on this floor, says the proposed change means extravagance, I must believe him; and if this proposition is to punish him for helping us defeat the Morrison tariff bill let us defeat it. If the Committee in the past has acted as a check upon jobbery and waste and extravagance, we need it now, especially since the President's message threatens a deficit of twenty-four millions." [1]

Joseph G. Cannon also backed Randall. He was a man of singular ability and energy, destined to longer service than any member living or dead, and to long service as Speaker. His parliamentary training had been perfected before its success was generally acknowledged, but long before the Forty-ninth Congress opened his faculties had become so well drilled that he could use them at any given moment to their fullest stretch. Moreover, his conspicuous work for twelve years upon Post-Offices and Appropriations gave him great prestige. It enabled him to speak from experience, and in accents of subdued, mellifluous benignity, with a face that suggested soft, bland benevolence, he presented arguments logically cogent and expressive of his own deep convictions. He declared that each of the five committees involved, under the distribution plan, would magnify its work, regarding it of more importance than that of all others combined, and thus, by confusing possible future needs with present demands, would sub-

[1] 49th Cong., 1st Sess., *Record*, pp. 319–20.

stitute a jingo extravagance for a patriotic economy. It meant experiments, the adoption of fads, the vagaries of theorists, and a wide-open Treasury with no one authorized to close the door. "I would rather bunch appropriations again in Ways and Means," he declared, with startling emphasis, "than pass them around."

This rattling speech, made by one whose service already covered more years than any other member present save Randall, Holman, Cox, and William D. Kelley, brought Reed to his feet. In 1880 he had declared that "the effect of distribution will be to add to the expenses of the Government more than the Holman rule ever saved." This was Randall's argument now. But Reed like Morrison had a grievance. For several years he had chafed under the Committee's control of the House and had resented its abandonment of what to him seemed vital to the Republic's welfare, until he was ready to sacrifice consistency, declaring his former attitude a "youthful effort," taken when "I actually believed" that the Committee, under the rules then adopted, would transact business in a sensible way. "But for three Congresses," he continued, "members have been in irons. It has left us without a fortification, without a navy, and without the transaction of any business except that of the Committee itself." This savage attack, including the period covered by the chairmanship of Atkins, Hiscock, and Randall, added life to the debate, and, if judged by applause, expressed the sentiment of the House. Like all sweeping statements, however, this caustic condemnation was not wholly just. The building of a modern navy, which had long engaged

England in expensive and unsatisfactory experiments, had already begun, four armored cruisers being then under construction.[1] Nor had coast defenses been overlooked. Although nothing had happened to arouse the country's attention to their immediate need, the Endicott Board had selected twenty-six places to be fortified at an estimated cost of $122,000,000.[2] Strange that one accustomed to accuracy of statement should overlook these facts at such a time. It increased the surprise, too, that his argument ignored Cannon's warning; avoided Holman's estimated cost to the Government; and failed to consider Randall's comparison of river and harbor appropriations before and after the removal of the Committee's check upon such expenditures. In fact, aside from his pungent criticism, he added nothing except that more members needed the knowledge gained in committee activities, and that "distribution" would raise the average of intelligence. In illustration of enlightenment thus teaching economy, he cited the merchant who could fix a price to meet competition the better he knew his business. At all events, he said, with a penetrating glance at Herbert, "it is better to give liberally with knowledge than niggardly in ignorance." [3]

The indication that the tide ran strongly against the Committee on Appropriations was verified by the vote of 227 to 70 in favor of distribution. Its one-sidedness

[1] These were the Atlanta, Boston, Chicago, and Dolphin, authorized in 1883 under Hiscock.

[2] The Endicott Board was authorized March 3, 1885, under Randall.

[3] 49th Cong., 1st Sess., *Record*, p. 210.   The entire debate is found on pages 168-76, 197-210, 225-41, 278-98, 310-38.

surprised even Morrison. He counted upon the opposition of "Randall and his forty thieves," but he did not expect the support of two thirds of the Republicans. An analysis of the arguments and the vote makes it plain that a get-even spirit actuated Morrison and his low-tariff followers, while resentment of the Committee's tyranny, especially under the construction given the Holman amendment, largely governed others.

Legislation shaped in such temper is not likely to tolerate high principle or to result satisfactorily even to those who framed it. In this instance repentance came early, for the system introduced soon verified Randall's prediction. Under it each of the eight appropriation committees, acting independently, without restraint, and without regard either to its fair proportion or to the amount of available revenue, reported whatever it deemed desirable, apparently indifferent to an abnormal increase in appropriations or to the creation of a treasury deficit. This has resulted in such an alarming growth of public expenditures that some modification of the present plan seems essential to the future welfare of the Republic. Indeed, so enormous was the increase before the retirement of Speaker Reed in 1901, that he expressed to Joseph G. Cannon deep regret for his action. With equal frankness Joseph D. Sayers, of Texas, one of the least sentimental and the most unaffected of men, who followed the lead of Morrison and later retired to become governor of his State, "indulged the hope that the Committee would be again charged with all the appropriations of whatever character. Until this is done much cannot be accomplished in the direction of economy." [1] In corroboration of this statement James A. Tawney, of Minnesota, for several years chairman of the Committee on Appropriations, reported that during the Sixty-first Congress his committee cut seventeen millions from the estimates, while other appropriating committees added twenty-eight millions, thus proving that committees which appropriate for a single department acquire a special bias which begets extravagance. [2] In discussing this subject John J. Fitzgerald, of New York, Tawney's successor as chairman of Appropriations, startled the country with a comparison of the appropriations made from 1875 to 1885 with those made from 1901 to 1912. This showed a total increase in twelve years of over six billion dollars, or 270.8 per cent. Upon the same basis of comparison the population of the United States increased 70.9 per cent, and its wealth, based upon a "true valuation of real and personal property," 80 per cent. [3] During these later years committees appropriated without restraint. Occasionally a party's need of a record for economy, voiced privately by the Speaker or publicly by the chairman of the Committee on Appropriations, whose duty it is to review the disposition of public moneys, [4] effected temporary retrenchment. Not infrequently other and more tortuous methods were invoked. In 1901 Senator Carter, of Montana, defeated a river and harbor bill, carrying fifty million dollars, by continuing debate until

---

[1] 63d Cong., 1st Sess., *Record*, p. 2460.
[2] 61st Cong., 3d Sess., *Record*, p. 2630.
[3] 63d Cong., 1st Sess., *Record*, p. 2458.
[4] 63d Cong., 2d Sess., *Record*, p. 7034.

Congress expired.[1] But such savings, made for use in a political campaign or to preserve a treasury balance, do not belong in the realm of legislative economy, since extravagance is only deferred.

Indeed, so enormous is the waste under the present method of making appropriations that little if any division of sentiment exists as to the need of a change. In the Sixty-second Congress Swagar Sherley, of Kentucky, with a display of pluck indicative of his independence, pronounced the system absolutely unscientific, "because we consider the individual bills separately and apart from their relationship to the whole expenditure." [2] With equal spirit John J. Fitzgerald, of New York, a cold economist, basing his convictions on several years' activity as chairman of Appropriations, declared that "while such an illogical, unscientific, and universally condemned system prevails, attempts at reform will be futile and an effective remedy for the resulting evils is impossible." [3] Other members of long experience have spoken as decisively.

It is probable that any method which the Government might adopt for reducing expenses would prove less effective than if operated by a great corporation controlled by a single head. Even the boasted English budget system, originally formulated if not fully developed by William Pitt, needs improvement.[4] But that some plan will soon be devised for avoiding excessive

[1] Soon after President McKinley appointed him to the board of commissioners of the Louisiana Purchase Exposition, of which he became chairman.

[2] 62d Cong., 2d Sess., *Record*, p. 5132.

[3] 63d Cong., 1st Sess., *Record*, p. 2454.

[4] Sir Courtenay Ilbert, *History of Parliament*, p. 109.

expenditures cannot be doubted. It is suggested that greater scrutiny and further revision of the items placed in the Book of Estimates, submitted to Congress by the Secretary of the Treasury, would be a long step in the right direction.[1] Though prepared with ample details and in strict accordance with law, it is stuffed with excessive amounts reported by ambitious bureau chiefs whose action is final. In transmitting these estimates the Secretary is simply a messenger. He is not only powerless to revise them, but without authority of law to notify the President of their amount unless in excess of the estimated revenue. It is likewise suggested that more modern and economical methods be substituted for the present archaic departmental system. Although big business has long demonstrated the large saving made by central purchasing agencies, no government official, until President Taft appointed a commission on

[1] Estimates of appropriations for the next fiscal year are prepared by the head of each department and bureau of the public service, who must specify their sources and indicate the conjectural from those established. References must also be given to laws or treaties which authorize such expenditures. If such estimates vary materially from those formerly proposed or contain new items, reasons must be set forth. These various estimates are submitted to the Secretary of the Treasury, who must add statements showing appropriations made in the previous year, the number and class of employees with their pay, and an estimate of all revenues likely to be received during the next fiscal year. This information, forming a Book of Estimates of three hundred or more pages, is printed, indexed, and arranged under the heads of Civil Establishment, Military Establishment, Naval Establishment, etc., and transmitted to the Speaker of the House, who refers it to the several committees making appropriations. If the estimated appropriations exceed the estimated revenue, the Secretary of the Treasury must notify the President, who may, in his message to Congress, indicate how such appropriations may be reduced, or recommend loans or new taxes to cover the deficiency.

economy and efficiency, ever recommended that one bureau, representing the several departments, be authorized to make repairs, to prevent duplication of work, and to purchase all supplies.

To the end that the House may exercise greater economy, Fitzgerald advocates enlarging the Committee on Appropriations to include the chairmen of other appropriating committees and restore its control of all supply bills.[1] This desire to return to the procedure of 1866 is not surprising, since its abandonment so speedily brought the predicted evils; but it may well be doubted if other committees will ever consent, even in the interest of economy, to sacrifice their right to appropriate. Another plan, presented by Swagar Sherley, of Kentucky, attracts equal attention. It provides for a Committee on Estimates and Expenditures, to consist of the chairman and one or more members of Rules, Ways and Means, and each of the eight appropriating committees, who shall determine the available revenue and apportion it to each of the several appropriating committees. In ascertaining these amounts it is proposed that the Committee, avoiding details of routine estimates, shall simply determine policies, such as the number and type of battleships, public buildings, and coast defenses, the extent of river and harbor improvements, and important changes respecting the army and navy, thus ascertaining in advance how much the House is willing to expend over and above the ordinary upkeep of the Government. After the House adopts the report, no committee may modify it.[2] Although it is objected that this Committee,

[1] 63d Cong., 1st Sess., *Record*, p. 2459.
[2] 62d Cong., 3d Sess., *Record*, pp. 5132–38.

in fixing the amount of each supply bill, must practically absorb the functions of the appropriating committees, it is said in reply that the chairman and several members of each of these committees, with full knowledge of the estimates, will be present to urge the needs of their respective departments, while each one can be heard as fully as now whenever the report of the Committee on Estimates and Expenditures is before the House. Other difficulties are presented which may, perhaps, be removed, for experience often avoids parliamentary obstacles that seem to block the way. It is favorable to its adoption that it not only maintains the integrity of all appropriating committees, but permits members to exercise the highly valued prerogative of increasing estimates, or making appropriations not covered by estimates, so long as apportioned amounts are not exceeded or adopted policies modified.

CHAPTER XIII

THE COMMITTEE OF THE WHOLE

THE Committee of the Whole is not a committee in the sense used in the preceding chapter. In early years the House employed it for the consideration of such important questions as the tariff, the creation of executive departments, the President's annual messages, propositions relating to land gifts, and proposed amendments to the Constitution. Very often its deliberations resulted in an agreement upon the details of a measure, leaving nothing to a committee of reference except the mere labor of drafting a bill. Because of this practice John W. Taylor, an exceptionally able and acute Speaker, decided that the Committee of the Whole belonged to the regular committee system.[1] But the more modern view holds that it is simply the House itself doing business under a special and less formal procedure, by means of which the entire membership is enabled to participate in the consideration of a bill, unhampered by roll-calls or the intervention of motions to adjourn, to refer, to postpone, for the previous question, and the like.

To most members the procedure is a favorite one. The absence of roll-calls avoids record votes, while debate under the five-minute rule, so called from the time limit of the speeches, becomes intensely interesting and often critically analytical, the freedom and informality

[1] 19th Cong., 1st Sess., *Debates*, p. 1358.

of explaining and opposing amendments adding a zest which is absent in more formal discussions. At such times the House is at its best. It takes nothing for granted. It ridicules an explanation that does not explain and quickly punctures a proposed panacea. "The key to the difficulties of most unsettled questions," says Bagehot, "is commonly in their undiscussed parts";[1] but under the five-minute rule as it now exists there are no undiscussed parts. If ably led on either side such a debate compels men to comprehend, and destroys prejudice by driving it from shelter. Many floor leaders have shone in these discussions, but "no one during the present generation," says Mr. Blaine, "has rivaled Robert C. Schenck's singular power in this respect. He was an intellectual marvel. The completeness and clearness of his statement, the facts and arguments which he could marshal in that brief time, were a constant surprise and delight to his hearers. He was able in every form of discussion, but his peculiar gift was in leading and controlling the Committee of the Whole."[2]

This Committee has a long history. It originated in the time of the Stuarts, when taxation arrayed the Crown against the Commons, and suspicion made the Speaker a tale-bearer to the King. To avoid the Chair's espionage the Commons met in secret, elected a chairman in whom it had confidence, and without fear of the King freely exchanged its views respecting supplies. The informality of its procedure survived the occasion for secrecy, but to this day the House of Commons keeps

---

[1] *The English Constitution*, p. 207.
[2] *Twenty Years of Congress*, vol. I, p. 499.

up the fiction of concealment, the Speaker withdrawing from the hall when the Committee convenes, and the chairman occupying the clerk's desk.[1]

From the outset the American House contemplated a Committee of the Whole House, and a Committee of the Whole House on the State of the Union. The latter got its title from the "Committee of the Whole House on the State of America," used by the Continental Congress, its prototype being the English "Committee of the Whole House on the State of the Nation." When adopting its title the House also appropriated its functions, employing it, as stated above, for the informal consideration of highly important matters before their reference to select or standing committees. This was the procedure in 1789 when Madison raised the question of tariff duties. Meanwhile bills favorably reported from select or standing committees were referred to a "Committee of the Whole House." Originally this committee also bore the title of the "Committee of the Whole on Ways and Means," [2] the former being used for ordinary bills and the latter for appropriation and revenue measures. A similar practice still obtains in the House of Commons. It has a Committee of the Whole on Supply, or the "Committee of Supply," and the Committee of the Whole on Ways and Means, or, in common parlance, the "Committee of Ways and Means." If engaged in considering Indian revenue accounts, such subject gives the Committee another and different title. In other words, the British Committee of the Whole, although

[1] In early years this was the practice in the House of Representatives.

[2] 14th Cong., 1st Sess., *Journal*, pp. 298–99.

the same body, is really four or more distinct committees, each confined exclusively to its own business, so that before other matters are taken up it must rise and give way to another class of legislation.

Early in its history the American House sought a similar arrangement. The reference of all reported bills to a Committee of the Whole House gave rise to much wrangling as to which should have precedence, and to relieve the trouble the House, in 1817, provided that not more than three bills, which must be analogous in nature, should be referred to the same Committee of the Whole. While this apparently created several such committees, it really did nothing more than divide reported bills into various classes, each class to be disposed of before another could be taken up. A further rule, adopted in 1820, limited these divisions to (1) private Senate bills reported by a House committee; (2) private House bills reported; (3) public bills reported; (4) Senate bills unfavorably reported; and (5) reports unfavorable to petitions. This arrangement segregated private and public bills, and although the House refused to limit the number of Committees of the Whole to three, as proposed in 1822 and again in 1824, the practice soon established the custom.

Meanwhile, opposition to exploiting matters in the Committee of the Whole on the State of the Union which belonged primarily to standing committees, became more and more pronounced. The open procedure, it was claimed, invited publicity, consumed too much time, embarrassed members by exciting the country, and presented no good reason why all questions should not first be considered by standing or select committees. The settlement of this matter proved decidedly virulent. Madison favored the widest publicity, and in the art of political advocacy he had no equal. Never aspiring, but ever adequate to great affairs, he possessed a power of detail and a didactic precision that laid bare all the weak points of an opponent. He thought that in an age of important business, when an unusual number of great topics awaited discussion, the House itself should first digest such subjects, unless prevented by want of time or the necessity of examining documents. On the other hand, the Federalists, led by Theodore Sedgwick, favored legislative initiative only through standing or select committees. This gave members little skilled in diversified argument, but capable of forming an accurate judgment, an opportunity of expressing opinions without being compelled to argue, or to persuade, or even to defend their position. Such an advantage, peculiar to all small committees, hastens business, and as the affairs of the House rapidly multiplied, the custom of considering matters in Committee of the Whole on the State of the Union, other than bills regularly referred to it from reporting committees, gradually became obsolete. In 1833 it was declared "a usage of the past." Meantime, the practice was established of using this Committee for the consideration of bills involving a tax or charge upon the people, while private bills of a like character were considered in Committee of the Whole.

Although the original rule, adopted in 1794, that every "motion or proposition for a tax or charge upon the people shall first be considered in a Committee of the

Whole House," sufficed for more than half a century, it did not always cover the refinements of its spirit. Thus, Speaker Cobb held that a bill directing a claimant to be paid did not go to the Committee of the Whole unless it actually appropriated the money. Other Speakers decided that the rule did not include "an appropriation hereafter to be made," or "to be paid out of an appropriation already made." To cover these evasive phrases an amendment was adopted in 1874. The revision of 1880 extended it to relief of sureties on a bond, and in 1896 the House added the reference of claims to the Court of Claims. Under the present practice, therefore, "all motions or propositions involving a tax or charge upon the people, and all appropriations of money, or bills making appropriations of money or property, or requiring such appropriations to be made, or authorizing payments out of appropriations already made, or releasing any liability to the United States for money or property, or referring any claim to the Court of Claims, must first be considered in a Committee of the Whole." [1] In other words, a bill which sets in motion a train of circumstances destined ultimately to involve certain expenditures must run the gantlet of the five-minute rule, unless it comes up by unanimous consent, by special order, or under suspension of the rules, the effect of such motions being to discharge the Committee and bring the bill before the House itself. Nor does the rule apply to a conference report, which must be accepted or rejected as an entirety without amendment; [2] or to Senate

[1] Rule xxiii, sec. 3.
[2] 41st Cong., 3d Sess., *Globe*, p. 1916. The early practice allowed it. See 27th Cong., 2d Sess., *Globe*, p. 868.

amendments that merely change the amount, or to bills in which an appropriation is incidentally but not necessarily involved, or is a mere matter of speculation, or is not to be borne by the Government, or is simply changed as to the mode of expenditure. Speaker Reed held that expenses paid from the House contingent fund did not come within the rule, although Carlisle and Crisp decided otherwise. In holding that expenses for printing, paid out of the contingent fund, did not go to the Committee, Speaker Keifer reasoned that the right of the Committee on Printing to report at any time carried with it the right of present consideration in the House.

Consideration of other than appropriation bills is permitted in Committee of the Whole. The President's annual messages and articles of impeachment are uniformly referred to it. Under its unrivaled procedure the general revision of the rules in 1880 received notable care. In general, any subject the House desires to study with searching fidelity may be referred to it. When attending an impeachment trial the House appears as in Committee of the Whole.

The ceremony of passing from the House to the Committee of the Whole requires but a moment. A member moves that the House resolve itself into the Committee of the Whole House for the consideration of bills on the private calendar, without designating any one; or the Whole House on the State of the Union for the consideration of revenue or general appropriation bills, or a particular bill designated by its number and title. This motion is neither debatable nor amendable, and, if carried, the mover or another reserves all points of order on paragraphs not germane or within the reporting committee's jurisdiction. The length of general debate is also usually limited at this time. After these preliminaries the Speaker designates a chairman, ordinarily selected in advance, to whom he politely extends the gavel. Prior to the Third Congress the House chose him by ballot. In the House of Commons he is nominated by the Ministry, ceases to be a partisan, and rules as impartially as the Speaker himself. In the American House, on the contrary, the chairman remains a partisan. He not only represents his party, but his selection is often based upon his known disposition to rule in favor of the bill under consideration. If it is to be stoutly contested, he usually knows in advance the points upon which he must rule, and his decisions not infrequently are prepared before his appointment.

The chairman's duties begin when he declares the House in Committee of the Whole. With matters immediately preceding he has nothing to do. Nor does he control admission to the floor, or leave to print, or matters for the *Record*, although he may exclude disorderly words. Under the rules he maintains order, recognizes members for debate, decides points of order, and directs the Committee to rise whenever members become unduly turbulent, since punishment belongs to the House. Indeed, at such times the Speaker may of his own volition resume the chair. When John Bell, of Tennessee, one of the ablest and most distinguished members, was assaulted by a colleague, Speaker Polk rushed to the desk, declaring that he "had taken the chair without an order to bring the House into order," citing Jefferson's

Manual as his authority.[1] Three years later Speaker White reached the chair while Henry A. Wise, of Virginia, and Edward Stanly, of North Carolina, were exchanging blows.[2] On one occasion when James S. Sherman, of New York, was presiding as chairman of the Committee, he, of his own motion, sent for Speaker Reed to resume the chair for the purpose of bringing to order an unruly member who had defied the chairman and persisted in his disorder. After a mollifying lecture from the Speaker on the necessity for mutual coöperation to secure orderly procedure and maintain the dignity of the House, the skies were cleared and the Committee resumed its session.

The effect of the Speaker's sudden appearance under such conditions is often humorous, sometimes resulting in loud laughter, for angry scenes quickly change to exhibitions of mock harmony. Since such disturbances usually occur in the heat of debate, a manly apology, promptly made, ordinarily satisfies. During the nervous tension immediately preceding the declaration of war with Spain in 1898, an intense excitement, raised by the charge of liar and the drawing of a knife, subsided so suddenly on the appearance of the mace, borne by the sergeant-at-arms, that it provoked no official notice. Only once in the history of Congress has a Speaker threatened to call the Capitol police. This record is the more remarkable, perhaps, if one may credit the statement of James H. Hammond, of South Carolina, respecting the Speakership contest in 1859. "I believe," he wrote, "that every man is armed with a revolver —

---

[1] 25th Cong., 2d Sess., *Globe*, p. 422.
[2] 27th Cong., 1st Sess., *Globe*, p. 445.

some with two and a bowie knife." Before the Civil War it was not unusual for members to bear concealed weapons. Speaking of his experiences in the fifties, former Speaker Grow tells of a revolver slipping from a member's hip pocket and falling noisily to the floor in front of the Speaker's desk. In answer to a request from the Chair, its owner explained that he had carried it the night before as a protection against vicious dogs and forgot to remove it from his pocket. This explanation raised a roar of derisive laughter, but the matter received no further notice. "It is doubtful," added Grow, "if a revolver has been carried in the House for forty years." [1]

Although one hundred constitutes a quorum in the Committee of the Whole, it may proceed with a less number until the chairman is notified of the fact. He then directs a roll-call, and if a quorum fails to respond, the Speaker resumes the chair while the chairman reports the absentees for entry in the Journal. When a quorum finally appears, the Committee resumes its session. As it cannot adjourn or transact business other than that before it, it frequently rises that the House may receive a message from the Senate or the President. A motion to rise is not debatable. Nor is it in order if a member has the floor in debate, or pending a demand for tellers, or the announcement of a vote; but it has precedence of a motion to amend. The chairman of his own volition may direct the Committee to rise at an hour previously fixed by the House for an adjournment, or to rise informally to receive a message; but a message

[1] Conversation with the author.

from the President, received after the Committee rises, may not then be laid before the House without unanimous consent.

When in Committee of the Whole House members participating in debate are confined strictly to the topic under consideration, but during general debate in Committee of the Whole House on the State of the Union any subject, however irrelevant, may be discussed. Two members of opposing views apportion the time, giving preference to members of the reporting committee. Promptly at the close of general debate, which must be fixed by vote in the House, the clerk begins reading the bill.[1] At the end of any paragraph a member who gets the floor may raise a point of order, move to strike out the enacting clause, or offer an amendment. A motion to strike out precedes one to amend, while the right to explain or oppose precedes a motion to amend an amendment. The proponent of an amendment is allowed five minutes to explain and an opponent five minutes to reply. This ends debate on that amendment; but similar privileges are permitted on other amendments, on amendments to an amendment, and on the *pro-forma* amendment to "strike out the last word." Points of order are decided by the chairman, while debate on an appeal is limited as in the House. One fifth of a quorum is required to order tellers, but yeas and nays are not taken or pairs announced.

Although a disposition rarely manifests itself to close the five-minute debate immediately, the Committee

[1] Revenue and appropriation bills are divided into paragraphs; other bills into sections.

may, after one speech of five minutes, cut off all debate on the pending section; but this does not preclude offering and disposing of amendments without debate. Indeed, no way exists to take a bill from the Committee until read through by paragraphs or sections except by a special order, or by striking out the enacting clause. The latter course, should the House non-concur, recommits the bill to the Committee as unfinished business.

It took nearly a century to perfect this felicitous system, so responsive to the majority and so tolerant to the minority. Originally speeches were unlimited, and so long as this vicious handicap continued the procedure profited little by other benefits. Finally, in 1841, the Committee on Rules, taking advantage of its privilege to report "at all times," submitted a rule that whenever a bill had been read for amendments without debate, the Committee of the Whole might report to the House.[1] During the struggle the House not only adopted the rule, but it limited all speeches to one hour both in the House and in Committee of the Whole. In reviewing this historic conflict one wonders that many very sensible persons, including John Quincy Adams, should have opposed such a needed reform as the limitation of speeches. No doubt the manner of bringing it about goaded the minority into violence, but it soon proved a satisfactory compromise. Not as much could be said of the exclusion of debate on amendments. In fact, the rule amounted to burlesque, since it needs discussion to amend wisely, and to obviate the defect privilege was granted in 1847 to explain each amendment in one

[1] 27th Cong., 1st Sess., *Globe*, p. 155.

speech of five minutes. Contrary to expectation, however, this increased obstruction by inviting scores of amendments which were withdrawn as soon as read and explained. An additional provision, adopted in 1850, permitted one speech in reply, but denied the right to withdraw amendments except by unanimous consent. Although this proved a long step toward perfecting the five-minute rule, anti-slavery advocates demonstrated that it in no wise lessened obstruction.

This became alarmingly evident pending the consideration of the Kansas-Nebraska Bill in 1854. One irreverent abolitionist declared that the heavens and earth may pass away, but the Missouri Compromise shall not pass away, and to prevent such an inexcusable betrayal of a sacred agreement the Free-Soilers consumed several months with an endless number of amendments. Finally, Alexander H. Stephens moved to strike out the enacting clause, citing Rule 119 as his authority. In appearance Stephens resembled John Randolph, his attenuated body seeming scarcely able to support his massive head, while his amiable disposition and gentle manners exaggerated his physical frailty. But his vigorous mind and clear voice, as he explained his historic motion, quickly dispelled the idea of weakness. Without displaying the slightest feeling he evinced a subtle charm of manner that explained his power as a popular speaker. Should the enacting clause be stricken out and the House refuse to concur, he said, the bill, which will then be in the House, can be voted upon directly. "I make this motion now," he added, "because the measure has been under consideration for five months and in this way we shall get rid of these endless amendments." [1]

Israel Washburn, of Maine, quickly took the floor. He was a new member, just entering his second term, and like Stephens belonged to the milder men of the House. But his knowledge of the rules and his readiness to apply them had already attracted attention, and he now made the point of order that under the unbroken practice for many years such a motion must be made in the House. To this the chairman retorted that the practice had been in violation of the rule. Thereupon Washburn denounced the proceeding as "the most flagrant attempt ever made to trample on the constitutional rights of a minority of the representatives and of a majority of the people." [2]

Stephens understood the practice as Washburn did. The motion to strike out the enacting clause had long been recognized, and Rule 119, adopted in 1822, gave it preference over one to amend; but it had distinctly been held in 1842 that this motion could not be made in Committee before the bill was read through for amendments, and the practice had conformed to that decision.[3] Stephens maintained, however, that Rule 119 did not belong among the rules relating to the Committee of the Whole, but was in fact a part of the rule prescribing the precedence of motions admissible when a question was under debate, whether in the House or in Committee, and that therefore it was not subject to the limitations imposed by the ruling of 1842.

---

[1] 33d Cong., 1st Sess., *Globe*, p. 1241.   [2] *Ibid.*
[3] 27th Cong., 2d Sess., *Globe*, pp. 244–45.

Years afterward Speaker Blaine pronounced this explanation "a parliamentary fraud"; adding, "and I measure my words when so describing it." [1] It was certainly a fictitious device, and by means of it a ruling of the Chair, sustained on appeal by a majority vote, accomplished what would otherwise have required a suspension of the rules by a two thirds vote. But like all sudden and radical changes in the parliamentary procedure of the House, it was the product of party necessity. It belongs in the same category with the action of the Whigs in 1841; with the abolition of dilatory motions in 1882; with the adoption of a special order by a majority vote in 1883; and with the counting of a quorum in 1890; and although it was a counterfeit contrivance, entirely lacking the constitutional basis and broad application of the extraordinary innovations established by Reed, the curious eye will search through parliamentary history in vain for anything more adroit and unexpected. A bomb dropped from the clouds into the midst of the Free-Soilers could not have created greater consternation, and in their unsuccessful efforts to escape the destructive blow they exhausted all the devices known to obstructionists.

Although the means adopted to repeal the Missouri Compromise were bitterly denounced at the time as subversive of the rights of the minority, the precedent became an accepted practice of the House for several years. It proved too useful to be willingly given up. If it helped one party in 1854, Banks used it to aid his side in 1857; but the cunning play did not belong in a parlia-

[1] 43d Cong., 2d Sess., *Record*, p. 899.

mentary code, and in the revision of 1860 Washburn destroyed its sting by providing that whenever the House refused to concur in a report striking out the enacting clause the bill should automatically return to the Committee. As this deprived the House of the right to refer it for reformation to another committee, an amendment adopted in 1870 restored the privilege, with the reservation that whenever the bill "is again reported to the House it shall be referred to the Committee of the Whole without debate." [1] Washburn also destroyed the evil of unlimited discussion of amendments by clothing the Committee with power, after the five-minute rule begins, to close debate upon any section, further amendments being decided without debate. Thus was perfected the present admirable procedure under the five-minute rule.

A bill being read through for amendments the Committee's work concludes with a motion to rise and report with recommendation that the measure be passed, or referred, or laid on the table, or postponed. Thereupon the chairman, returning the gavel to the Speaker, resumes his place on the floor and reports in form as follows: "Mr. Speaker, the Committee of the Whole House or the Whole House on the State of the Union, having had under consideration the bill [giving number and title] has directed me to report the same with amendments with the recommendation that the amendments be agreed to and that the bill do pass," or otherwise as the recommendation directs. This brief report includes all the information the House can possess. If

[1] Rule XXIII, secs. 6 and 7.

another than the chairman seeks to add a further statement, even though he claims the floor on a question of personal privilege, the Speaker declines to hear him, since no such matter is before the House.[1] This ironclad rule occasionally becomes a cover to wrongdoing,[2] but the House, if so disposed, can correct any high-handed action by non-concurring in the report.

[1] 56th Cong., 1st Sess., *Record*, p. 4730.
[2] 29th Cong., 1st Sess., *Globe*, August 10, 1846.

CHAPTER XIV

THE MAKING OF A LAW

WHEN a member introduces a bill he endorses it with his name and the committee to which in his opinion it belongs, and delivers it to the clerk, who enters it by number and title in the Journal and the *Record*. The Speaker or his secretary then indicates the committee to which it goes. An error in the reference of a private bill must be corrected, otherwise it cannot be reported; but a committee to which a public measure is improperly referred acquires jurisdiction if the mistake remain unrectified. If a bill falls within the jurisdiction of two committees, it may be sent to either; if portions belong to several committees, it may be divided among them, or the entire bill referred by the House to any committee. But if a bill be for the payment or adjudication of a private claim, it requires unanimous consent to refer it elsewhere than to the committee of original jurisdiction. Errors of reference not involving contested jurisdiction are usually adjusted without the attention of the House.

After reference a bill is sent to the printer, who makes six hundred and twenty five copies of a public measure and two hundred and sixty copies of a private bill. These are sent to the committee of reference and to the House and Senate document rooms. If the demand warrants it the secretary of the Senate and clerk of the House may print one thousand additional copies. If more are needed the House must order them by resolution.

A committee cannot change the subject or the title of a bill, but it may draft a new measure based upon bills relating to the same subject, or frame a bill of its own. Such bills take a new number and often bear the chairman's name, as the "McKinley Bill," the "Dingley Bill," or the "Underwood Bill." When a committee reports a bill the chairman certifies that a majority favored it, a quorum being present, after which it is filed with the clerk, who enters it by title, number, and date on the Private Calendar if it be a private bill, on the House Calendar if a public bill without an appropriation, or on the Union Calendar if a public bill carrying an appropriation. A report, accompanied with the views of the minority, is also filed. Both bill and report then go to the printer. A general appropriation or other privileged bill, although reported from the floor, is also filed with the clerk, who lists it on the proper calendar and sends it with the report to the printer.

A bill, previous to its passage, must be read three times, the first and second readings (the first by title and the second in full) occurring when it is taken up in the House. The question, "Will the House now consider it?" may then be demanded by any member. This question of consideration, as elsewhere stated, is the means by which the House protects itself from business it does not at the time wish to consider. It cannot be debated or reconsidered, and after being moved neither the previous question nor a point of order can prevent its being voted upon. But it cannot be raised after debate has begun, or after the previous question is ordered, or against a bill to which the President has filed objections, or which goes to the Committee of the Whole, or is taken up by unanimous consent, under a suspension of the rules, or by a special order which provides for immediate consideration. If the question be negatived, the bill remains as unacted upon. If decided in the affirmative, the bill is open for debate, amendment, and a third reading.

If a bill involves a tax or charge upon the people it goes to the Committee of the Whole House, or the Committee of the Whole House on the State of the Union.[1] If it carries no appropriation it is usually taken up by unanimous consent, under suspension of the rules, by special order, by privilege, on fixed days of the week, or on call of committees; or it may be considered in Committee of the Whole. In each case the procedure varies. Unanimous consent avoids the question of consideration, and as the purpose of the bill is ordinarily clearly outlined before consent is given, it soon reaches a vote. Should a disposition be manifested to amend or unduly debate it, a demand for the previous question would quickly pass or reject it.

A motion "to suspend the rules and pass the bill," when seconded by a majority of a quorum, bars the question of consideration, limits debate to twenty minutes on a side, excludes amendments other than those authorized by the reporting committee, and avoids intervening motions. At the close of the forty minutes' debate a vote is taken, and if two thirds of a quorum

[1] See chap. XIII, p. 260.

vote in the affirmative the bill is passed. The passage of a bill convoyed by a special order is not less direct, since the Committee on Rules usually specifies the length of general debate, the manner of considering amendments, the time for ordering the previous question, and the hour for taking the final vote. In other words, the adoption of a special order avoids all moves for compassing the delay of a bill. Indeed, its consideration becomes little more than a stage play, since the debate, however strenuous and noisy it may be, cannot modify its course.

A privileged bill, as well as one taken up on fixed days of the week or on call of committees, if not sent to a Committee of the Whole, is open to the question of consideration, and, "when under debate," to motions to adjourn and to lay on the table. Although the motion to adjourn has the highest precedence and nothing may intervene to prevent a vote, it cannot interrupt a member who has the floor, or stop a vote, or be used for dilatory purposes. A more drastic motion is to lay on the table. Under the old practice it put the bill aside temporarily, but since 1841 the House has used it to dispose finally of a bill without debate. Moreover, the motion, if it prevails, carries all amendments to the table with it; or, if moved on an amendment, it carries the bill with it. If Senate amendments to a House bill be laid on the table the bill also goes to the table. "This is upon the very sensible ground," said Speaker Reed, "that you cannot go on with an amendment when the main subject is no longer before the House, and cannot go on with the main question when there exist amendments liable to be called up at the pleasure of the House." [1] Speaker Randall held that a motion to lay a particular section on the table, if decided affirmatively, carried the whole bill to the table, and Speaker Boyd, as early as 1853, held that it carried to the table all pending motions connected with it. Speaker Reed further extended its power by holding that the motion might be made even though a member entitled to prior recognition held the floor for debate.[2] Thus, it became possible for one who inadvertently failed to raise the question of consideration to repair the mistake by moving to lay the bill on the table.

If the motions to adjourn and to lay on the table are negatived, the previous question, if ordered, carries the bill through the amendment stage until engrossed and read a third time. The previous question as used in the House is the only motion for closing debate. Under the present rule it may be asked and ordered upon a single motion, a series of motions, or an amendment or amendments, or it may be made to embrace all authorized motions or amendments and include the bill to its passage.[3] After it is ordered, a motion to lay on the table, to postpone, or to refer cannot be applied to it or to the main question. In other words, it brings the House to a direct vote upon the immediate question, unless no debate has occurred on it, in which case forty minutes are allowed. But this applies only to the main question and not to incidental motions. Nor does it matter how slight the prior debate may have been. Even the utter-

---

[1] *Parliamentary Rules*, p. 83.
[2] 55th Cong., 1st Sess., *Record*, p. 744.   [3] Rule XVII, sec. 1.

ance of an explanatory sentence is held to be "debate."[1] Thus, in April, 1898, when the celebrated House joint resolution authorizing and directing President McKinley to intervene and stop the war in Cuba came from the Senate with a substitute as an amendment, Speaker Reed ruled that after the previous question was ordered, although the object of the forty-minute rule was solely to prevent a proposition being rushed through without debate, the pending substitute could not be discussed, since its subject-matter had already received such debate as the House saw fit to give it before the resolution went to the Senate.[2]

Until the previous question is ordered, however, debate continues, and the intervening motions to postpone to a day certain, to refer, to amend, and to postpone indefinitely, are allowed in the order of their recital. The purpose of these motions is usually to delay or defeat the bill. The motion to postpone to a day certain, for illustration, gives opportunity, without permission to debate the merits of the main question, to plead for time to study the measure. In like manner the motion to refer affords a further chance to sidetrack it by insisting that more time than the House can then give is needed to investigate it. If the motion be to refer with instructions, the scope of the debate is extended to the merits of the bill. But the most insidious motion is to postpone indefinitely, because it avoids a direct vote on the bill, opens the whole question to debate, and, if carried, defeats the measure.

[1] 54th Cong., 1st Sess., *Record*, p. 5649.
[2] 55th Cong., 2d Sess., *Record*, p. 4062.

In actual practice, however, these intervening motions are rarely used, for when a bill reaches the amendment stage the previous question is usually ordered. In that event the Speaker states the question to be, "Shall the bill be engrossed and read a third time?" If decided in the affirmative, the bill is again read by title, unless its reading in full is demanded. At this stage the Chair recognizes an opponent of the measure for a motion to recommit. Unless precluded by the previous question, this motion may be amended, as by adding "with instructions," and if recommitted and subsequently reported again, another motion to recommit is allowed. If the motion be "to recommit with instructions that the committee report forthwith," the Chair reports at once without awaiting action by the committee and the bill is again before the House for its immediate consideration.

In presenting the reason for this peculiar procedure, which originally excited much adverse criticism, Speaker Reed said: "The rules provide that after a bill is ordered to a third reading — that is, after it passes the amendment stage — the House shall look at it as amended. It might happen that the majority does not favor two apparently conflicting amendments, and to give opportunity to remedy it this motion 'to recommit with instructions that the committee report forthwith' is permitted. It takes the form of a peremptory instruction to the committee, and it seems proper that the chairman of the committee should promptly obey the orders of the House. It is true the chairman is only the mouthpiece of the committee, but the committee itself is the agent of the House and the House has a perfect right to order the committee to do its will in whatever fashion it sees fit. . . . When it orders the committee to report 'forthwith,' that expression carries with it the right of immediate consideration, thus enabling the House to finish the business upon which it has entered. . . . Nor can the substitute, if it belonged to the Committee of the Whole, be sent there for consideration, for the whole subject has been considered by that Committee and the House has disagreed with its report so pointedly that it has directed the committee originally in charge of the matter to report to the House 'forthwith' another bill."[1]

If the motion to recommit be defeated, the bill is passed *viva voce*, or by the yeas and nays, if demanded by one fifth of a quorum. The title of the bill, which becomes important in case of doubt or ambiguity, is then amended, if necessary, without debate. But the bill is not "out of the woods" until a motion to reconsider is disposed of. Under the rule this motion may be made at any time on the same or succeeding day, after which it cannot be withdrawn except by consent of the House, but may be called up by any member, "provided, that such motion, if made during the last six days of a session, shall be disposed of when made." [2] While this motion is pending, therefore, a bill is not considered passed. Nor will the Speaker knowingly sign it, for if the bill has gone to the Senate or reached the President the motion may still be entertained. It has precedence of all other questions except a motion to adjourn and the consideration of a conference report, and may even

[1] 51st Cong., 2d Sess., *Record*, p. 3505.   [2] Rule xviii, sec. 1.

be made after the previous question has been ordered
on a bill to its passage. When once entered it remains
pending until the end of a Congress unless sooner disposed of, and whenever agreed to it reopens the entire
proposition.

This motion, apparently so disturbing to parliamentary action, has had a curious and interesting history.
Originally it was unlimited. It could be moved at any
time regardless of the whereabouts of the bill, which
might in the mean time have reached the Senate or the
President. But in 1811 the House restricted the motion
to "the same or succeeding day," and so it remained
until 1828, when Speaker Stevenson, in one of his
famous autocratic rulings, restricted it to the hour on
those two days devoted to the presentation of motions.
The House quickly resented this limitation, and at the
instance of Philip P. Barbour, of Virginia, whom President Jackson subsequently appointed Associate Justice
of the Supreme Court, it declared that on either day the
motion "shall take precedence of all other questions
except a motion to adjourn." [1] A little later Stevenson
crippled it with another shot, holding that a member
could withdraw his motion even though the time had
elapsed for another to make it. This ruling continued
until 1848, when the House adopted the present provision
preventing its withdrawal without the consent of the
House. Meantime, however, members of the Twenty-
third Congress (1839) had stumbled on a way to avoid
its sting. A sharp contest over a memorial relating to
the abolition of slavery in the District of Columbia had

[1] 20th Cong., 1st Sess., *Journal*, p. 1041.

ended in an order directing the clerk to print it. Such respect had rarely if ever been shown petitions of this character, and Henry A. Wise, of Virginia, moved to reconsider the resolution, "which gave rise," says Adams, "to a snarling debate." [1] After this a motion followed to lay the motion to reconsider on the table. Just what this would accomplish nobody seemed to know, but Speaker Bell ventured the opinion that the clerk could not print the memorial, as the motion to lay on the table, if carried, might subsequently be taken from the table, when the question would recur on the motion to reconsider. Of course such a disposition of the matter satisfied the distinguished Virginian, and the motion to reconsider went to the table. At a later day, when a member sought to take the motion from the table, he found his unprivileged effort thwarted by a single objection which could be overcome only by a suspension of the rules. This meant that tabling a motion to reconsider virtually killed it. Thus was established the practice, whenever a motion is carried or lost, of immediately moving to reconsider and to lay that motion on the table.[2] The present custom of the same member making the double motion came a little later.[3]

A bill being passed and the question of its reconsideration being disposed of, the clerk certifies the fact at the foot of it and delivers it to the Committee on Enrolled Bills, where it is engrossed; that is, printed on paper. The clerk then sends it by a messenger to the Senate,

[1] *Diary*, vol. IX, p. 206.
[2] 27th Cong., 2d Sess., *Globe*, p. 11; *Journal*, p. 406.
[3] 32d Cong., 1st Sess., *Globe*, p. 1560.

who, at a proper moment, is introduced by the sergeant-at-arms with the words, "Mr. President, a message from the House of Representatives." Thereupon the messenger bows and addresses the presiding officer as "Mr. President," who, in turn, addresses the messenger as "Mr. Clerk." The messenger, in a distinct voice that all may hear, responds: "I am directed by the House of Representatives to inform the Senate that the House has passed the following bill [indicating it by number and title], in which the concurrence of the Senate is requested." The bill is handed to the sergeant-at-arms and the messenger retires. If the Senate amends it, it is returned with like formality, the messenger, after presentation by the doorkeeper, addressing the Chair as follows: "Mr. Speaker, I am directed by the Senate to inform the House of Representatives that the Senate has passed the bill of the House [indicating it] with the accompanying amendments, in which the concurrence of the House is requested." The bill then goes to "the Speaker's table" and is subsequently referred to the proper standing committee. On being reported it follows the course previously taken, except that it need not go to the Committee of the Whole if the amendments do not involve new and distinct appropriations.[1] In such cases the House not infrequently disagrees to all amendments and asks at once for a conference.

The Speaker, under the modern practice, usually appoints three conferees or managers, — the chairman of the committee in charge of the bill, the member next in

[1] An increase or decrease of an amount is insufficient to send it to the Committee of the Whole.

rank, and the ranking member of the minority, who continue to act to the end. Conferences are held in the room of the Senate committee having jurisdiction of the bill. No reason exists for this and the custom is often resented. "Why should we go over there to listen to their reasons for amending our bill," complainingly inquired Samuel J. Randall, "when the House asks the conference and holds possession of the papers?" Other famous chairmen have voiced similar protests. But so far as known only one conference in half a century has occurred in the House wing of the Capitol. Though entirely informal, conferences are ordinarily conducted behind closed doors. There is no presiding officer, although the first-named manager in each body assumes to lead his section. In settling points of difference members of both Houses frequently appear, often upon invitation. The privilege of making statements is a courtesy that sometimes disarms opposition. Nor is it uncommon to invite a representative of the Government, whose expert knowledge is of value. The President, also, is frequently consulted as to his views and wishes. In one case formal hearings, attended by witnesses and attorneys, aided in eliminating difficulties. Not infrequently resort is had to the most amusing schemes for securing a unanimous report. Senator Hoar, of Massachusetts, cites an instance of reaching an agreement by striking out, hit or miss, every alternate amendment.[1] Indeed, it has been charged that laws are made in the conference room. "By our practice," said John Sherman, of Ohio, "we have gradually extended

[1] *Autobiography*, vol. II, p. 99.

the powers of conference committees until a proposition
to send a bill to conference sometimes startles me. I feel
that both Houses ought to make a stand against the
attempt to transfer the entire legislative power of Congress to such committees." [1] The text to which both
Houses have agreed cannot in the slightest particular
be changed in conference, but a harmless amendment is
sometimes inserted for the purpose of admitting modifications which will emasculate or defeat the bill. The
danger of the House being deceived into concurrence
is minimized, since the rules require that the report of
the managers shall be accompanied by a detailed statement sufficiently explicit to inform the House what
effect any amendments or propositions will have on
the measure to which they relate; nor can any conference report be considered until such report and the accompanying statement shall have been printed in the
Record. But this rule does not apply during the six days
preceding the end of a session. [2]

A conference report is highly privileged. It may be
presented at any time when the Journal is not being
read or a vote taken. It has precedence of a motion to
adjourn, and the only business allowed to intervene is
a recess previously fixed, or a question of privilege which
relates to the integrity of the House as an agency for
action. When recession is reported to have reached its
limit, the House may pass the bill, but it cannot submit
matter to its managers not originally submitted to them,
or instruct them to do what they might not have done

---

[1] 48th Cong., 1st Sess., *Record*, pp. 3974, 4098.
[2] Rule xviii, secs. 1, 2.

in the first instance. Nor is it wise to instruct them not to agree to an amendment, otherwise the Senate may decline to confer and ask a "free conference"; that is, one unfettered by instructions.[1] Usually the House approves the work of its managers, who thereafter often meet a more yielding spirit. If each House sincerely desires to pass a bill an agreement seldom fails.

When a House bill has passed each body, the clerk prints it on parchment and delivers it to the Joint Committee on Enrolled Bills, who compares it with the engrossed bill and reports it to both Houses. Thereupon it is signed by the Speaker in the presence of a quorum and by the President of the Senate in like manner, after which the chairman of the Committee on Enrolled Bills presents it to the President, the date of such presentation being entered upon the Journal of each House. If the President fails to approve or to return it within ten days, Sundays excepted, it becomes a law unless Congress prevents its return by adjourning. When approved the President indicates the calendar day and hour of signing,[2] notifies the body in which it originated, and sends it to the Secretary of State, who deposits it in his office for publication and preservation. It is usual for the President, when a bill becomes a law without his signature, to inform the House in which it originated. To facilitate the approval of bills on the last day of a Congress, the President ordinarily occupies the room assigned him in the Senate wing of the Capitol, although

---

[1] 51st Cong., 2d Sess., *Record*, pp. 3745, 3768, 3860.
[2] Prior to the Fifty-ninth Congress he indicated the legislative day, which does not always correspond with the calendar day.

enrolled bills pending at the close of a session may be treated at the next session of the same Congress as if no adjournment had occurred. So a bill signed during a recess becomes a law if the President acts within the ten days' limitation. After a bill goes to the President and before its approval, it may be recalled by a concurrent resolution, or, if an error exists, corrected by a joint resolution.[1]

A bill disapproved by the President must be returned to the body in which it originated and the objections entered on the Journal. Thereupon, if a quorum be present, the House usually, although not invariably, proceeds to consider the matter, the Speaker putting the question, "Will the House, on reconsideration, agree to pass the bill, the objection of the President to the contrary notwithstanding?" If the previous question be ordered, the issue is at once determined by a call of the yeas and nays, an affirmative vote of two thirds of the members present being sufficient to pass the bill over the veto. If so passed, it is sent, together with the President's objections, to the Senate. On the other hand, if it appears that two thirds of the members are indisposed to overrule the veto, a motion is made in the first instance to refer the bill, with or without the message, or to lay it on the table. This procedure is held allowable within the constitutional mandate that the House shall enter the President's objections on its Journal, "and proceed to reconsider it."[2] In practice such action, when taken, is seldom disturbed.

[1] 39th Cong., 1st Sess., *Globe*, pp. 3241, 3357.
[2] Constitution, art. I, sec. 7.

CHAPTER XV

DEBATE AND DEBATERS

WHEN not voting the House is talking. Points of order, appeals, motions, methods of procedure, questions of privilege, considerations of reports and bills and resolutions — all create differences and provoke debate. But under the present rules it is easily controlled. Adams complained that every member is so hemmed in by rigid rules that he cannot open his lips without leave.[1] He meant, of course, that one could neither take the floor without recognition, nor keep it unless in order. The Speaker controls debate on points of order, and whenever ready to rule he may decline to hear further argument. The House controls debate on appeals, on privilege, on procedure, and the like, and whenever it has heard enough the cry of "Vote! vote!" is usually effective. Debate on resolutions and bills considered under suspension of the rules is limited to forty minutes, divided equally between the mover and the one demanding a second, who apportion the time. If one asks unanimous consent for the immediate consideration of a bill a long dialogue may continue pending objection, but if none be made the debate can be limited by the previous question, which is the only motion used for closing debate in the House as distinguished from Committee of the Whole. Thus debate, whenever or however it occurs,

[1] *Diary*, vol. IX, p. 135 (1834).

is dominated by clearly defined and well-understood rules, and although members may not obtain recognition whenever they seek it, opportunity to speak, dependent upon the condition of business and the age of the session, is usually given when the House goes into Committee of the Whole for the consideration of general appropriation bills. Several hours are then set apart for "general debate," and members may discuss any matter however foreign to the measure before the Committee. This custom is borrowed from the House of Commons. "The second reading of an appropriation bill," says Lucy, "plays the part of the seven baskets in the parable, all the elocutionary or disputatious fragments which remain after the feast being picked up and crammed within its ample fold." [1]

"General debate" is often a dreary performance. The contentiousness is not close enough or rapid enough to hold the interest. One set speech follows another, and although recognition alternates from one side to the other, the answering speech seldom bears directly on the points of the preceding speaker. Besides, busy men who care for nothing except the vital question involved weary of generalities or the repetition of familiar principles. Whatever interest attaches to these speeches, therefore, grows out of the manner of delivery, or the sharp, striking presentation of the subject-matter. Too often at such times speeches are recited from memory or read from manuscript in a monotonous tone, not infrequently to less than a dozen persons who remain out of compliment to the participants. Nevertheless, the House is the

[1] H. W. Lucy, *Peeps at Parliament*, p. 217.

most indulgent of audiences. It smiles at feeble jokes, encourages with occasional applause, and conceals an inclination to laugh if an impassioned orator upsets an inkstand or sends a glass of water flying over his neighbor. Even the bore is held sacred lest in the struggle for relief from tiresome talk the right of free speech be lost.

In early years members occasionally attempted to silence tedious speakers by noisy interruptions,[1] but in its wildest moments the House never adopted the intolerant treatment which the British Commons accorded Mr. Gladstone in 1885 upon his introduction of the first Home Rule Bill. He pathetically complained that "it struck a fatal blow at the liberties of debate and at the dignity of Parliament." [2] When objection was taken to the Colonial Secretary answering questions on Chinese labor, addressed directly to the Premier, the Opposition prevented his speech by yelling continuously for one hour.[3] Such demonstrations are wholly unknown in the American House.

The custom of printing undelivered speeches in the *Record* affords additional opportunity for presenting one's views. Indeed, readers of the *Record* can no longer know what is really said on the floor, since many undelivered speeches indicate applause never given and questions never asked, while the right to revise delivered speeches permits omissions and additions. "The petty practice," says McCall, "of editing the report of speeches by inserting 'applause' and 'laughter' in the

---

[1] John Quincy Adams, *Diary*, vol. IX, pp. 118, 152.

[2] *Hansard*, May 15, 1885.

[3] Lucy, *Memories of Eight Parliaments*, p. 372.

printed version has made the House appear to be a very stupid sort of body, going wild with enthusiasm over eloquence the cheapest and most fustian, and convulsed with 'laughter' over jokes the point of which years of subsequent study have failed to disclose " [1] *Hansard*, the official publication of the British Commons, designates revised remarks by a star. A similar use of the asterisk would improve the integrity of the *Record*, for much that is spoken is never printed and much that is printed is never spoken. "Gales sent me the manuscript of his reporter," wrote Adams, "and I wrote almost the whole of it over again." [2] It is not surprising, perhaps, that the sarcastic "old man eloquent," in his cooler moments, deemed revision wise, but a star should have noted the change.

The five-minute debate in Committee of the Whole, as stated elsewhere, is at times highly enjoyable. Too often, however, it becomes mere routine work — a transference to the floor of differences developed in the committee room, which the House hears and then decides. This sort of teamwork has led a distinguished critic to charge that "in form, committees only digest the various matter introduced by members and prepare it for the House; but, in reality, they dictate the course to be taken. The House sits not for serious discussion, but to sanction the conclusions of its committees, so that it is not far from the truth to say that Congress in session is Congress on public exhibition, whilst Congress in its committee rooms is Congress at work." [3] To an ob-

[1] *Life of Thomas B. Reed*, p. vii.   [2] *Diary*, vol. VIII, p. 437.
[3] Woodrow Wilson, *Congressional Government*, p. 79 (published in 1885).

server in the gallery this would often appear to be true. With manifold interests and limited time legislators must specialize as well as members of other professions. Thus each committee becomes a specialist in legislation, and the House, in disposing of private and minor public bills which constitute two thirds of its business, relies upon information presented by its committees. It sits as a court, so to speak, and approves or disapproves. In the case of private pension bills it often acts perfunctorily, passing one or two hundred measures in as many minutes. The House of Commons conserves its time by similar methods. It appoints four standing committees, each composed of sixty to eighty members representing parties in proportion to their number, to which are referred all measures except money bills and those conferring provisional orders. In these committees, whose work supersedes action in Committee of the Whole, twenty is a quorum and forty an average attendance. Their sessions are public or private as each committee directs, and their reports go directly to the House, which perfunctorily approves. But in the American House, as in the Commons, measures of public interest, especially those involving revenue and appropriations, ordinarily receive thorough consideration. In the House of Representatives members often range themselves in concentric circles about the debaters, who are frequently encouraged by loud applause.

Possessors of correct and complete knowledge are nowhere more willingly heard than in the House, and if one has a good voice it deepens the interest. "Genius is not important," said Thomas B. Reed. "On the con-

trary it is a disqualification. Men are wanted who have
knowledge, the ability to sift estimates, to ascertain
the law, and to present recommendations for the consideration of the House." [1] The truth of this statement
is happily illustrated by the manner in which William
B. Washburn, of Massachusetts, a clear-headed, sound
business man, eager to do justice and determined to
do right, disposed of the cloud of war claims that so
heavily burdened Congress after the close of the Civil
War. His thorough investigation, lucid reports, and
sane recommendations quickly gained the confidence
of the House. "Beneath his plain courtesy," says Senator Hoar, "was a firmness and fairness which Cato
never surpassed."

It frequently happens that the chairman of a great
committee submits to the House a complicated bill of
one hundred or more printed pages, divided into sections, each paragraph presenting a different state of
facts. To retain control of its form and substance
through all the vicissitudes of its consideration, especially if it be of a controversial character, he must not
only know the history, purpose, and need of every item,
and with tact and good temper answer questions without
wobbling, but quickly distinguish amendments harmful
if not fatal in their tendency, and indicate by timely and
conciliatory suggestions the way out of tangles created
in the heat of discussion. Mr. McKinley's ability to do
this rested upon perfect knowledge gained in committee
or by midnight study, and it made him an ideal chairman of Ways and Means.

[1] 49th Cong., 1st Sess., *Record*, p. 208.

The House usually possesses a corps of able debaters, noticeably limited to members upon whom fall the burden of much talking. It is practice that makes an acceptable parliamentary speaker. "A parliamentary orator," says Justin McCarthy, "is one who can employ the kind of eloquence and argument which tell most readily on Parliament. But it must not be supposed that the parliamentary orator is necessarily a great orator in the wider sense. Some of the men who made the greatest successes as parliamentary debaters have failed to win any genuine reputation as orators of the broader and higher school. Disraeli first rose to fame as a great debater during the debate on the abolition of the Corn Laws, but he never succeeded in being more than a parliamentary orator." [1] Burke says that by slow degrees Charles James Fox became the most brilliant and powerful debater ever heard in Parliament, and Fox himself attributed his success to the habit of speaking, well or ill, at least once every night. Macaulay thinks it would be difficult to name any great debater whose knowledge of the science of parliamentary defense resembles an instinct. It is often observed that a new member, though he has gained high reputation as a speaker in other fields, struggles piteously with parched tongue in his early attempts to address the House. Morley tells of Gladstone, at the beginning of his parliamentary career, offering up a silent prayer before rising to speak. "I made a few remarks to-day," wrote John Quincy Adams, soon after entering the House in 1831. "I am so little qualified by nature for an extemporaneous orator that I was not a

[1] *A History of our Own Times*, vol. I, pp. 303–04.

little agitated by the sound of my own voice." [1] Yet, eleven years later, when bent with age and trembling with palsy, he stood in his place for an entire week, pending Wise's resolution to expel him, and cowed an angry majority into a body of deeply interested listeners, whose verdict was nearly three to one in his favor. With sarcasm always on tap, he seemed to spare no one. Although he never attained first rank as a parliamentary debater, he not only possessed marked dramatic power, but his habit of seizing upon and repeating slowly, with a rising and falling inflection, a single word used by an opponent, created a "raw" as horsemen say.

Members are rare who, with lightness of touch and inbred courtesy, wield a polished blade, smiting gently and filling the great hall with ripples of laughter as they drive home arguments which are the despair of their opponents. A distinguished preacher once attempted it and failed. A lecturer, with rounded periods well memorized, failed to attract after the second effort. A noted afterdinner speaker who captivated well-fed audiences seemed out of place in serious debate. An orator, well groomed, with raucous voice and stage stride, held attention like an actor on the opening night, but repetitions drew small houses. Indeed, it is difficult to tell just what the House will like. Macaulay's description of the Commons applies to it. "The House of Commons," he says, "is a place to which I would not promise success to any man. I have great doubt about Jeffrey. It is the most peculiar audience in the world. I should say that a man's being a good writer, a good orator at the bar, a good mob orator,

[1] *Diary*, vol. VIII, p. 424.

or a good orator in debating clubs, was rather a reason for expecting him to fail than for expecting him to succeed in the House of Commons. A place where Walpole succeeded and Addison failed; where Peel now succeeds and where Mackintosh fails; where Erskine and Scarlett were dinner bells; where Lawrence and Jekyll, the two wittiest men, or nearly so, of their time, were thought bores, is surely a very strange place." [1] Mr. Blaine, in his eulogy of President Garfield, says: "There is no test of a man's ability in any department of public life more severe than service in the House of Representatives; there is no place where so little deference is paid to reputation previously acquired or to eminence won outside; no place where so little consideration is shown for the feelings or failures of beginners. What a man gains in the House he gains by sheer force of his own character, and if he loses and falls back he must expect no mercy, and will receive no sympathy. It is a field in which the survival of the strongest is the recognized rule, and where no pretense can survive, and no glamour can mislead. The real man is discovered, his worth is impartially weighed, his rank is irrevocably decided." [2]

The House often tires of talk. Yet floor leaders, like faithful sentinels, fearful that something may occur to demand their presence, sit day after day listening to "the dreary drip of pointless twaddle." Often between seven and eight o'clock, says Lucy, "when the House was almost empty and some unimportant, unattractive member found his chance, Mr. Gladstone sat with hand

[1] Trevelyan, *Life and Letters of Lord Macaulay,* p. 57.
[2] Delivered in the House of Representatives, February 27, 1882.

to ear. During the interminable Home Rule debates he formed a habit of moving to the gangway end of the Treasury Bench, sitting there by the hour listening to members whose measure of attraction was indicated by the emptiness of the benches." [1] A similar sight may often be witnessed in the American House. It relieved the disappointment of strangers, when visiting an empty House in the seventies, to find Randall and Garfield patiently attentive. Their names had become household words and their presence gave warmth to the great chamber. For years with boldness and matchless force they convinced the country that its deliberative assembly was under worthy guidance, and their constant attendance suggested the importance of the questions arising in the years immediately succeeding the Civil War. At a later period Thomas B. Reed, tireless, unfaltering, ruthless, held the weary watch. It meant that no point was too minute for his criticism or too large for his virile grasp, while his presence encouraged the hope that at any moment his clear, penetrating voice might change the House from a dull, half-weary body to an expectant public meeting. When he rose, a hundred members, catching the words "Mr. Speaker," hastened from their seclusion and settled into an attitude of attention. Without notes and perhaps without scruples he restated the point at issue, rubbed off the paint, picked an apt illustration, forgot and forgave nothing, and in a few minutes, with well-phrased sentences, sometimes steeped in sarcasm or flashing with wit, disclosed the weakness of an opponent. Such a

[1] H. W. Lucy, *Peeps at Parliament*, p. 178.

speech banishes fatigue like a night's refreshing sleep. That is what the House likes.

The high-principled orator, dignified in manner and unfailing in courtesy, who gives rhetorical finish to his sentences, is deeply appreciated by the House; but the real leader is the original, daring debater, who seizes the opportune moment, and, without apparent preparation, hurls his forceful, compact sentences, loaded with destructive arguments, into the midst of his adversaries. Many historic speeches have come thus unannounced. In a few minutes Henry L. Dawes, by advocating a free breakfast table and tactfully moving the previous question, completely wrecked a revenue reform measure which sacrificed the protective interests of New England.[1] Perhaps the most notable instance of such readiness occurred in 1879, when a majority of the House, chafing under federal laws governing elections, attempted to force their repeal by refusing to make appropriations. Day after day the debate dragged tediously, until James A. Garfield, prodded by impudent questions and angered by satirical laughter, launched into a thirty-minute speech, charging that the former enemies of the Government, having failed to shoot it to death, now proposed to starve it to death! The effect was electrical. It gave purpose to the debate, threw the House into wild excitement, and so deeply stirred the country that the appropriations were passed and the session hurriedly closed.[2]

Years after as sudden a change occurred when the

[1] 43d Cong., 2d Sess., *Record*, p. 4480.
[2] 46th Cong., 1st Sess., *Record*, pp. 115–18.

House levied a duty on products coming from Porto Rico, the sum so collected to be returned to the Island. In his message President McKinley had advocated free trade, the press of the country supported the policy, and the majority party approved it. But in the discussion Sereno E. Payne, of New York, chairman of Ways and Means, spoke with such fullness of knowledge, illustrating the effect of recent storms upon the Island and showing the need of immediate funds for roads and schools, that he persuaded his party in a single speech to adopt the policy so beneficial to the impoverished people. With equal thoroughness James R. Mann, of Illinois, turned the chamber into a great chemical laboratory, and without mystery or magic opened a way for the passage of the Pure Food Bill by demonstrating with simple experiments the various processes of adulterating food products with enormous profit. There was nothing sensational. His readiness in blending and mixing amazed his hearers, while peals of laughter greeted his versatility in manufacturing whiskey out of water and drugs. It was the triumph of preparedness.

The House is rarely if ever without a few effective debaters. As stated above, veteran members who talk much usually learn to talk well. But as one studies the great debates of the past century, the fact appears that speakers who have commanded the country's attention come in groups. Indeed, it may be said that the congressional firmament reveals constellations of genius as clearly as the heavens disclose brilliant star clusters. The jewels in Orion's belt never shone more brightly than did Fisher Ames, of Massachusetts, the transcendent orator and profound lawyer; Elias Boudinot, of New Jersey, the accomplished and benevolent statesman; and James Madison, the Constitution-maker, who served in the first two Congresses under President Washington; while about them, like the three collinear stars, clustered Elbridge Gerry, Roger Sherman, and George Clymer, the trio of distinguished "signers." These men represented a country staggering under a mountain of debt inherited from the Revolutionary struggle, and without waiting for the inauguration of a President or the creation of a Treasury Department, they prepared and passed a revenue bill before the organization of the Government was announced to foreign nations. "It is a circumstance of curious interest," writes Mr. Blaine, "that nearly, if not quite, all the arguments used by the supporters and opponents of a protective system were presented at that time with a directness and an ability which have not been surpassed in any subsequent discussion. The 'ad valorem' system of levying duties was maintained against 'specific' rates in almost the same language employed in recent years. The 'infant manufactures,' the need of the 'fostering care of the Government' for the promotion of 'home industries,' the advantages derived from 'diversified pursuits,' the competition of 'cheap labor in Europe,' were all rehearsed with a familiarity and ease which implied their previous and constant use in the legislative halls of the different States before the power to levy imposts was remitted to the jurisdiction of Congress." [1]

The light of these patriots had scarcely disappeared

[1] *Twenty Years of Congress*, vol. i, p. 183.

when Robert Goodloe Harper, of South Carolina, John Randolph and John W. Eppes, of Virginia, and George W. Campbell, of Tennessee, dwarfed the fame of colleagues by their supremacy in debate. Under their management, and especially that of Randolph, was established a national judiciary which proved so wise that the execution of law within the jurisdiction of federal courts, although enlarged from time to time, remains to this day substantially the same as in the beginning. After them came the famous quintet of bold, aggressive young men — Henry Clay, John C. Calhoun, William Lowndes, Langdon Cheves, and Richard M. Johnson, whose militant patriotism forced the War of 1812. In this brilliant constellation also shone Daniel Webster, John W. Taylor, and Henry R. Storrs, of New York, Philip P. Barbour, of Virginia, and James Buchanan, of Pennsylvania. It was a period of strong wills and commanding intellects, when the Missouri question suddenly arrayed the North and the South in a violent and absorbing conflict, which as quickly subsided upon the adoption of the Missouri Compromise.

The organization of the Democratic and Whig parties, constructed on the ruins of the old Republican party that Jefferson created and dominated for a quarter of a century, brought into the congressional heavens an entirely new star cluster, which attracted the country's attention during the Speakership of Stevenson and Polk (1827–39). Rufus Choate and Edward Everett adorned the earlier part of it. For a single term Sergeant S. Prentiss, of Mississippi, Thomas F. Marshall, of Kentucky, and Richard H. Menifee, a young man of great promise, flashed their meteoric light. William Pitt Fessenden, caustic and stern, also tarried for a term before passing to the Senate, while Franklin Pierce, with fine rhetoric, handsome features, and charming manners, impressed John Y. Mason and Dixon H. Lewis with his steadfastness and future availability for President. But the stars whose light shone the most steadily during the struggles over the right of petition, the principle of a protective tariff, and the nullification movement, were John Quincy Adams of daring courage; Samuel F. Vinton, of Ohio, whose rare endowments identified him with all the vital issues; George Evans, of Maine, incomparable for masterful argument and graceful thrust of rapier; Thomas Corwin, of keenest wit and oratorical power; John Bell, of Tennessee, a Titan in offensive and defensive debate; and Henry A. Wise, before whose malicious sarcasm even the Speaker quailed.

A small star cluster of the first magnitude appeared in the forties, when the Walker Tariff Bill, the annexation of Texas, the Mexican War, and the Clay compromises divided Congress and the country. From the South came Alexander H. Stephens, with frail body and massive head; Howell Cobb, of Georgia, faintly indicating leadership proportions; and Robert Toombs, the fiery apostle of an unhappy policy. From the North, Joshua R. Giddings, of Ohio, massive and muscular in physique, who continued the fight that John Quincy Adams had provoked and stubbornly maintained; Robert C. Schenck, of the same State, an ideal parliamentary talker; Robert C. Winthrop, a graceful, highly cultivated orator, though never an effective debater;

Edward Dickinson Baker, then of Illinois, a man of extraordinary gifts of eloquence; and Stephen A. Douglas and Thaddeus Stevens, destined to be without living rivals as dominating political leaders. Although a native of New England, Douglas in action was of a Western type. Schouler, the historian, thus describes him: "He had a small, compact frame, whence issued a surprisingly stentorian voice, and his type of eloquence at once startled the House by its novelty. As he warmed up in speech his grave face became convulsed, his gesticulation frantic, and while roaring and lashing about with energy, he would strip off his cravat and unbutton his waistcoat to save himself from choking, until his whole air and aspect, as he stood at the desk, was that of a half-naked pugilist hurling defiance at the presiding officer. But all this gave at once to his person that picturesqueness which goes halfway toward making one a figure in public life."

Early in the next decade the vital issue suddenly changed. Although the Whig party, weakened by personal strife and hopelessly divided on questions of principle, suffered a crushing defeat in 1852, the South was dissatisfied. The Mexican War had added Texas as slave territory, but it had also given to the Union the great free Commonwealth of California, while the growing West and Northwest threatened to present other States with like sentiments. Unless this rich territory could be opened to slave labor the far-seeing Southern leaders saw but one result to the battle between freedom and slavery, and to gain such an advantage they forced the repeal of the Missouri Compromise. Leading this tragedy were Stephens, of Georgia, George S. Houston, of Alabama, Linn Boyd and John C. Breckinridge, of Kentucky, William Barksdale, of Mississippi, John S. Phelps, of Missouri, Thomas L. Clingman, of North Carolina, William Aiken, James L. Orr, and Lawrence M. Keitt, of South Carolina, and Thomas S. Bocock, of Virginia. Of the Southern stars in the House only John S. Millson, of Virginia, and Thomas H. Benton, of Missouri, opposed the proposition. Simultaneously there appeared, rising slowly above the horizon, a Northern constellation that blazed the brighter the nearer it approached the zenith. Galusha A. Grow and Schuyler Colfax; the two Washburns, Israel and Elihu B.[1]; Henry Winter Davis, of Maryland; Anson Burlingame, Nathaniel P. Banks, and Henry L. Dawes, of Massachusetts; John Sherman and John A. Bingham, of Ohio; Justin A. Morrill, of Vermont, and Reuben E. Fenton, of New York. All were not orators or even effective debaters. Nor did any, perhaps, possess the imagination that lifts speeches into an atmosphere above the level of the *Record*. But proud of soul and weighted with patriotic responsibility, they championed their cause with buoyant readiness. Thomas B. Reed, who heard Banks in the campaign of 1856, presents a vivid picture of him: "Banks that day was in the prime of vigor and personal comeliness. Dressed in blue, with closely buttoned coat, his well-chosen language, his graceful figure and gesture, and his aggressive way carried with him the whole audience." [2]

[1] Although brothers, Elihu spelled his name with a final " e " and Israel without it.

[2] S. W. McCall, *Life of Thomas B. Reed*, p. 13.

The opening of the Thirty-eighth Congress (1863) presented another remarkable cluster. Notable, indeed, would it have been if limited to William B. Washburn and George S. Boutwell, of Massachusetts; William B. Allison and John A. Kasson, of Iowa; Francis Kernan and John A. Griswold, of New York; and John A. J. Creswell, of Maryland, and William R. Morrison, of Illinois; but the addition of James G. Blaine, James A. Garfield, and Samuel J. Randall gave it a character that surpassed in brilliancy and commanding intellect even the famous galaxy headed by Clay and Lowndes in the Twelfth Congress. Nor did it lose its luster during the entire decade, for as one after another disappeared Michael C. Kerr, of Indiana, Benjamin F. Butler, of Massachusetts, Eugene Hale and William P. Frye, of Maine, and Joseph G. Cannon, of Illinois, filled the gaps. Others also gave it *éclat*. Proctor Knott, of Kentucky, made dullness feel ashamed; Henry J. Raymond, of New York, although too confident of his splendid gifts, evoked high compliment by ready and effective speech; while Roscoe Conkling, whose "affluent and exuberant diction was never surpassed in either branch of Congress, unless, perhaps, by Rufus Choate," [1] seemed supreme in everything he chose to do.

The laws of the Reconstruction period, trampling too heedlessly, perhaps, upon men's prejudices, for a time suppressed the brightest minds of the South; but when statutes ceased to oppress, a brilliant star group again appeared from the Southland, including Stephens and Benjamin H. Hill, of Georgia; Roger Q. Mills and John

[1] Blaine, *Twenty Years of Congress*, vol. I, p. 328.

H. Reagan, of Texas; Eppa Hunton and John Randolph Tucker, of Virginia; John G. Carlisle and John C. S. Blackburn, of Kentucky; and John D. C. Atkins, of Tennessee. It was a notable coincidence that just at this time no less remarkable an assemblage appeared from the North, headed by Thomas B. Reed, William McKinley, Frank Hiscock, of New York, George D. Robinson, of Massachusetts, and Benjamin Butterworth, of Ohio. Though the *Record* is evidence that some of these newcomers did little more than "rattle a defiant drum," several showed the power and genuine inspiration in debate which mark the highest forensic success.

The period of Cannon's Speakership (1903–11) was especially distinguished for its members of long continuous service. Never in the history of the House did so many men of large parliamentary experience appear. The so-called Clay Congresses (1811–25) mustered at no time more than twenty members who had served five terms each, while from 1789 to 1860 only forty exceeded six terms. After the Civil War the average term of service gradually lengthened, although during the administrations of Speakers Blaine and Kerr and Randall and Carlisle the longest consecutive service rarely exceeded twelve years. Constituents did not seem to appreciate the value of experienced legislators. But of those who assembled in December, 1905, thirty-eight had served fourteen years or better, and seventy-eight from ten to twelve years each. In that experienced body one could count many excellent talkers and several most effective debaters. Of this type were Jonathan P. Dolliver, of Iowa, eloquent and aggressive; Champ Clark, of Mis-

souri, always delightfully interesting and decidedly
human; Theodore E. Burton, of Ohio, a master of clear
statement and a dispenser of unchallenged information;
Samuel W. McCall, of Massachusetts, scholarly and
scrupulously fair; and John Dalzell, of Pennsylvania,
proud of soul, but of good temper, who was preëminently
fitted by nature to hold high place in the councils of his
party. In this group belonged Oscar W. Underwood, of
Alabama, James R. Mann, of Illinois, and John S.
Williams, of Mississippi.

Among other members who engaged the interest of
the public were Charles H. Grosvenor, of Ohio, and
William P. Hepburn, of Iowa. Side by side they sat,
two veterans of the Civil War, gray with age, but ever
adequate, listening with a chip on the shoulder, and ever
and anon, with silver-trumpet voice, a perfect articula-
tion, and a splendid diction, delighting the House with
the vigor and freshness of their speeches, bristling with
sarcasm and political raillery.

Of equal interest were Robert R. Hitt, of Illinois, and
Marlin E. Olmsted, of·Pennsylvania. Hitt was cradled
among statesmen. He reported in shorthand the Lin-
coln-Douglas debates in 1858 — something of a feat in
that day; as secretary to Oliver P. Morton, the War
Governor of Indiana, he met the master-spirits of the
war; and as a member of the American Legation at Paris,
after the downfall of Napoleon III, he came into more or
less intimate associations with the men worth knowing
in Europe. On his return he joined Mr. Blaine in the
Department of State, served as Commissioner to the
Hawaiian Islands, and for twelve years headed the Com-

mittee on Foreign Affairs. All parties greatly esteemed him. He was a man of high principle and amiable character, whose calm earnestness, avoiding extravagance and yielding nothing to fiery nonsense or provincial prejudice, impressed the House as a champion of the dignity and honor of his country. Like Hitt, Olmsted had a calm, meditative intellect, often coldly analytical, but never artificial or ineffective. He was not eloquent. He lacked the imagination if not the enthusiasm of an orator. As an effective reasoner, however, he was without a rival. In revising the laws governing the Philippine Islands, a labor covering most of one session, he patiently and cleverly met opposition with a gentle, unprejudiced intelligence that won respect and rarely failed to secure assent.

Among these various groups were men whose genius especially fitted them for the work of the House. Their leadership seemed indigenous to the soil. It required the tumult and excitement of large membership rather than the frigid silence of a smaller body clearly to exhibit their poise as they calmly rose to every occasion, phrasing sentences and selecting words that conveyed without anger and without offense their aggressive, belligerent attitude. One can hardly imagine John Quincy Adams or Joshua R. Giddings serving in another legislature. Their places in parliamentary history could have become distinguished only in the House. In a crisis, when colleagues wavered and agitation threatened the support of a violent change in administrative policies, Thaddeus Stevens was exactly the man to seize boldly and adroitly on the critical moment. His radicalism represented the views of multitudes of people whose representatives promptly answered to his trumpet call, and with audaciously powerful sarcasm he maintained the lofty tradition founded by Adams in the House as much as did Disraeli that founded by Pitt and Fox in the Commons.

It is not easy to think of Samuel J. Randall and Thomas B. Reed serving elsewhere than in the House. They were leaders of men. They could brighten the driest details, inspire implicit confidence in their views, and arouse the admiration of the indifferent until their appeals divided members into two hostile camps; but they could also hold their alignment without the loss of a vote and crush a less confident man who dared to offend. Morrison, of Illinois, used to say in jest that no man "can be quite so wise as 'Sam' Randall looks." Although Reed voluntarily withdrew from the splendid arena in which he had so long played a brilliant part, and Randall died a member of the House, neither left any intimation that a seat in the Senate attracted him. Probably no member of the House ever refused an election to that exalted body. Relief from the biennial campaign, with its many harassing features, would of itself commend the change. When increasing age begins to shy at the more strenuous life, the desire for a shift becomes even more potent. This was Disraeli's reason for not resisting the glittering lure of a coronet. He was no longer as young, he said, in his farewell speech at Aylesbury, as when forty-three years before he had addressed the electors of Buckinghamshire in that same place. But he lives in history only as the great leader of the Commons. Men have likewise passed to the Senate whose brilliant parliamentary careers are remembered solely because of their service in the House. Whoever thinks of John Randolph, or John Quincy Adams, or Blaine, or Carlisle as senators? It is interesting to note, also, the long list of notable members of the House who never served in the Senate. Among them are Presidents Madison, Polk, Fillmore, Lincoln, Hayes, Garfield, and McKinley, and all the Speakers for the past century save Clay, Bell, Hunter, Blaine, and Carlisle. Indeed, of the array of brilliant members mentioned in this chapter, two thirds never served in the Senate.

It is difficult to get away from the men composing these various groups, for whenever subjects of national interest have engaged the attention of the House their speeches adorn the pages of the parliamentary annals. Ranged on either side, they have alternately carried their points, and, although the legislation of one decade has been modified in the next, a glance through a century of lawmaking history clearly shows that policies which made for the speedy transaction of business, for better government, for larger liberty, and for the greatest good to the greatest number, have slowly progressed. In fact, the tariff is the only question of nation-wide interest which has not in some measure yielded to argument, and although the theory of protection has dominated the country most of the time in the last half-century, the differences of opinion as to the best mode of levying duties on imports are as wide to-day as in the beginning.

It is doubtful if even the best speeches upon questions of vital interest are much read except as presented through the press. When delivered, the country care-

fully watches the progress of a debate, as it did when
Congress repealed the Missouri Compromise and ham-
mered into shape the fourteen tariff acts which have
followed at too frequent intervals the Act of 1816; but
after their passage few persons other than the historian
re-read the debates. Details are tedious, banter is un-
gainly, sarcasm seems blunt, denunciation loses its
attractiveness, and arguments condensed into a single
article are more accessible. Indeed, little is remembered
of a law in the making except choice bits of rhetoric —
the literature of debate — which find their way into
books of eloquence and form material for declamation
in school and college work. Nevertheless, parliamentary
debate will ever continue to attract. The clash of mind
against mind reveals not only personality, but the roots
of the division which are traced discriminatingly from
cause to effect. It is a field contest. In modern phrase
it is "team play," in which the art of finesse becomes a
necessary part of the debater's equipment, and every
maneuver to gain a superior position belongs to the
struggle.

Moreover, touches of genius in the shape of calm,
didactic exposition, or the more elaborate sentences of
the rhetorician, half conversational and half oratorical,
are certain to get into the fusing pot, out of which the
law is finally drawn. Apropos of this, many still living
will recall the close of the debate on the Wilson Tariff
Bill in 1894. Thomas B. Reed broke his record of thirty
minutes by speaking two hours, while William L. Wilson,
an accomplished orator, took account of time no more
than did the audience which filled the great hall. In

this debate there was nothing volcanic — no trace of gushing, or overpowering, spontaneous eloquence. The thoughts, too, were calm. But there was vigor of language, extreme readiness, a versatility that amazed men at its extent, a blending of details into concrete propositions that dazzled and battered, and now and then a sentence of scintillating wit or impinging sarcasm that touched off peals of applause. "To achieve this with contested facts in a combative life," says Bagehot, "is among the rarest operations of a rare power." No one changed his mind, however. Lines were then strictly drawn and the result known in advance; but the interest was not less intense than in the days when Lowndes argued for the Act of 1816, or Henry Clay gave reasons for presenting the Bill of 1833.

Interest is added to these spectacular occasions by the presence of a full House, sitting in martial array. If it happens to be evening the illuminated ceiling of the chamber throws a soft, rich light upon the scene, the crowded galleries catch the spirit that reigns upon the floor, and for the moment the salvation of the country seems to hang upon the voting down or up of the measure.

CHAPTER XVI

CONTESTED ELECTION CASES

THE constitutional provision that "each House shall be the judge of the elections, returns, and qualifications of its own members" gives a majority the right to dispose of contested election cases as party interest determines.[1] There is neither appeal nor review. Although precedents be ignored, statutes neglected, and the rules of evidence disregarded, there is no redress. Conscious of this power the House, for a century and a quarter, has been rendering partisan judgments.

Early in its history it evinced a desire to treat such cases impartially. Its first Committee on Elections, headed by George Clymer, of Pennsylvania, recognized the sacredness of titles to seats, and in presenting the facts, uncolored by partisan influences, it enabled the House to act fairly and justly. The disposition of the famous case of Anthony Wayne, the Revolutionary hero, is a notable illustration of this loyalty to principle. It is easy to imagine the influence of Wayne's patriotic services. The memory of his conduct at the battles of Brandywine and Germantown and Monmouth, and his brilliant achievement in carrying Stony Point with the bayonet at midnight, deeply affected his colleagues. To members from the South his courage in saving Lafayette in Virginia and his superb skill in aiding at the siege of

[1] Constitution, art. I, sec. 5.

Yorktown, especially commended him. But the testimony in his case revealed gross errors, if not criminal suppression of the returns. Thereupon the House, by a unanimous vote, declared the seat vacant, although it seemed to hold Wayne guiltless of any wrongdoing, since it soon after supported President Washington's recommendation that he be appointed general-in-chief of the army.

To guide it in the settlement of contests the House, in 1791, appointed Fisher Ames, of Massachusetts, chairman of a committee to prepare a uniform mode of procedure. His admirable report, which fixed the time for taking depositions and prescribed rules for governing the procedure, formed the basis of the Statute of 1798. This gave the settlement of disputed titles the character of a judicial proceeding. But a violent antagonism between the Federalists and Anti-Federalists, revealed in the case of Joseph B. Varnum, of Massachusetts (1795), early established the rule that might makes right. In his first campaign for Congress, Varnum, who was destined to become Speaker, left a trail of questionable doings behind him. It appeared from a memorial submitted by Theodore Sedgwick, the Federalist leader, that the board of selectmen in Varnum's home town, of which Varnum himself was a member, had returned sixty votes more than the town was entitled to, thus giving him eleven majority. In the debate Sedgwick asked that testimony be taken under the procedure established by the Ames report, since the House alone could compel the contumacious town clerk to produce the record containing the names of the illegal voters. To this Varnum strenuously objected. Such a procedure, he insisted, would make the House a party to the investigation, a precedent which, if once established, must greatly harass sitting members. He thought the complainants should first present the names of the voters alleged to be illegal, and when told that his co-conspirator, the town clerk, refused to produce the records, without which the spurious names could not be discovered, he introduced evidence that the methods practiced by the other side disclosed the only reprehensible conduct. Nevertheless, the Anti-Federalists, who happened to be in control, sustained Varnum's objection to summoning the town clerk, and later adopted a resolution declaring "that the charges against him are wholly unfounded, and that his conduct appears to have been fair and unexceptional throughout the whole transaction." [1] Thus, amidst an outburst of derisive laughter, the incident closed like a harlequinade.

This case, so unblushingly violative of all principles of equity, tended to make decisions in election contests more and more indefensible. The failure to reënact the Statute of 1798, which expired by limitation in 1804, indicated a growing disposition to treat such contests entirely from a party standpoint. The Kentucky case of Letcher vs. Moore (1833) illustrated the length to which well-meaning members often allowed their personal prejudices or party fealty to govern in such matters. By willfully withholding a poll-book a sheriff of one of the five counties composing the district prevented the issue of a certificate to Letcher, who had received a

[1] 4th Cong., 2d Sess., *Journal*, p. 659.

majority of all the votes. No one believed Moore entitled to the seat, but the absence of a certificate presented a chance to challenge Letcher's title, and by the very close vote of 112 to 114 the House refused to seat him, declaring the place vacant.[1] "The House stultified itself," wrote Adams, "by shrinking from the decision which had been forced upon it." [2]

This astonishing result, obtained by setting aside valid returns without the slightest excuse, encouraged members in the next Congress to dispose of the North Carolina case of Newlands *vs.* Graham with even less regard for the proprieties.[3] Graham's certificate showed seven majority, but the House, without the slightest examination, "excluded the rightful member and came within one vote of admitting the intruder." [4]

If a majority, without need of recruits, wantonly unseats opponents simply to gratify partisan prejudices, it is certain to disregard all semblance of fairness when control of the House hinges on its action. This truism was illustrated in the Mississippi case of Prentiss and Word *vs.* Claiborne and Gholson (1837). In response to President Van Buren's call for an extra session, the governor, under the general authority of the Constitution to fill vacancies, issued writs for a special election to choose Representatives to serve "until superseded by the members chosen at the regular election on the first Monday and Tuesday in November." Under this proclamation Claiborne and Gholson were duly elected and

[1] 23d Cong., 1st Sess., *Debates*, pp. 2130-60.
[2] *Diary*, vol. ix, p. 445.
[3] 24th Cong., 1st Sess., House Rep. no. 378.
[4] John Quincy Adams, *Diary*, vol. ix, p. 445.

took their seats in September. The evidence of a political reaction throughout the country, induced by the "hard times" of that year, suggested the advisability of retaining the sitting members throughout the entire Congress, and early in October, on the plea that the governor had exceeded his power in limiting their service, the House declared them elected for the full term. Thereupon Claiborne and Gholson to escape defeat at the polls, cunningly renounced their candidacy for reëlection in November. This left the field open to Sergeant S. Prentiss and Thomas J. Word.

Prentiss had already won a nation-wide fame as an orator, and his contest crowded the floor and galleries with Washington's intellectual life, eager to hear the extraordinary Mississippian with "the big towering head" and a voice resembling "the sweet, strong tones of a great organ." In the argument Claiborne denied the governor's authority to limit his term, held the action of the House in October *res adjudicata*, and declared the voters of Mississippi knew nothing of the limitation, their intention being to elect for two years instead of two months. Prentiss, claiming that the voters understood the limitation, pronounced it infamous to charge the people of a great State with ignorance. He also stigmatized the October action of the House as a gross legislative usurpation. If the governor had no right to limit the term, he said, the House had no power to extend it. Congress may seat or exclude, but it cannot elect, a member. Prentiss spoke two hours a day for three consecutive days, and at its conclusion took his place among the greatest orators of his time. Mr. Webster declared that "no one can equal him." John C. Calhoun pronounced it "splendid, splendid, splendid!" with additional emphasis on each repetition of the word. John Quincy Adams, who rarely commended and never flattered, thought it "full of spirit and of argument, and seldom surpassed as a specimen of eloquence." Sixteen years afterward President Fillmore wrote: "It was the most brilliant speech I ever heard."

It proved more than brilliant, however. The argument that the House may seat or exclude, but cannot elect, captured the legislative mind, and the October edict was rescinded and the would-be usurpers unseated.[1]

This should have opened the door to Prentiss and Word, whose credentials, regular in form, sufficient in law, and representing an unimpeached majority, were based upon the November election. But the loss of control loomed big in the eyes of Administration supporters, and the vote refusing them admittance resulted in a tie, 117 to 117.[2] This gave Speaker Polk the casting vote. As elsewhere related, Polk was an able, bold, ambitious politician, who measured men and means according to their value in advancing his personal interests, which just then centered on the governorship of Tennessee, and although his hesitation, and finally his whispered "Aye," faintly heard in a House profoundly silent, indicated that the famous orator had captured his reason, he preferred to obey the voice of selfishness. No applause followed the announcement. Men recognized it as a Pyrrhic victory. "This has been one of the most remarkable

[1] 25th Cong., 2d Sess., *Globe*, p. 158.   [2] *Ibid*.

conflicts between honest principle and party knavery
that I ever witnessed," wrote Adams. "The result is a
parti-colored composition between right and wrong —
half honest and half knavish. The retribution upon
Claiborne and Gholson is signal." [1] But Prentiss and his
colleague were not defeated. The voters of Mississippi
shared the indignation of the country, and at a special
election, called immediately thereafter, both received an
overwhelming majority. [2] On presenting himself before
the Speaker to be sworn, Prentiss claimed his seat by
virtue of the November election, holding the more recent one to be unconstitutional. To this Polk made no
answer. But at the close of the Congress, when the
Speaker's friends sought to pass the usual vote of
thanks, Prentiss's brilliant and caustic summary of
Polk's uninviting character as a presiding officer forced
a speech of glorification and pique. [3]

The stinging reproof administered by the people of
Mississippi in no wise modified the House procedure.
Partisan influences not only dictated decisions, but contests without merit found encouragement for the purpose of controlling the organization of the House. To
such an extent was this practiced that in the next Congress (1840) a hold-over clerk became the chief con-
spirator in the famous New Jersey contest known as the
"Broad Seal case." [4] Attempts to reform such practices
finally resulted in the Act of 1851, which governs the

[1] *Diary*, vol. IX, p. 488.
[2] 25th Cong., 1st Sess., *Globe*, p. 95; *Ibid.*, 2d Sess., *Globe*, pp. 104,
150, 158, and Appendix pp. 68, 93, 124, 127.
[3] See chap. v, p. 72.
[4] See chap. II, p. 14.

present procedure.[1] It provides that a contestant must serve within thirty days an "intelligible" notice, specific in its allegations, which the contestee must answer within thirty days; that testimony must be taken during the next ninety days, the contestant being entitled to the first forty and the last ten; that either party may apply for subpœnas to any state or federal judge, or to any mayor, recorder, notary public, or register in bankruptcy, and in their absence to any two justices of the peace within the district; that if consent be given in writing the parties may, without further notice, take depositions before any authorized officer, but witnesses must be subpœnaed five days in advance and are not required to leave their county. The testimony, including papers and ballots, after being duly attested by witnesses, must be transmitted by the officer taking it to the clerk of the House, who, within twenty days thereafter, must notify the parties to appear and select such portions as they desire printed, the pleadings and an index being a part of the record. Within sixty days after printing the parties must exchange briefs, which, with the record and all unprinted testimony, are filed with the Committee on Elections.

In its investigation the Committee may examine ballots, and in case of doubt or ambiguity as to votes, it may take testimony, especially where wrongly written ballots or the mistakes of returning officers appear, provided such errors contribute to change the result. The House never presumes fraud, however glaring and widespread, so that a contestant must invalidate the con-

[1] 29 Stat. L., p. 568.

testee's title by proving his own. The mere showing of enough illegal votes to change the result will not suffice. The fact must affirmatively appear that the contestee benefited by them. But the burden of proof shifts to the sitting member whenever the Committee ascertains that the credentials originally belonged by right to the contestant. Where notices of election fail to reach a town and no votes are cast, proof is required of the number of voters thus disfranchised in order to show that title would continue in the returned member if all such votes had been cast against him. It is of no consequence that a contestant receives fewer votes than the head of his party ticket. Nor does the candidate receiving the next highest number take the seat if the one having a majority dies or is excluded.

In the House, during the consideration of an election case, both parties are heard, the contestant opening and closing the debate. Counsel was occasionally allowed in earlier years, but since 1856 the practice has been discontinued. When a delegate who could neither speak nor understand English appeared from the Territory of New Mexico, the Committee represented him on the floor.

The provisions of the Act of 1851, however, have never governed the House. Israel Washburn, of Maine, declared it directory, not binding. "By the Constitution," he said, "each House is made the sole judge of the returns, qualifications, and election of its own members, and each body must and can judge for itself. The law of 1851 is simply the advice or suggestion of reasonable and just men as to the proper course to be taken and nothing more." [1] Unfortunately, a disposition to ignore the act has long controlled the House. It often waives specifications when a notice is vague, or unrelated to vital questions, or defective as to the number of illegal votes. In one case it heard a contest upon the merits, although the notice was too imperfect to support a decision. At another time it ignored the fact that the first notice was irregular and that the supplemental notice was filed after the time required by law. One House insisted upon considering a question not raised in the notice, and another, after ruling a notice insufficient, permitted the contestant to amend orally. On the other hand, because a contestant did not demand it in his notice, the House refused to count the votes of one precinct, although the testimony justified it.

Discretion is likewise exercised in taking testimony. The House sometimes specifies the character and often fixes the time and place of taking it, especially if the provisions of the law exclude or prevent its being taken in time to secure a decision. The evidence being imperfect or insufficient, the House has frequently authorized the Committee to take additional testimony. In one instance it prescribed a course of procedure for serving a notice and taking testimony. On the other hand, it has as often ignored testimony on mere technicalities. One House rejected important testimony-in-chief because taken in the time allowed for rebuttal; another refused to allow additional newly discovered testimony, although the supporting affidavits disclosed a deliberate and carefully planned conspiracy to seat the contestee.

[1] 35th Cong., 1st Sess., *Globe*, p. 452.

Indeed, so many contrary precedents have been established that whatever the majority desires to accomplish, whether honest or dishonest, can be supported by precedent. Or, to state it in another form, it may be said that adherence to or departure from precedents and statutory procedure occurs whenever it will subserve the interest of the majority. "The decision of election cases," says Thomas B. Reed, "invariably increases the party which organizes the House and appoints the Committee on Elections. Probably there is not an instance on record where the minority benefited." [1] Reed himself had had a contest. The charge, based upon the intimidation of voters, was supported by such indifferent proof that it invited ridicule rather than serious consideration. "I can only say," he wrote, in concluding a brief of less than three pages, " that my experience with the Democracy of my district does not lead me to regard them as cowards. If I could scare them as easily as the contestant seems to think and by means as inadequate as he has proved, I have certainly been recreant in a plain duty. I ought to have scared more of them." Nevertheless, inconsequential as the case was, he recognized that he retained his seat simply because his party happened to control the House.

When asked what were party questions, George D. Robinson, of Massachusetts, afterwards governor, facetiously replied, "I know of none except election cases." Upon entering the room of the Committee on Elections of which he was a member, Thaddeus Stevens inquired the point in the case under investigation. "There is not

[1] *North American Review*, vol. 151, p. 114.

much point to it," replied his colleague; "they are both damned scoundrels." "Well," said Stevens, "which is the Republican damned scoundrel? I want to go for him." [1] When privilege was sought to prepare and publish a digest of contested cases adjudicated in the Fifty-first Congress, John H. Rogers, of Arkansas, facetiously moved an amendment that "any member who referred to them hereafter as an authority should be sentenced to penitentiary for life." [2] George F. Hoar, of Massachusetts, who served on the Committee on Elections during the Forty-second Congress, confesses that "whenever there is a plausible reason for making a contest the dominant party in the House almost always awards the seat to the man of its own side." [3] He might with pardonable propriety have omitted "almost," for of three hundred and eighty-two cases of contest submitted up to and including the Fifty-ninth Congress (1907), only three persons not of the dominant party obtained seats.

These partisan settlements have enormously multiplied contests. Their number in early Congresses, when the membership was comparatively small, often occasioned surprise, but since the Civil War the number not infrequently aggregates twelve to fifteen in a single Congress. In the Forty-seventh Congress (1881) it reached twenty-one, and in the Fifty-fourth (1895), thirty-one, of which twenty-six came from the Southern States. From 1865 to 1905 two hundred and ninety-two

---

[1] George F. Hoar, *Autobiography*, vol. I, p. 268.
[2] 51st Cong., 2d Sess. *Record*, p. 2334.
[3] *Autobiography*, vol. I, p. 268.

cases were filed, of which one hundred and eighty-seven came from the South.

The increasing number of contests has correspondingly augumented the cost. The law allows each party in interest $2000 for expenses, based upon a sworn detailed statement, with a voucher for each item.[1] But double this amount is often voted. In the celebrated Pennsylvania case of Curtin *vs.* Yocum, which arose in the Forty-sixth Congress (1879), the House allowed each party $8000, which defrayed only a fraction of the expense. Ten cases in the Forty-sixth Congress mulcted the Government $59,567, and the twenty-one cases filed in the Forty-seventh, of which all were not prosecuted, cost $71,285. During the eight Congresses succeeding the Forty-second, eighty-four cases cost $318,000, or an average of nearly $40,000 for each Congress or $4000 per case filed. In 1903 a contestant from Missouri got his seat the last week of the Congress, drawing $10,000 salary, while the contestee had drawn as much. In addition each received $2000 for expenses.

The swelling of testimony, which often fills hundreds of pages, adds enormously to the labor of examination and decision. Nothing can be excluded which either party desires inserted in the record. Objection may be noted, but the testimony is taken. Only those who incur the expense can really appreciate this burden. Besides, a fiercely contested election at the polls is not unlikely to be continued for another year with equal fierceness

[1] Witnesses fees are limited to seventy-five cents per day and five cents a mile for travel. Fees of officials employed in taking testimony are governed by the laws of the State wherein the service is rendered.

at Washington. Indeed, comparatively few contestants appear except those belonging to the party which organizes the House. This accounts for the absence of contests from the South during the administration of Speakers Kerr, Randall, Carlisle, and Crisp, and the phenomenally large number presented during the Speakership of Keifer and Reed.

Although three Committees on Elections are now appointed instead of one as formerly, members often find it physically impossible, with their other duties, to give to the many cases the study necessary to their proper disposition. In the House their consideration is no less burdensome. Six cases in the Forty-eighth Congress consumed thirteen days, four cases in the Fiftieth took nine days, and nine cases in the Fifty-first occupied sixteen days, or one ninth of the entire session. Yet after the toil, the expenditure of money, and the consumption of so much time, the decision, whatever it may be, is discredited as partisan. No better illustration of this practice need be cited than the West Virginia case of Smith *vs.* Jackson, arising in the Fifty-first Congress (1889), and made famous by the action of Speaker Reed, who, to secure its consideration, initiated the counting of a quorum. The governor gave Jackson, the sitting member, a certificate based on a plurality of three votes. Smith, the contestant, claimed a plurality of twelve votes. The law of West Virginia made it the duty of the commissioners of county courts in each congressional district to transmit to the governor a certificate of the result of elections within their respective counties, in which the number of votes received should be set forth in words. The commissioners of Pleasant County certified that Jackson "received eight hundred and *twe* votes." Of course, "t-w-e" was intended for "two," the clerk having omitted to close the "o." But the governor treated it as an abbreviation of "twelve," although no one ever before recognized such an abbreviation, which might stand for "twenty" as well as "twelve." Moreover, "twe," under the law, stood for a written number, and no number of three letters beginning with "tw" is or ever was known to the English language except "two." Besides, the records of the Pleasant County clerk showed Jackson's vote to be 802. This correction gave Smith seven majority. Nevertheless, the decision was denounced as grossly partisan.[1]

Although Committees on Elections are usually made up of able and conscientious members, their work has neither lessened the number of cases nor decreased expenses. In the presence of such a record it is so obvious that something essentially vicious exists in this settlement that one naturally turns to the procedure in the House of Commons. Originally it disposed of contests in the American fashion. When the system became intolerable, it adopted in 1770 what it was pleased to call a "reform measure," under which thirty-three members were chosen by lot. Subsequently each party struck off eleven names, leaving a committee of eleven to whom were referred all contests. In 1839 Adams spoke of this arrangement as "complicated," adding: "The ultimate result is chance which is a more impartial arbiter than

[1] 51st Cong., 1st Sess., House Rep., no. 19; Rowell, p. 13; *Record*, pp. 1025–43; *Journal*, pp. 187–90.

will." [1] In 1848 the English substituted a Committee on Elections, appointed by the Speaker and approved by the House. This proved so unsatisfactory that in 1868 the Commons turned the whole matter over to the judges of the Queen's Bench, the Common Pleas, and the Exchequer, with power to establish a procedure for determining the facts and principles of law. Under this system each case is assigned to a judge, who visits the election district at once, examines witnesses, and determines the facts on the spot, with the result that comparatively few contests now arise, while expenses are greatly reduced. Indeed, so satisfactory is the English plan that Thomas B. Reed advised Congress to establish a similar tribunal, expressing the belief that its decisions, if acquiesced in for a few years, would create a dominating sentiment sufficient to compel their acceptance. Acting on his advice, the Committee on Elections in 1895 reported a bill giving United States District Courts jurisdiction. But nothing came of it. To the objection that such assignments impair the usefulness of judges, it is urged that English courts have not so suffered, while publicity safeguards impartiality.

The existence of such a tribunal in 1887 must have greatly benefited Speaker Carlisle, who suddenly became a contestee. After serving notice of contest and examining ten witnesses, the contestant moved the Committee on Elections to appoint a subcommittee to take further testimony, supporting his motion by affidavits affirming the contestee's admission of defeat; a midnight conference of the contestee and his friends for

[1] *Diary*, vol. x, p. 170.

the purpose of securing the election by fraud; the absence in most counties of tickets bearing the contestee's name; the presence of poll-books in which the names of scores of voters appeared in the same handwriting; and the existence of many certificates bearing the name of the same official signed in different handwriting. In excuse for his failure to cover these points in the original notice, the contestant pleaded betrayal by his attorney and the contestee's admission of enough illegal votes to more than offset his alleged majority. The majority report, presented by Charles F. Crisp, refused the motion because it did not appear by satisfactory evidence that the contestant could prove title to the seat even if allowed to reopen the case. On the other hand, the minority, although admitting that the contestee's affidavits completely refuted the specifications, thought that grave charges of fraud should not be hastily dismissed on the mere presentation of *ex-parte* affidavits. "It believes that a reasonable showing having been made by the contestant, he should, in all justice and fair dealing, be allowed to establish by legal and competent evidence, if he can, these allegations of fraud." Accordingly it presented a resolution referring all papers in the case to a subcommittee, with instructions to investigate carefully. At the conclusion of the debate the resolution was defeated — yeas, 125; nays, 132.[1]

It is not surprising, perhaps, that Speaker Carlisle's party, in view of the long-established custom of deciding such questions wholly from a partisan standpoint, declined to go into a long, expensive, and possibly doubtful

[1] 50th Cong., 1st Sess., *Record*, pp. 590–606, 629.

trial. Yet Carlisle's alleged admission of defeat and of hundreds of illegal votes, coupled with a mass of alleged forgeries and the questionable conduct of the contestant's attorney, provoked criticism and aroused a distrust that pained the Speaker's admirers. Had a federal judge entered the district as soon as notice of contest was filed, an indelible stain on an otherwise creditable record must have been avoided.

CHAPTER XVII

IMPEACHMENT PROCEEDINGS

In seeking to remove public officials by impeachment Congress in the main has confined its efforts to members of the judiciary. The attempt to impeach President Johnson advertised its great prerogative and engrossed its whole attention; but of the thirty-four cases which have come within its scrutiny twenty-nine were judges of United States courts. This is not surprising, perhaps, since other appointive officers are subject to dismissal and members of Congress to expulsion. Only the President, Vice-President, and judges are inaccessible except by impeachment.

The Constitution alone governs cases of impeachment. It provides that "the President, Vice-President, and all civil officers of the United States shall be removed from office on impeachment for, and conviction of, treason, bribery, and other high crimes and misdemeanors." [1] It further provides that "the House shall have the sole power of impeachment," and "the Senate shall have the sole power to try all impeachments." [2] In other words, the House indicts as a grand jury and prosecutes as a district attorney; the Senate hears and pronounces judgment as a court. "No person shall be convicted without the concurrence of two thirds of the members present. Judgment shall not extend further than to removal from office and disqualification to hold

---

[1] Art. II, sec. 4. [2] Art. I, secs. 2 and 3.

and enjoy any office of honor, trust, or profit under the United States; but the party convicted shall nevertheless be liable and subject to indictment, trial, judgment, and punishment according to law." [1] If the President be tried, the Chief Justice presides. At other trials the Vice-President, the president *pro tem*, or some senator chosen for the purpose, may officiate.[2]

In the House impeachment proceedings are set in motion by petition, memorial, a letter of complaint, or upon an oral or written statement of a member. The first impeachment, charging William Blount, a senator from Tennessee, with conspiracy to invade the territory of a friendly power, was based upon a letter transmitted to the House by President Jefferson. In the case of Samuel Chase, an Associate Justice of the Supreme Court, John Randolph, of Virginia, rose in his seat, and, without resolution or specific charges, moved the appointment of a committee to consider the propriety of impeachment. Although a general investigation as to the execution of the laws preceded the impeachment of President Johnson, the House finally voted to investigate his conduct on charges made by a single member on his own responsibility. To become privileged a proposition to impeach, as distinguished from one to inquire, must be presented; but the House, having once consented to hear the matter, disposes of it as it sees fit. If one House refuses to impeach, another may act. In the case of Judge John C. Watrous, of Texas (1852), three consecutive Houses passed upon the same petitions without result.

[1] Art. I, sec. 3.   [2] *Ibid.*

Under the approved practice the House refers complaints to the Judiciary Committee, which, if the matter seem sufficiently serious, appoints a subcommittee to investigate, with authority to send for persons and papers. Although respondents in the earlier days did not always appear at such inquests, the later practice invites them to be present in person or by counsel, with the privilege of presenting and examining witnesses and submitting oral or written statements. When heard in his own behalf, however, a respondent is not obliged to answer or produce proof. Rules of evidence are ordinarily observed, unless the respondent, as in the case of Judge Blodgett, of Illinois (1879), demands the most liberal latitude. Of the thirty-four cases examined by the House, twenty-five did not reach the Senate. Of these, fifteen disclosed no cause of action, two were referred to other tribunals for prosecution, and eight respondents resigned pending the investigation. Of the nine officials tried by the Senate, Judges Pickering, of New Hampshire (1803), Humphrey, of Tennessee (1862), and Archbold, of Pennsylvania (1913), were convicted.

Whenever the House indicts it appoints a committee, usually of two members, to notify the Senate of its action. A committee is also appointed to prepare articles of impeachment. After their adoption five or more members are selected by ballot or designated by the Speaker to act as managers, upon whom rests the entire responsibility of conducting the prosecution. The House, if it attends the trial, appears as in Committee of the Whole. During the trial of Justice Chase, of the Supreme Court

(1804), and of President Johnson (1868), it appeared daily in the Senate. It also accompanied its managers when articles of impeachment were filed against Judges Peck, of Missouri (1826), and Humphrey, of Tennessee (1862). But with these exceptions it disclosed no special interest in such trials. Nor do respondents always appear in person. At the time of their trial Judge Humphrey served the Confederacy; Judge Pickering was insane; Senator Blount remained at his home in Louisiana; and President Johnson deemed an array of five distinguished attorneys sufficient representation. Justice Chase, Judge Swayne, of Florida (1904), Judge Archbold, of Pennsylvania (1913), and Secretary of War Belknap (1876) appeared, although Belknap absented himself on the day the Senate voted.

The Senate is a tribunal of first instance and of last resort. No appeal lies from its decisions and no precedent may govern its action. In preparation for the event senators take the oath,[1] prescribe ceremonies, originate forms, adopt rules, and, at an appointed day and hour, receive the House managers, who read and file the articles of impeachment, duly signed by the Speaker and attested by the clerk. The Senate also issues a writ of summons to the respondent and fixes the time for filing his answer. In conjunction with the House managers a day is agreed upon for beginning the proceedings, when, if the respondent fails to appear in person or by counsel, the trial proceeds as on a plea of not guilty.

---

[1] The oath is ordinarily administered to the secretary of the Senate by some qualified official, who administers it to the presiding officer, who in turn administers it to the senators.

At the suggestion of Vice-President Burr the Senate made elaborate preparations for the trial of Samuel Chase, an Associate Justice of the Supreme Court. Senators sat on crimson benches arranged on either side and in line with the Vice-President; boxes were assigned to managers and respondent's counsel on the right and left of the Chair; the floor of the Senate, reserved for members of the House, was flanked with boxes, set apart for foreign representatives and officers of the army and navy; while above a temporary platform, handsomely furnished, provided room for ladies, those of distinguished families finding accommodations in boxes at either end. Only doors of the permanent gallery opened to all comers. Over this brilliant array stood the marshal of the District of Columbia as the preserver of order. This arrangement, affecting the scene in the great hall of Rufus at the impeachment of Warren Hastings, created a mad rush for seats, which seriously disturbed the proceedings, and early in the trial the spectacular became impracticable. Finally, when the respondent, then an old man, a father of the Republic, and second in ability to none in the chamber, received a triumphant acquittal, the crimson benches disappeared with the violent party spirit that initiated the proceedings. Nevertheless, the House retained its pompous title of "the great inquest of the nation," while the Senate remained a "high court of impeachment."

Preliminary to the trial of President Johnson, the Senate, perhaps fearing the influence of Chief Justice Chase, manifested a disposition to rid itself of the character of a judicial body. The claim that the ordinary restrictions of judicial process had no more application than the guarantees accorded to the accused in jury trials was strengthened by the fact that no right existed to challenge a member of the Senate for any cause, or to appeal to any court, or to any law save the Constitution. Others argued that the presence of the Chief Justice fixed its status as a court. Moreover, the Constitution, by empowering the Senate to "try" impeachments, contemplated the form of a judicial action. The peculiar character of the oath administered to senators, as well as an adherence to the technical terminology of the law in the use of the words "conviction" and "judgment," contributed to this conclusion. Precedent, too, had established its judicial character. The Senate, however, decided that it sat as a "constitutional tribunal," convened "to inquire into and determine whether Andrew Johnson, because of malversation in office, is longer fit to retain the office of President, or hereafter to hold any office of honor or profit." [1]

Having settled its status the Senate declined to require the Chief Justice to be sworn. It also questioned his right to decide on the admissibility of evidence. Some maintained that he acted not as a presiding judge, but simply as the mouthpiece of the Senate. He could decide nothing. No one not a senator could take any part in the trial save as a ministerial agent. This view did not satisfy the more conservative, and by a vote of 31 to 19 the Chief Justice received permission not only to decide all questions of law and evidence, subject to appeal if any senator demanded a roll-call, but to give the casting

[1] *Report of Trial*, p. 30.

vote in case of a tie. It emphasized the judicial character of the body, too, when the Chief Justice, arrayed in his robe, appeared at the door of the Senate, attended by an Associate Justice, who subsequently administered the oath to him.

In the trial of impeachment cases it was very early contended that the rigid rules of evidence which governed the practice of courts of law did not apply. William Wirt, in the Peck case, quoting the *Federalist* in support of the proposition, argued that proceedings in the Senate should at least be conducted as liberally as in courts conversant with the civil law. In general, however, the rules of evidence governing inferior or *nisi prius* courts have been recognized. Thus, witnesses are required to state facts instead of opinions, and to present the best evidence procurable. Conversations with third parties, not in the presence of the respondent, are ordinarily excluded as well as cumulative testimony as to the respondent's intent, although the respondent's declarations of intent, made at the time of the act, are admissible.

Questions of jurisdiction have also perplexed Congress. Pending the preparation of articles of impeachment in the case of William Blount the Senate expelled him. Thereupon counsel raised the inquiry whether he could be punished a second time by impeachment. He did not contend, counsel said, that an officer could avoid impeachment by resigning, but denied that the respondent could be tried and disqualified for the same offense for which he was expelled. Thereupon the Senate, by a vote of 14 to 11, declared that "the court is of opinion

that the matter alleged in the plea of defendant is sufficient in law to show that this court ought not to hold
jurisdiction of the said impeachment, and that it is dismissed." [1] The case of Schuyler Colfax, growing out of
the Crédit Mobilier scandal in 1873, presented the question whether a Vice-President could be impeached for a
wrongful act committed while Speaker of the House.
The Judiciary Committee held it material to allege that
the accused still exercised the duties of the office in
which the wrong occurred.[2] Benjamin F. Butler, of
Massachusetts, John A. Bingham, of Ohio, John A.
Peters, of Maine, and other admittedly able lawyers concurred in this report. Clarkson N. Potter, of New York,
dissented. The House took no further action presumably for the reason that Colfax in a day or two would
retire. When Edward H. Durrell, District Judge of
Louisiana, resigned pending investigation (1874), Butler
thought the proceeding might go on for the purpose of
disqualification, but he doubted its propriety because of
Durrell's advanced age. Thereupon the House, by a
strict party vote, laid the resolution of impeachment on
the table — yeas, 129; nays, 69.[3] Similar disposition was
made of the case of Richard Busteed, District Judge of
Alabama, who resigned pending impeachment proceedings.[4]

The case of Secretary Belknap presented the same
question. Belknap resigned as soon as an investigation
exposed his crime, and when the cause reached the Senate

[1] *Annals*, pp. 2318–19.
[2] 42d Cong., 2d Sess., *Record*, pp. 324–26.
[3] 43d Cong., 2d Sess., *Record*, pp. 319–24.   [4] *Ibid.*

his counsel held that the Constitution contemplated impeachment and removal of a civil "officer" only while he held the office, the sole purpose being promptly to arrest his power to do wrong. "When an officer resigns and becomes a private citizen, is he still an officer?" counsel asked facetiously. "Who is the President? An ex-President? When we speak of the President do we refer to anybody except the incumbent of that office? The Constitution declares that when a President is impeached, the Chief Justice shall preside. Who would preside if an ex-President was impeached? An ex-Chief Justice? This puzzle arises out of the absurdity of impeaching an ex-President! The Constitution says, also, that upon conviction the President and all other civil officers shall be removed. How can a man be removed who holds no office? And if removed, how can the sentence be made effectual except by disqualification? Although the President cannot pardon the convicted offender, he may reinstate him the next morning. To prevent this was the object of the disqualification clause. Removal and disqualification cannot be separated. You cannot remove without disqualifying and you cannot disqualify without removal, because the Constitution requires the Senate to pronounce a judgment of removal *and* disqualification — not removal or disqualification." [1]

George F. Hoar, of Massachusetts, a House manager, declared that English precedents and the history of the Constitution pointed irresistibly to the conclusion that the power of the Senate over official wrongdoers to interpose by its judgment a perpetual barrier against their

[1] 44th Cong., 1st Sess., *Record of Trial*, pp. 70–74.

return to office does not depend upon the consent of the
culprit, or the accidental discovery of the crime before
his term of office has expired. It is a perpetual power,
hanging over the guilty officer during his life. The
history of the formation of the Constitution, he continued, shows that the clause making civil officers re-
movable on conviction is there as an exception to clauses
which had previously determined the tenure of those
offices. The power of impeachment is not defined in the
grant in the Constitution. It is conferred as a general
common-law power. No limit of its application to persons is inserted in the grant. But removal by impeachment is inserted as a subsequent limitation on the tenure
of office to guard against the argument that officers,
whose term is fixed in the Constitution, cannot be
removed under the power of impeachment, just as impeachment is excepted in the clause securing the right
of trial by jury and in the clause conferring the power of
pardon. But suppose the phrase "all civil officers" was
inserted as a definition of the persons who may be
reached by this process, does it apply to them at the
time the offense is committed or at the time of the
punishment? If a statute enact that all wrongdoers
may be punished, it is clear that liability to punishment attaches when the act is committed. The whole
constitutional provision can be summed up in two sentences which precisely state the contention. The managers claim that the Constitution in substance says that
"the Senate shall have the sole power to try impeachments, and civil officers shall be removed on conviction."
Counsel for defendant put it that "judgment in case of

conviction shall be removal from office and disqualification, if the defendant is willing. If unwilling, he resigns." [1]

Over this question the Senate deliberated in secret
session for two weeks and finally, by a vote of 37 to 29,
held the respondent amenable to trial. Among those
voting "yea" were George F. Edmunds, of Vermont,
Allen G. Thurman, of Ohio, Joseph E. McDonald, of
Indiana, James A. Bayard, of Delaware, John Sherman,
of Ohio, Justin S. Morrill, of Vermont, Henry L. Dawes,
of Massachusetts, and Francis Kernan, of New York;
while Oliver P. Morton, of Indiana, Richard J. Oglesby,
of Illinois, William B. Allison, of Iowa, John J. Ingalls, of
Kansas, Lot M. Morrill, of Maine, George S. Boutwell,
of Massachusetts, William Windom, of Minnesota, and
Roscoe Conkling, of New York, voted "no." It was a
division of notable men of acknowledged gifts, whose
sincerity was voiced by the final roll-call, those holding
"want of jurisdiction" generally voting "not guilty."
This reduced the affirmative vote below the required
two thirds, thus practically amounting to an acquittal,
although Belknap's guilt was admitted. In reporting
the result, the House managers declared that the trial
had at least settled the question "that persons who have
held office are impeachable." [2]

At the trial of Robert W. Archbold in 1913 the question again arose. Archbold served as judge of the
Eastern District of Pennsylvania from 1901 to 1911,
after which he became a circuit judge and a member of

---

[1] 44th Cong., 1st Sess., *Record of Trial*, p. 57.
[2] *Record of Trial*, p. 357.

the Court of Commerce. Impeachment articles 1 to 6 related to offenses committed as circuit judge and article 7 to 12 as district judge, while article 13 included acts of misconduct while district as well as circuit judge. In its decision the Senate convicted for crimes committed as circuit judge and acquitted for alleged misconduct as district judge, several senators holding that the Senate was without jurisdiction of such misconduct. On the thirteenth article nearly one third answered "not guilty," notwithstanding "the charge contained was sustained by wrongful acts committed while holding the office of circuit judge." [1] In view of this vote it cannot yet be affirmed with certainty that persons who are not in office can be impeached for misconduct committed while in office, although the Archbold case settled the practice that in pronouncing sentence after conviction the Senate may remove and disqualify, or remove without disqualifying.

What constitute "other high crimes and misdemeanors" has been a more perplexing question. These words were copied into the Constitution from British constitutional and parliamentary law, and for more than a century eminent authorities have differed as to what offenses are subject to impeachment. One theory is that the Constitution adopted the English system of impeachment only as a mode of procedure, and that no offense is impeachable which is not subject to indictment under a statute of the United States or the common law. Thus, counsel in the Chase case (1804) held that "other high crimes and misdemeanors" meant offenses which are

[2] *Record of Trial*, p. 1675.

violations of law, exposing the violaters to punishment, these terms being synonymous, except that "crimes" refer to felonies, while "misdemeanors" include lesser offenses; but that in order to prevent impeachment for petty crimes, the Constitution limits them to "high misdemeanors." Moreover, misdemeanor is a legal and technical term, well understood and defined in law as an act committed or omitted in violation of a public law, and when interpreted in connection with "treason, bribery, and other high crimes," to be tried in the same manner and subject to the same penalties, it becomes something vastly more than an alleged breach of legal ethics. The House, counsel continued, cannot make an act impeachable at its will or pleasure; otherwise public officials must be the tools or the victims of the victorious party. Nor is the Senate to become a court of honor to punish breaches of politeness or to mark the precincts of judicial decorum. A respondent must be judged by some known law of the country, and the only offense described by the Constitution is the violation of some statute of the United States, or of a State, or of a provision of the common law. In the exercise of its power, therefore, Congress must be governed by the rules that limit the action of courts or grand juries, and if no law is violated, the House cannot impeach or the Senate convict.

In the first attempt of the House to impeach President Johnson (1867), the chairman of the Judiciary Committee, James F. Wilson, of Iowa, declared that it could not be presumed that the framers of the Constitution, after indicating such offenses as treason and bribery, intended to remove all further restraint by using the words "other high crimes and misdemeanors," thus allowing the House to impeach for any conduct which the whims, caprices, and passions of a majority might magnify into crimes. Wilson not only adopted the argument presented in the Chase case, holding these words to mean indictable offenses, but he contended that impeachment must follow the doctrine of the Supreme Court, that the Federal Government, having no jurisdiction of offenses at common law, can exercise no criminal jurisdiction which is not given by statute, since courts which are created by written law and whose jurisdiction is defined by written law, cannot transcend that jurisdiction.[1] In other words, no offense is impeachable which Congress has not made so by statute. To the suggestion that this was narrower than the limitation contended for in the Chase case, Wilson replied that the doctrine cited had not then been laid down by the Supreme Court.[2]

In the trial of President Johnson the able counsel for respondent adopted this argument, holding that impeachable offenses are "only high criminal offenses against the United States, made so by some law of the United States existing when the acts complained of were done." [3] In the Swayne case (1904), Marlin E. Olmsted, of Pennsylvania, a House manager, declared that such limitation renders the constitutional provision practically a nullity, since Congress has defined by statute comparatively few offenses. Even murder, he said, is not

---

[1] United States vs. Hudson and Goodwin, 7 Cranch, 32; United States vs. Coolidge et al., 1 Wheaton, 415; Ex parte Ballman and Swartwout, 4 Cranch, 95; United States vs. Lancaster, 2 McLeans R., 433.

[2] 40th Cong., 1st Sess., House Rep. no. 7.   [3] Ibid.

defined by any act of Congress. To which reply was made that every difficulty may be easily surmounted by appropriate legislation. "What right has the House and Senate to sleep on their undisputed legislative powers," asked James F. Wilson in the Johnson case, "and then resort to the common law of England for the punishment of civil officers, when no civil court of the United States can punish a citizen or foreigner for any crime except it be first prescribed by an act of Congress?" [1]

Another theory represents impeachment as not a mere procedure for the punishment of indictable crime, but that the phrase "high crimes and misdemeanors" is to be taken in a much broader sense and interpreted in the light of parliamentary usage, so as to include grave political offenses, maladministration, arbitrary and oppressive conduct, and even gross improprieties. Thus, in the trial of Justice Chase (1804) the House managers asserted that as "good behavior" limits a judge's term of service, he is liable to removal for "misbehavior," such as delivering an opinion on the law before counsel is heard, or making political harangues from the bench, or impeding important business by unnecessarily adjourning court, or ordering a defendant to trial when good grounds are presented for postponement, or making a decree not sanctioned by law, or delivering opinions unwarranted by precedent, principle, or legislative act, even though he do not violate positive law, provided senators are convinced, from a concurrence of circumstances, that he erred through design even if not corrupted by a bribe. The managers admitted that "mis-

[1] 40th Cong., 1st Sess., House Rep. no. 7.

demeanor" in a court of law meant an offense against a statute, but before the Senate, charged with the sole power of removal, it refers to official misconduct whether against a positive law or unwarranted by law.

In the case of James H. Peck (1830), the managers maintained that any official act committed or omitted by a judge which violated "good behavior" became an impeachable offense. So, preceding the formal impeachment of President Johnson, George S. Boutwell, of Massachusetts, representing the majority of the Judiciary Committee, argued that "high crimes and misdemeanors" include all cases of misbehavior whether known to statute law or not, the object of impeachment being to remove an official whose moral delinquency an ordinary tribunal is inadequate to reach. A President, he said, may ignore the law or impeach the power of Congress by nullifying its acts or denying their authority, thus being guilty of offenses calculated to subvert the Government without being liable to indictment.

The House, in formulating articles of impeachment, has included indictable and non-indictable offenses. Even in the Johnson case, after it had charged specific violations of the Tenure-of-Office Act, the Reconstruction and Conspiracy Acts, the Appropriation Act of March 2, 1867, and the Constitution, it interjected article 10, charging the President with bringing the office into contempt by his speeches at Cleveland and St. Louis during the "swing around the circle" in 1866. While the practice of the House, therefore, is unsettled, the judgments of the Senate have established the rule that convictions must be limited at least to acts having the character of a crime. The Chase and Peck and Swayne cases enunciate this principle. In the Johnson impeachment it happened that the Senate did not vote upon article 10, but of the twenty-two senators who subsequently filed statements, seventeen declared that the charge did not amount to official misconduct. Senator Ferry, of Michigan, who voted "guilty" on other articles, thought the speeches vain, foolish, vulgar, and unbecoming, "but the Constitution does not provide that a President may be impeached for these qualities." [1]

While senators have generally agreed that the violation of a statute constitutes ample ground for conviction, the seven recusant Republicans in the Johnson case denied that the President had violated any statute. Senator Trumbull, of Illinois, declared that the Tenure-of-Office Act did not forbid the removal of Secretary Stanton or the *ad-interim* appointment of General Thomas. Nor did the record contain, he said, "a particle of evidence" of the violation of the other acts cited. "If the question was, Is Andrew Johnson a fit person for President? I should answer, no! His speeches and the general course of his administration have been as distasteful to me as to any one. But to convict or to depose a Chief Magistrate when guilt is not made palpable by the record would be fraught with far greater harm to the future of the country than can arise from having him in office." [2]

Cases considered with a view to impeachment have too often disclosed partisan or personal bias. Hildreth,

---

[1] 40th Cong., 1st Sess., *Report of Trial*, p. 451.
[2] 40th Cong., 2d Sess., *Globe*, Supplement, p. 420.

the historian, declared the Chase case "without sufficient foundation in fact or in law." [1] Adams pronounced it "a party prosecution." The Pickering impeachment belongs in the same category. Pickering's habits unfitted him to perform his duties, but the disregard of testimony proving insanity illuminated the animus of the proceeding. Fearful of its influence the majority wickedly substituted the question, "Is the respondent guilty as charged?" for the constitutional form, "Is the respondent guilty of high crimes and misdemeanors as charged?" An insane man's acts could not amount to "high crimes and misdemeanors," and to avoid the scruples of senators the incriminating words were omitted. Under the modern practice Congress retires such a sufferer without reproach by creating an additional judge, with the proviso that no successor to the existing incumbent be appointed.

Having convicted Pickering, Randolph immediately preferred charges against Samuel Chase, of Maryland. Of ardent passions, strong mind, and dominating temper, Chase's life had been turbulent and boisterous. He had signed the Declaration of Independence, and for his distinguished service in Congress, especially during the early period of the Revolution, President Washington appointed him to the Supreme Court. On his circuit, which included Maryland and Virginia, he did not cease his patriotic activities. Randolph and William B. Giles, of Virginia, had long desired his removal, and when the latter occupied a seat in the Senate, the twain conspired. While the former, as prosecutor, prepared articles of im-

[1] *History of the United States*, vol. v, p. 254.

peachment, the latter, as a judge, formulated rules for
the government of the Senate. They declared it the duty
of the House to impeach, and the right of the Senate to
remove, any judge who held an act of Congress unconstitutional, or sent a *mandamus* to the Secretary of State.[1]
To carry his point, Giles endeavored to frame rules of
procedure absolving the Senate from recognizing principles that restrain and bind courts of justice. But several
influences, notably the President's fear of Randolph's
increasing power, compelled the majority to present the
judgment question in its constitutional form, so that
of the twenty-five Republican senators who voted, six
answered, "Not guilty," a sufficient number to acquit.
Adams, who happened at the time to be a member of
the Senate, affirms that the six followed Jefferson's
directions.[2]

Judge Peck's impeachment was practically a party
proceeding. Peck disbarred and committed a St. Louis
barrister for contempt for publishing an article criticising
the court's decree touching certain land titles. Although
this action seemed high-handed, the House refused to
prosecute until James Buchanan became chairman of
the Judiciary Committee. Buchanan was an impressive
advocate, acquainted with all the arts that contribute to
popularity, and he used the case as a stepping-stone to
party preferment. He needed rehabilitation. Within
ten years he had left the Federalists, joined the Democrats, and quarreled with President Jackson. It added
to the interest of the trial that he was opposed by

---

[1] John Quincy Adams, *Diary*, vol. i, pp. 321, 323.
[2] *Diary*, vol. i, p. 372; vol. viii, p. 306.

William Wirt, then at the height of his fame, who appeared as the respondent's counsel.

The case turned on the point whether guilty intention must be established by proof. Buchanan claimed that if the commission of an unlawful act be proved, guilty intention followed as a necessary implication of law. Wirt declared that whatever it is material to charge it is material to prove. If the respondent knew the attorney's act was not a contempt and still punished it as one, it would be an intentional violation of law and an impeachable offense; but the intent must be proved, otherwise every mistake of law or error of judgment on the part of a judge would become a crime or civil injury for which he would be personally responsible. "I have examined the various cases of impeachment of judges both in England and in the United States," said the distinguished counsel, "and I have not heretofore observed that any counsel, even under the severest stress of evidence, has taken refuge in so bold a proposition as that error of judgment is an impeachable offense." [1]

It is not unlikely that Buchanan relied more upon the partisanship of thirty-eight Democratic senators than upon the strength of his proof, but when the vote of twenty-one to twenty-two for acquittal was announced, Adams inferred that Buchanan miscalculated the influence of the President. "Jackson's aversion to him," wrote Adams, "arises from a dirty intrigue to sacrifice me by purchasing Clay, which Buchanan disclosed, seemingly unconscious of moral turpitude in the avowal, and with a dullness of intellect equally un-

[1] 21st Cong., 2d Sess., *Report of Trial*, pp. 485–97.

conscious of the javelin he was thrusting into Jackson's side." [1]

The display of party feeling in the impeachment of President Johnson surpassed, if possible, the rancor exhibited in the trial of Justice Chase. At times the Senate Chamber disclosed the deep, earnest activity of a national party convention. Butler and Boutwell, to whom the President was a "monstrous malefactor," played the part of John Randolph, while Sumner, who spoke of Johnson as the "enormous criminal of his age," displayed the hostility of William B. Giles. Sumner thought impeachment a political and not a judicial proceeding, since the Constitution gave the Senate sole power to try. In his opinion the Senate was not confined to the "rigid rules of common law," because "its rules, unknown to ordinary courts," reverse the rule giving the accused the benefit of the doubt. "If on any point you entertain doubts," he said, "the benefit of those doubts must be given to your country. This is the supreme law." [2] He argued, also, that in order to avoid delay all testimony not trivial should be received, yet he refused to vote when the respondent offered to prove that several cabinet members advised him of the unconstitutionality of the Tenure-of-Office Act, although the Chief Justice held such an offer admissible on the question of intent. Other Republican leaders were not more punctilious.

After submission of the case a system of coercion existed to bring doubtful senators into line. Letters

[1] *Diary*, vol. VIII, p. 307.
[2] 40th Cong., 1st Sess., *Report of Trial*, pp. 473–80.

threatened, the press criticized, and colleagues censured. Nevertheless, the resistance of the seven recusant Republicans set an admirable example to their successors. "The glory of the trial," says Rhodes, "was the action of these seven senators. Only after great inward trouble could they come to their determination. It was so easy to go the other way, to agree with the thirty-five, most of whom were honest men and some of whom were able lawyers, who interpreted the evidence and the law in favor of conviction. The average senator who hesitated finally gave his voice with the majority, but these seven in conscientiousness and delicacy of moral fiber were above any average, and in refusing to sacrifice their ideas of justice to a popular demand, which in this case was neither insincere nor unenlightened, they showed a degree of courage than which we know no higher. Hard as was their immediate future they have received their meed from posterity, their monument in the admiring tribute of all who know how firm they stood in an hour of supreme trial." [1]

[1] *History of the United States*, vol. VI, p. 156.

CHAPTER XVIII

THE PRESIDENT AND THE HOUSE

THE Senate and the House, for the purpose of counting the electoral vote for President, meet in joint session on the second Wednesday in February succeeding the election in November. The presiding officer of the Senate, who receives the returns from the governors of the several States, opens and hands them to the tellers to be read and tabulated, after which he announces the result. During this joint session no debate is allowed, but if the two Houses disagree as to the counting of any vote, they separate, each body being allowed two hours for debate. No recess can continue after ten o'clock of the next calendar day, Sunday excepted, and if the count be not concluded before the fifth calendar day further recessing is disallowed.

The person having the greatest number of votes, if it be a majority of the electors appointed, becomes the President; otherwise the House withdraws and immediately proceeds to choose by ballot from the three persons having the highest number, each State being allowed one vote. A quorum consists of two thirds of all the States, a majority being necessary to a choice. In 1801, when the electoral count disclosed no choice for President, the House, after returning to its own chamber and excluding every one except its officers, adopted rules to continue in session without adjournment or interruption by other business until a choice was made, all questions to be decided by States without debate. When each State had ascertained its choice by ballot, the name of its candidate, or, if equally divided, the word "divided," was written on duplicate ballots and deposited in different boxes, the ballots in each being counted by different tellers appointed from each State. When the balloting, which lasted with postponements for several days, finally gave Thomas Jefferson a majority, the Speaker announced his election and immediately notified the President and the Senate. The proceeding in 1825, resulting in the election of John Quincy Adams, in no wise materially differed except that the rules admitted members of the Senate. If the House makes no choice before the 4th of March, the Vice-President becomes President.[1]

On March 4, or, if it falls on Sunday, on March 5, the President is inaugurated. Originally the ceremony occurred in the hall of the Senate or House as the President elect indicated; but in 1817, because Speaker Clay objected to the red morocco chairs of the Senate being substituted for the plain democratic seats of the House, the committee "retired somewhat huffed," as Clay expressed it, and held the function on the east portico of the Capitol.[2] This eligible place, affording all the people an opportunity to witness the spectacle, at once became the favorite locality, and except in 1821 and 1825, when the ceremony occurred in the hall of the House, and again in 1909, when inclement weather pre-

[1] 24th Cong., 2d Sess., *Globe*, p. 212.

[2] Constitution, Amendment xii. See, also, Act of January 19, 1886, 24 Stat. L., p. 1.

vented, and the ceremony occurred in the Senate Chamber, the oath has been administered and the address delivered on the spot immortalized by the two inaugurals of President Lincoln.

For a time the House, because it ceases to exist as an organized body before the event, had no official connection with the inauguration of the President; but for many years a joint committee has perfected the arrangements, members of the House, during the inauguration of the Vice-President, occupying seats on the floor of the Senate, with the Speaker at the right of the presiding officer. On the march to the portico of the Capitol they are preceded by the Supreme Court, ambassadors and ministers of foreign countries, and members of the Senate. Following them are members of the Cabinet, the Admiral of the Navy, the General of the Army, governors of States, and other officials invited to the floor of the Senate.

Although the Constitution fixes the time for the assembling of Congress on the first Monday in December, the President may convene it or either House at an earlier day and at a place other than the seat of government. Such special session ends, however, on the day the regular session begins. After its organization the House informs the President of the presence of a quorum and its readiness to receive his message. The election of a Speaker amounts to an organization, and in 1860 notification preceded the selection of a clerk; but usually it follows the choice of all its officers. It is customary, also, though not an invariable rule, for the House to notify the President of the election of a Speaker *pro tem*. When near the close of a session it likewise notifies him of its approaching adjournment, and if the two bodies disagree as to the time he may adjourn them.

The President presents a message at the opening of each annual or special session, and at such other times as he may desire to make a communication. Besides a discussion of the routine affairs of the Government, such messages may include reports from heads of departments, the promulgation of the ratification of constitutional amendments, communications or petitions from foreigners, and letters impeaching the conduct of federal civil officials. Presidents Washington and John Adams, flanked by the Vice-President and Speaker, presented their annual messages in person. Subsequently the Vice-President, attended by the Speaker and members of the two Houses, proceeded to the President's audience chamber and presented a joint address in reply. President Jefferson preferred to communicate in writing, a custom which continued until President Wilson (1913) revived the earlier practice. Although one way is as proper as the other, the applause which greets the Chief Executive, especially after he has appeared several times in person, is likely to be confined to one side of the chamber, giving the ceremony something of a partisan character, which occasions a subtle embarrassment. If a message be transmitted in writing, it is promptly received by the House, the Committee of the Whole, if it be in session at the time, informally rising for the purpose. If presented before the organization of the House, it remains in the custody of the clerk. If of a confidential character, a rule of the House, though not invoked since 1843, provides for a secret session. An annual message is formally laid before the House at a time prescribed by the order of business. It is then read in full, entered in the Journal, printed in the *Congressional Record*, and referred to the Committee of the Whole House on the State of the Union, which, on motion of the chairman of Ways and Means, distributes the various topics to appropriate standing or select committees with or without instructions. Special messages, however, even when relating to matters of great importance, are ordinarily referred to committees by the Speaker without reading or debate. To lay a communication from the President on the table, other than a veto message, is considered a mark of disapprobation.

All enrolled bills and such resolutions as are legislative in effect, except those proposing amendments to the Constitution, go to the President for his approval, and, if signed, are deposited with the Secretary of State for preservation and publication. If not signed or returned within ten days, they become laws, unless in the mean time Congress expires. It is doubtful, however, if adjournment for a recess invalidates. A bill returned with the President's objections is privileged, and if a quorum be present it is usually considered at once. It cannot be postponed indefinitely, but if returned too late in the session for consideration because of the absence of a quorum, it may be acted upon at the next session of the same Congress. To lay it on the table, or to refer it, is equivalent to agreeing to the President's objections. If passed in both Houses by two thirds of those present it goes directly to the Secretary of State.

As a rule Presidents have used the veto sparingly. In a measure this has been due to the watchfulness of Congress and the frankness of the Chief Executive, for members not infrequently obtain the President's views in advance. On more than one occasion President Roosevelt publicly announced a veto if a pending measure passed. The original purpose of the veto was to safeguard the Executive against the encroachments of Congress, but for many years it has been exercised to defeat measures objectionable in principle or in probable results. President Lincoln, speaking of executive influence, said: "By the Constitution, the Executive may recommend measures which he may think proper, and he may veto those he thinks improper, and it is supposed he may add to these certain indirect influences to affect the actions of Congress. My political education strongly inclines me against a very free use of any of these means by the Executive to control the legislation of the country. As a rule I think that Congress should originate as well as perfect its measures without external bias." [1]

President Cleveland regarded the right of veto as intended "to invoke the exercise of executive judgment and invite executive action." Of two hundred and sixty-five private pension bills heretofore vetoed by all the Presidents, he disapproved two hundred and sixty. Washington used the veto but twice, and Adams, Jefferson, John Quincy Adams, Van Buren, William Henry Harrison, Taylor, Fillmore, and Garfield, not at all. Lincoln vetoed three. Johnson was not so modest. He thought ten bills unconstitutional and many others in-

[1] Speech at Pittsburg, February 15, 1861.

advisable. McKinley disapproved fourteen bills; Roosevelt, forty; Taft, twenty-five; and Wilson (thus far, 1915), four. Up to the end of Roosevelt's Administration two hundred and seventy-six measures other than private pension bills had suffered veto, of which sixty-eight were deemed unconstitutional. That Congress did not ordinarily differ widely from the views set forth in veto messages is evidenced by the fact that only twenty-nine of the five hundred and forty-one were re-passed, and of these fifteen were bills vetoed by Johnson.[1]

Among the "certain indirect influences" to which Lincoln referred is the questionable practice, severely criticized of late by many members of both Houses, of letting it be known that certain bills originated in the White House. The President has no express power to submit the text of a measure and ask Congress to enact it, and the cases are probably few in which he has done so. But the heads of departments have often drawn bills of the highest importance and have caused their introduction by some member friendly to the object sought. The second Bank Act of 1816 and the Walker Tariff Act of 1846 are early and conspicuous instances of this practice. That President Grant suggested the drafting and passage of the Electoral Commission Act in 1877 is common knowledge. It is equally well known that President Roosevelt was largely instrumental in the enactment of the Transportation Act of 1907. Nor is it a secret that President Taft insisted upon significant changes in the Tariff Act of 1909. Indeed, since the

[1] Of the bills passed over a veto, one was disapproved by Tyler; five by Pierce; fifteen by Johnson; four by Grant; one by Hayes; one by Arthur; and two by Cleveland.

time of President Cleveland the Chief Executive has not hesitated to influence legislation by special messages, through the public press, and by direct appeal to individual members.

The House has always exercised its right to make requests of, and to express its opinion to, the President. In the early days the joint address adopted by the two bodies and presented by the Vice-President became the medium of such communications. Since the abandonment of that practice it has spoken through resolutions. In 1807 it asked him to inquire into charges against the chief of the army. So, in 1856, it requested that military protection, if necessary, be afforded to a committee charged with the investigation of affairs in the Territory of Kansas. Indeed, it has not hesitated to ask him to reduce executive estimates, to transmit proposed amendments to the Constitution, to investigate river and harbor improvements, to inquire into the culpability of executive officers, and to negotiate treaties. With questionable propriety it has ventured to bestow praise and censure.

Resolutions of inquiry are the usual method of obtaining information of the Executive. When addressed to the President the word "request" is inserted; if to a cabinet officer, the less conciliatory term "direct." Such resolutions, especially when relating to foreign affairs, usually, though not invariably, contain the clause, "if not incompatible with the public interest." Ordinarily such resolutions are fully answered, but the difficulty and delay in securing their adoption by the House raised the question as early as 1792 of allowing cabinet ministers permission to occupy seats in the House and to participate in the proceedings. Mr. Jefferson as Secretary of State had already appeared before the House at its request (1789), and President Washington and Secretary of War Knox had visited the Senate (1789).[1] Fisher Ames and Elbridge Gerry, of Massachusetts, argued that such an arrangement would facilitate public business and give the public a clearer idea of the inside workings of the departments. But James Madison, whose potent influence largely governed in such matters, pronounced it contrary to the spirit of the government scheme, which sought to keep the legislative and executive branches absolutely distinct. The House supported his objection, and there the matter rested until 1864, when a committee favorably reported a bill providing that cabinet members participate in debate upon questions relating to their departments and appear at stated times to answer questions. The discussion stressed the point that executive expression would be open instead of secret, thus avoiding misunderstandings and misrepresentations. On the other hand, it was suggested that the head of a department, speaking for the Administration, would become a target of an active Opposition to cross-examine, to assail with charges, to pick to pieces, and in effect to hide what he had to say in controversial detritus. Moreover, that he would be at a disadvantage in a great popular assembly, with its own privileges, prejudices, and notions, and among members of whose standing and qualities he was ignorant; that although he might be an able speaker in a courtroom or on the platform, he would

[1] 1st Congress, 1st Sess., *Annals*, pp. 51, 66.

rarely, without previous legislative experience, be able to stand the hurly-burly of a House, where only legislative leaders of long training can always be relied upon to hold their patience or keep their heads, and not say too little or too much.

It was agreed that Congress had authority to pass such a law, yet the pros and cons, a cluster of surmises, light and vague, seemed to inspire a fear that the arrangement might do more harm than good, and so the subject was again dropped without action.[1] Eight years later (1872) Walter Bagehot, the distinguished English writer, declared that "tried by their own aims, the founders of the United States were wise in excluding the ministers from Congress." [2]

Meantime, resolutions of inquiry often occasioned strained relations between the House and the Executive. Although no legislation existed requiring the latter to respond, the House maintained its inherent right to all information relating to subjects within the sphere of its legitimate powers, and while it recognized that the demand for papers and documents should be carefully limited to those already on file and relating to cases imperatively required by the public interest, it intimated that an official who should exclude from the files a paper of a public character because he considered it private would be liable to an accusation with a view to impeachment.[3]

A more vigorous assertion of this right was promulgated in 1842, when President Tyler held that, pending

[1] 38th Cong., 2d Sess., *Globe*, pp. 419-24, 437-48.
[2] *The English Constitution*, p. 95.
[3] 24th Cong., 2d Sess., House Rep. no. 194.

an investigation respecting frauds practiced upon the Cherokee Indians, the Executive, as a coördinate and independent branch of the Government, possessed a discretionary right to furnish or withhold the information sought. To this the House replied that while the Constitution makes each coördinate branch independent of the other, and assigns to the President alone certain functions, such as pardons, appointments to office, and negotiation of treaties, it authorizes the House to investigate all abuses for the prevention of their recurrence by proper legislation, and in the exercise of this function it has a right to all information wherever it exists. This right belongs to its character, is one of its attributes, derived not alone from its power to impeach, but from its character of "grand inquest of the nation," which is a permanent right inherent in it; and in demanding information from the departments for the purpose of performing this legislative function, it neither invades, impairs, nor suspends any right, power, or function of the Executive. Nor does it follow, continued the report, that information communicated to the House must be made public, since nothing prevents it from observing secrecy. For this reason court rules, which exclude particular evidence on the ground of public policy, do not apply to parliamentary tribunals. Nor can the rule which relieves a witness from producing private papers that would criminate himself apply to the President, for official information spread upon the records or contained in the files of departments is neither private nor privileged.[1]

[1] 27th Cong., 3d Sess., House Rep no. 271.

Nevertheless, the President has resisted the right of the House to inquire into alleged corrupt or illegal violations of duty by the Executive except as an impeaching body, and has even then refused to furnish evidence which might be used for impeachment purposes against himself or the heads of departments. Thus, in 1837, President Jackson vigorously resisted an attempt to secure his assistance to investigate his Administration. "In open violation of the Constitution and that well-established maxim that 'all men are presumed to be innocent until proven guilty,'" he said, "you request myself and heads of departments to become our own accusers and to furnish the evidence to convict ourselves." [1] In 1860 President Buchanan insisted that a resolution, authorizing the House to inquire whether the Executive or any officer of the Government has sought to influence the action of Congress by money, patronage, or other improper means, amounted to a charge of high crimes and misdemeanors, and declared that, since it possessed no power to investigate except as an impeaching body, its accusations should be definitely set forth and first considered by the Judiciary Committee. [2] Again, when the House, in 1876, sought information respecting the performance of executive acts at a distance from the seat of government, President Grant replied that the inquiry did not necessarily belong to the province of legislation. "If it be requested in view or in aid of the power of impeachment, it is asked in derogation of an inherent, natural right, recognized in this country by a constitu-

[1] 24th Cong., 2d Sess., House Rep. no. 194.
[2] 36th Cong., 1st Sess., House Rep. no. 394.

tional guarantee which protects every citizen, the President as well as the humblest in the land, from being made a witness against himself." [1]

The House yielded to the contention of President Jackson that it could investigate only with impeachment in view,[2] and upon receiving President Grant's reply, it concluded to drop the matter. But in 1860 it maintained at great length that the practice of investigating the acts of the Executive was coextensive with the existence of the Government, and that the House could proceed as it saw fit, its power to investigate acts of the President not being limited to impeachment. Under the Constitution, it said, the President possesses neither privilege nor immunity beyond that of the humblest citizen, and under the law he is left without shield or protection except such as is borne by all. He is amenable for all his acts, can make no plea denied to any other citizen, and is subject to the same scrutiny, trial, and punishment, with the hazards and penalties of impeachment superadded. The President and the citizen stand upon an equality of rights, the distinction between them simply arising from an inequality of duties.[3]

Requests of the House for information and papers relating to treaties with foreign nations have often been denied by the Chief Executive. In 1796 President Washington declared that to admit the right of the House to demand and receive as a matter of course all papers respecting a negotiation with a foreign power

[1] 44th Cong., 1st Sess., *Record*, p. 2158.
[2] 24th Cong., 2d Sess., House Rep. no. 194.
[3] 36th Cong., 1st Sess., *Globe*, pp. 997–98, 1434–40; House Rep. no. 394.

would establish a dangerous precedent. "It is essential to the due administration of Government," he said, "that the boundaries fixed by the Constitution between the different departments should be preserved, and a just regard to the Constitution and to the duty of my office, under all the circumstances of the case, forbid a compliance with your request." [1] Thereupon the House adopted a resolution declaring that it claimed no agency in making treaties; but it insisted that "when a treaty stipulates regulations on any of the subjects submitted by the Constitution to the power of Congress, it must depend for its execution, as to such stipulations, on a law or laws to be passed by Congress; and it is the constitutional right of the House in all such cases to deliberate on the expediency of carrying such treaty into effect, and to determine and act thereon as in their judgment may be most conducive to the public good." [2]

Alexander Hamilton, whom Mr. Jefferson regarded as the author of the President's message, afterward expressed his regret that a qualified answer had not been returned.[3] Nevertheless, in declining to comply with the request of the House for a copy of the instructions to the minister who negotiated a treaty with Mexico, President Polk relied (1848) upon the Washington precedent, although John Quincy Adams stubbornly supported the position of the House in 1796. No further action was then taken, but it illustrates the abiding faith in the principle, that the House, during the administration of President Grant, again asserted its right by readopting

[1] 4th Cong., 1st Sess., *Annals*, pp. 426–782.   [2] *Ibid.*, p. 782.
[3] 40th Cong., 2d Sess., House Rep. no. 37.

without debate or division the resolution of the Fourth Congress.[1]

Closely associated with this question is the view that a treaty often depends upon a law of Congress for the execution of stipulations which relate to subjects constitutionally intrusted to Congress. Thus, when a bill came up to conform American law to the provisions of the treaty "to regulate commerce between England and the United States according to the convention concluded on July 3, 1815," the House maintained its contention that while certain treaties could be executed without legislative consent, the rule did not apply to treaties which contain stipulations requiring appropriations, or which might bind the nation to lay taxes, to raise armies, to support navies, or to cede or acquire territory.[2] In the consideration of the bill to appropriate $7,200,000 for the purchase of Alaska in accordance with the treaty of March 30, 1867, it was conceded that the House would be justified not merely in withholding its aid, but in giving notice to foreign nations interested that a treaty would not be regarded as binding if it brought into the Union and conferred political powers upon large populations incapable of self-government; or alienated territory; or surrendered political power to any other Government; or reëstablished slavery; or annulled the institution of marriage; or changed the character of the Government.[3]

With equal assurance the House declared that the

[1] 42d Cong., 1st Sess., *Globe*, p. 835.
[2] 14th Cong., 1st Sess., *Annals*, p. 454, 473, 478, 482, 526.
[3] 40th Cong., 2d Sess., *Globe*, pp. 3620, 3658; House Rep. no. 37.

validity of a commercial treaty fixing rates of duty imposed on foreign commodities entering the United States for consumption must depend upon the law-making power; otherwise it would be an infraction of the Constitution [1] and an invasion of one of the highest prerogatives of the House. This principle was recognized in the reciprocity treaty with Mexico in 1886, and subsequently in those with Canada and Hawaii, the terms of which made their validity dependent upon the passage of appropriate legislation reducing the duties and making provision for carrying into effect their terms.[2] In its report upon a bill making effective a convention with the Republic of Cuba (1903), the Committee on Ways and Means declared that "foreign countries in making treaties with us are bound to take notice of this requirement of our Constitution, and, whether it is expressed in the treaty or not, the whole matter is subject to the necessary legislation by Congress." [3]

Whatever policy the President may have advocated, the House has been quick to voice its sympathy with people struggling to establish their liberty. As early as 1792 it expressed "sincere interest" in the adoption of a constitution by France, and in 1848 tendered through a joint resolution the congratulations of the American to the French people. Under the leadership of Henry Clay (1821) it voiced the "deep interest" of the American people for the success of the Spanish provinces of South America, and appropriated $100,000 to enable the President to give due effect to the recognition of their in-

[1] Art. I, secs. 7 and 8.
[2] 24 Stat. L., p. 988; 25 Stat. L., p. 1370.
[3] 58th Cong., 1st Sess., *Record*, p. 260.

dependence. The House also suggested acknowledging the independence of Texas (1846), recognized the independence of Haiti by a clause in an appropriation bill (1862), congratulated the people of Brazil on their adoption of a republican form of government (1890), and felicitated the people of Cuba on the appearance of a Cuban Republic (1902). Only when the House expressed its sympathy for the people of Mexico, struggling against the French invasion of 1864, did the Executive deny its authority to act. The House was unwilling that its silence on the subject should be accepted by the nations of the world as a manifestation of indifference to a violation of the Monroe Doctrine, and accordingly, on April 4, 1864, it passed by a unanimous vote a joint resolution declaring that the Congress of the United States "are not indifferent spectators of the deplorable events now transpiring in the Republic of Mexico; and they therefore think fit to declare that it does not accord with the policy of the United States to acknowledge a monarchical government erected on the ruins of any republican government in America under the auspices of any European power." [2]

Napoleon III did not relish the defiant tone of this pronunciamento, and a few weeks later the *Moniteur*, the official journal of the French Government, announced that "the Emperor's Government has received from that of the United States satisfactory explanations as to the sense and bearing of the resolution come to by the House relative to Mexico. It is known, besides, that the Senate has indefinitely postponed the examination of that ques-

[2] 38th Cong., 1st Sess., *Globe*, p. 1408.

tion, to which, in any case, the executive power would not have given its sanction." When this publication came to the knowledge of the House, it requested President Lincoln, "if not inconsistent with public interest," to communicate any explanations given the Government of France respecting the action of the House. In response he forwarded a copy of Secretary of State Seward's letter to William L. Dayton, American Minister to France, explaining that the subject of the House resolution "is a practical and purely executive question, and the decision of its constitutionality belongs not to the House nor even to Congress, but to the President. . . . While the President receives the declaration of the House with the profound respect to which it is entitled, as an exposition of its sentiments upon a grave and important question, he directs that you inform the Government of France that he does not at present contemplate any departure from the policy which this Government has hitherto pursued in regard to the war which exists between France and Mexico." [1]

Thereupon Henry Winter Davis, the powerful chairman of the House Committee on Foreign Affairs, presented an elaborate report, in which, after citing precedents and the attitude of former Presidents, he asserted that "no President has ever claimed such an exclusive authority. Nor can Congress ever permit its expression to pass without dissent. It is certain the Constitution nowhere confers such authority on the President. The precedents of recognition, sufficiently numerous in this revolutionary era, do not countenance this view. . . .

[1] 38th Cong., 1st Sess., House Ex. Doc. no. 92.

The declaration and establishment of the Spanish-American colonies first brought the question of the recognition of new governments or nations before the Government of the United States; and the precedents then set have been followed ever since, even by the present Administration. The correspondence now before us is the first attempt to depart from that usage, and to deny the nation a controlling, deliberative voice in regulating its foreign policy." [1] In conclusion he recommended a resolution declaring that "Congress has a constitutional right to an authoritative voice in declaring and prescribing the foreign policy of the United States as well in the recognition of new powers as in other matters; and it is the constitutional duty of the President to respect that policy, not less in diplomatic negotiations than in the use of the national force when authorized by law; and the propriety of any declaration of foreign policy by Congress is sufficiently proved by the vote which pronounces it; and such proposition, while pending and undetermined, is not a fit topic of diplomatic explanation with any foreign power." [2]

When the House, by a vote of 69 to 63, laid this resolution on the table, Davis promptly asked to be relieved of his chairmanship. It was a profound shock. Davis ranked in ability with Charles Sumner, head of the Senate Committee on Foreign Relations, and the House could ill afford to lose his services. But it recognized that one war at a time was sufficient, and that the Secretary of State was evidently playing a waiting game.

[1] 38th Cong., 1st Sess., House Rep. no. 129.
[2] 38th Cong., 2d Sess., *Globe*, pp. 48, 65.

Nevertheless, the President, with his usual disposition to avoid needless quarrels, saw no reason why the resolution might not pass. It could do no harm, since France was satisfied. Four days afterward, therefore, when Davis again presented it, the House, substituting "Executive Departments" for "President," adopted it — yeas, 119; nays, 8. In this connection it is interesting to recall that at the close of the Civil War, when General Sheridan occupied the Mexican border with an army of veterans, presumably to establish the Monroe Doctrine, the French hastened their departure, leaving Emperor Maximilian to be executed by the Republic of Mexico.[1]

When the President and the House are in political accord, the latter is slow to criticize or investigate the Executive. Between them is a common interest. The success of one makes for the good of the other. Besides, House leaders freely confer with heads of departments, and on important measures the President not infrequently presses his views upon chairmen and other influential members for whom he sends. Often intimate social relations strengthen the confidence and freedom of official intercourse. These influences account for the flaccid action of the House in 1837 and in 1848, when President Jackson protested against the investigation of his executive acts and President Polk refused to reveal the instructions used in negotiating a treaty with Mexico. For a similar reason it laid the Davis resolution on the table until President Lincoln *sub silentio* approved its adoption. On the other hand, when the Chief Executive and the House are of different parties, the latter, largely

[1] Philip H. Sheridan, *Personal Memoirs*, vol. II, pp. 227-28.

for political purposes, boldly and sometimes impudently presses its demands for information, and resents a denial of its authority in language indicating a high degree of feeling. It may well be doubted if the House, whatever its constitutional rights, would have made its savage reports in 1842 and in 1860 had it been in political accord with Presidents Tyler and Buchanan. Equally plain is it that the demand for information respecting President Grant's official acts when absent from Washington originated in the Opposition party.

When a disagreement between a friendly House and the President involves a principle which affects the integrity of the legislative branch, the attitude of the latter depends upon the spirit of its leaders. The respect and high esteem in which the House held President Washington did not restrain it from respectfully asserting its right to deliberate on and determine the expediency of a treaty which depended for its execution on a law to be passed by Congress; but when President Jackson extended the Washington precedent to a treaty with the Chickasaw tribe of Indians, it entered no protest. In one case, the House acted with spirit, conscious of its fidelity to principle; in the other, it showed a craven obsequiousness. Similar instances in its history might be multiplied, for types of leaders varied in different periods.

The choice of Speaker Macon, facilitated by the coalition between the South and the New York Democracy, which resulted in President Jefferson's election, rendered the House completely subservient to the Chief Executive. Even the appointment of chairmen of important committees, especially those which act as organs of communication with the President, were consented to, if not, as in the case of John Randolph, suggested by, the Administration. Nor did Speaker Varnum modify these conditions. He rid Ways and Means of Randolph over the wishes of Albert Gallatin, then Secretary of the Treasury, but not until the loquacious Virginian had become an object of dislike to the House and of distrust to the President. Indeed, during Jefferson's Administration the theory that the legislative and executive branches are independent of each other became a fiction, the supremacy of the latter being practically acknowledged. "Between you and myself," Jefferson wrote to Speaker Macon, "nothing but opportunities for explanation can be necessary to defeat the endeavors of an enemy who is sowing tares between us. At least, on my part, my confidence in you is so unqualified that nothing further is necessary for my satisfaction." [1] It should be added in defense of the House that at this time it had few if any men of sufficient prominence, except Randolph, to break the Jeffersonian spell under which Macon had fallen.

Henry Clay reversed this order of things. With a fearless nature and unrivaled powers he became a legislative leader, dominating President Madison during the War of 1812 and successfully opposing President Monroe. He stood for internal improvements, for a protective tariff, for recognition of the South American Governments, and for the Missouri Compromise, and carried them all through. But with the passing of Clay and

[1] Jefferson's MSS., March 22, 1806.

other leaders who gave character to the House, conditions dropped to the level of those existing under Jefferson; and although the strong will of Jackson roused antagonisms within as well as without his party, he absolutely dominated Speaker Stevenson and his committees. The margin was often meager, once being reduced to the Chair's casting vote, but it sufficed to control the investigation of the National Bank, and to secure a favorable report from the committee charged with an investigation of the Executive's acts. Though other Presidents prior to the Civil War lacked Jackson's dominating will power, it became the habit of a Speaker, if of the same faith, to subserve the interests of the Administration. His election meant subserviency. In fact, the slightest show of independence, either by President, Speaker, or Administration member, was deemed a breach of faith to the one supreme issue around which for twenty years the contentious waves broke angrily. As the contest over slavery grew in bitterness, the House passed more often into opposition, making the Speaker the rival of the President and his committees a check upon executive policies. Thus the House in opposition developed a power of initiative unequaled since the time of Clay, and which it never again entirely surrendered even under a President of its own political faith.

This independence was observable early in 1861, when the House, by a concurrent resolution, assumed the right to investigate the conduct of the war, authorizing a joint committee to send for persons and papers, and to sit during the session of either body. A more energetic manifestation of it appeared shortly after the death of

President Lincoln. Its excuse was the incredible and pertinacious folly of President Johnson, which first irritated and then exasperated his party. Finally, the House, led as fearlessly by Thaddeus Stevens as Henry Clay had marshaled its opposition to Madison and Monroe, took a position of open hostility, its resistance resembling somewhat that of the Commons in the days of the Long Parliament. Of course nothing so extreme had occurred before, or, let it be hoped, is likely to happen again; but even with the coming of harmonious relations under other Presidents, an unwillingness to part with the prerogatives and independence wrenched from the feeble hand of President Johnson occasionally exhibited itself in bold assertions that surprised its own leaders, mindful of the unceasing attrition of an Executive laden with a patronage that invites like the fleshpots of Egypt. Thus, in reaffirming, during the Administration of President Grant (1871), the attitude of its predecessor in 1796 respecting its constitutional right to determine the expediency of carrying a treaty into effect, it displayed a spirit of rare firmness. Courage as well as wisdom was likewise manifested in 1875, when, by a vote of 223 to 18, it resolved that any departure from the time-honored custom of limiting the Presidency to two terms would be unwise, unpatriotic, and fraught with peril to our free institutions.[1]

It was thought at the time an unusual display of self-reliance for a House of moderate, careful members, on the eve of an election in 1890, to ignore a proposition submitted by Mr. Blaine, then Secretary of State, re-

[1] 44th Cong., 1st Sess., *Journal*, p. 66.

leasing sugar duties in the interest of reciprocity. He had long considered the subject, had definite ideas and organized plans, and felt an eager interest in the smallest minutiæ of the mode of dealing with it. Indeed, many thought it a pity that McKinley himself did not propose it to help balance the elastic properties of other and newer schemes that appealed to his imagination, especially since any reciprocal advantages coming from Blaine to a House controlled by Speaker Reed, whose hostility to the Administration was outspoken, were certain to be pronounced incommensurate. President Cleveland's specific and urgent recommendations for the Wilson Tariff Bill (1894) met as cool a reception. He had won his election on the principle of a tariff for revenue only, and although disposed, apparently, to allow a very moderate measure of protection, the legislative leaders preferred an open break rather than yield to his demands. An exhibition of independence quite as intrepid occurred during the Buchanan Administration, when the House not only refused to comply with the President's request to impeach rather than investigate, but pointedly resented statements made in his message.

Nevertheless, the influence of the President in the House, whether controlled by his own party or another, is very far from negligible. The Constitution, as elsewhere stated, limits his duties to recommendations and the approval or disapproval of measures. To protect members from executive influence, the fear of which seems to have been constantly before its framers, it also provided that "No senator or representative shall, during the time for which he was elected, be appointed to any civil office under the authority of the United States, which shall have been created, or the emoluments whereof shall have been increased, during such time; and no person holding any office under the United States shall be a member of either House during his continuance in office." [1] In other words, a legislator was not to be induced to create an office, or to increase the emoluments of one, in the hope of an appointment; nor was the Executive able to appoint him while he continued in Congress. But in practice these constitutional limitations neither preserved the legislator's independence nor restrained executive influence. In fact, the President's possession of an ever-increasing patronage has enabled him at times to absorb the legislative branch of the Government. President Jefferson's manipulation to secure an appointment for Joseph H. Nicholson, of Maryland, for the purpose of crushing Randolph's opposition, furnished an early exhibition of such influence. But not until Jackson adopted Marcy's adage, "To the victor belong the spoils," did the President become a patronage broker, rewarding the obedient and punishing the contumacious. Although militant reformers, after years of patient struggle, have gradually exempted departmental clerks and other subordinates from the spoils system, an army of appointees still remains subject to the bargaining propensities of the Chief Executive.[2] Some have dispensed this patronage less conspicuously than others, but all have used it when conditions demanded.

[1] Art. I, sec. 6.
[2] The list prepared by a recent statistician includes over sixty thousand offices.

In the spring of 1864, after deciding upon an amendment to the Constitution abolishing slavery, President Lincoln, in order to secure its approval by three fourths of the States, found it necessary to create an additional Commonwealth, to be called Nevada. Strong opposition to its formation developed in the House, and to overcome it the President authorized Assistant Secretary of War Dana to secure three members who were reported as doubtful. "What do they want?" asked Dana. "I don't know. It makes no difference," replied Lincoln. "We must carry this vote or be compelled to raise another million of men and fight, no one knows how long. It is a question of three votes or new armies." "What shall I say to these gentlemen?" continued the Assistant Secretary. "I don't know," said the President; "but whatever promises you make I will perform." After learning that two wanted internal revenue appointments and the third a position in the New York customhouse worth twenty thousand dollars a year, Dana promised them "on the authority of the President." The next October, concludes the Secretary, the President signed the proclamation admitting Nevada as a State, and in the February following (1865) it ratified the Thirteenth Amendment.[1]

It is seldom that the application of such executive influence reaches the public even in the form of a reminis-

---

[1] The two received their places in the internal revenue service, but before the custom-house appointment was due to be made, President Lincoln was assassinated, and President Johnson refused to redeem the promise. "I have observed in the course of my experience," said Johnson, "that such bargains tend to immorality." (Charles A. Dana, *Recollections of the Civil War*, pp. 175–78.)

cence, but the results of such bargaining have from time
to time clearly appeared, as, for example, when Stephen
A. Douglas, assisted by President Pierce, forced the
repeal of the Missouri Compromise, and President
Cleveland constrained an unwilling House to repeal the
Sherman Silver Purchase Act. With consummate tact,
due as much to his delightful personality as to long
legislative experience, President McKinley not only
used the patronage at hand to sweeten the way of his
Philippines policy which Speaker Reed opposed, but increased the vast power of his office by appointing members of Congress to distinguished and lucrative places
on various commissions, authorized to negotiate treaties,
to locate boundaries, and to confer with foreign representatives respecting other matters.[1] It is not strange,
perhaps, that he should desire to select men whom he
personally knew to be qualified for such important diplomatic service. It was something of a shock, however,
that this gentlest of Presidents should presume to breach
the Constitution, for the line of demarcation was vague
and impalpable between the duties of such appointees
and those of regular diplomatic "officers" clothed with
dignity and authority. McKinley himself evidently
recognized the danger-line; otherwise he would scarcely
have submitted the names of the Hawaiian commissioners to the Senate, which wisely declined to take action.
"If these gentlemen are to be officers," asked one senator,

[1] These included arranging a standard of value by international
agreement; negotiating peace with Spain; settling the Behring Sea
controversy; establishing the boundary-line between Alaska and
Canada; arranging a treaty of commerce with Great Britain; and securing information upon which to base needed legislation for Hawaii.

"how can the President appoint them under the Constitution, the office being created during their term? Or, how can they hold office and still keep their seats in this body? If, on the other hand, they are not officers, under what constitutional provision does the President ask the advice and consent of the Senate to their appointment?" [1]

President Wilson did not tolerate McKinley's indefensible practice, but as an expert in securing legislation he in no wise suffers by comparison with the most dominating of all his predecessors. Soon after inauguration he became the legislative leader, dictating bills, demanding amendments, and forcing his views into statutes by the use of patronage, which filled with wonder and amazement veteran legislators who had served under eight different Presidents. The Speaker and floor leader could not baffle him, nor a union of disaffected leaders and a solid minority thwart him. "This was never better illustrated," said the New York *Sun*, "than last Saturday, when at four o'clock it became apparent that the senators from the cotton-growing States of the South had effected a coalition with the Republican side to kill the War-Revenue Bill or suspend it until legislation was put into the measure for the relief of the cotton planters. Immediately a strong arm was extended from the White House which promptly throttled the movement within thirty minutes after the fact of the revolt became known to Postmaster-General Burleson, with the immense post-office patronage of the country at his disposal. . . . When the test came, four hours later, three

[1] Hoar, *Autobiography*, vol. II, p. 47.

of the eight revolters faltered and the scheme collapsed." [1]

Although the press of the country has occasionally denounced such exhibitions of executive pressure as reprehensible, the President has always treated patronage as a legitimate instrument for influencing Congress. Indeed, not since the establishment of a departmental classified service has a Chief Executive suggested the elimination of this adventitious influence, until President Taft surprised the country and dismayed the average politician by recommending that almost the entire Federal establishment be taken out of personal and partisan politics and covered into the classified service. The language of this extraordinarily wise message is worthy of repetition: —

"I wish to renew my recommendation that all the local offices throughout the country, including collectors of internal revenue, collectors of customs, postmasters of all four classes, immigration commissioners, and marshals, should be by law covered into the classified

[1] October 18, 1914. Of the use of patronage President Wilson says: "There are illegitimate means by which the President may influence the action of Congress. He may bargain with members, not only with regard to appointments, but also with regard to legislative measures. He may use his local patronage to assist members to get or retain their seats. He may interpose his powerful influence, in one covert way or another, in contests for places in the Senate. . . . Such things are not only deeply immoral, but they are destructive of the fundamental understandings of constitutional government and, therefore, of constitutional government itself. . . . No honorable man includes such agencies in a sober exposition of the Constitution. . . . Nothing in a system like ours can be constitutional which is immoral or which touches the good faith of those who have sworn to obey the fundamental law. The reprobation of all good men will always overwhelm such influences with shame and failure." Woodrow Wilson, *Constitutional Government in the United States* (1908), p. 71.

service, the necessity for confirmation by the Senate removed, and the President and the others, whose time is now taken up in distributing this patronage, under the custom that has prevailed since the beginning of the Government, in accordance with the recommendation of the senators and congressmen of the majority party, should be relieved from this burden.

"I am confident that such a change would greatly reduce the cost of administering the Government, and that it would add greatly to its efficiency. It would take away the power to use the patronage of the Government for political purposes. When officers are recommended by senators and congressmen from political motives and for political services rendered, it is impossible to expect that while in office the appointees will not regard their tenure as more or less dependent upon continued political service for their patrons, and no regulations, however stiff or rigid, will prevent this, for such regulations, in view of the method and motive for selection, are plainly inconsistent and deemed hardly worthy of respect." [1]

Of course the House desired nothing of this kind; otherwise it would promptly have passed a constitutional amendment carrying it into effect. It never graciously approved the merit system, and although the President's use of patronage has become increasingly arrogant, often subjecting its leaders to humiliating defeat, it has never raised its voice in resentment. The reason lies on the surface. Under a custom as old as the Government, members

[1] 62d Cong., 3d Sess., *Record*, pp. 896, 947. The list affected by this recommendation included 59,237 postmasters, 122 collectors of customs, 67 collectors of internal revenue, 86 United States marshals, and 6 immigration commissioners.

of the majority party claim the right to name federal officers in their respective districts, and obedience to party and executive dictation insures them the privilege. Indeed, if a district is likely to resent a prescribed policy, a member, unless his vote is absolutely needed, is suffered to assume an attitude of "independence" and thus avoid trouble at home.

It is not surprising, therefore, that such a prerogative, held under such tolerant conditions, is highly appreciated, and although the distribution of patronage has its disadvantages, since the gratitude of appointees is not always as steady or influential as the hostility of the disappointed, a sacrifice of the means of building up a political machine does not commend itself to the average congressman any more than to most Presidents.

Upon the death of a President, Congress pays its tribute of respect. The decease of President William Henry Harrison, the first to die in office, occurred when the Congress was not in session (April 4, 1841), but when it assembled in the following December, John Quincy Adams, then a member of the House, presented a resolution that a committee of one member from each State be appointed, to join a committee on the part of the Senate, "to report by what token of respect and affection it may be proper for Congress to express the deep sensibility of the Nation to the event of the decease of their late President." In obedience to this mandate a joint resolution was adopted providing that the chairs of the President of the Senate and the Speaker of the House be "shrouded" in black during the residue of the session; that members wear the usual badge of mourning for thirty days, and that the President of the United States be requested, when transmitting a copy of the resolution to Mrs. Harrison, "to assure her of the profound respect of Congress for her person and character, and of its sincere condolence on the late afflicting dispensation of Providence."

Of the five Presidents who died in office the decease of Zachary Taylor (July 9, 1850) alone occurred when Congress was in session. On its announcement to the House several eulogies were immediately pronounced, the halls of the Senate and House were draped, appropriate resolutions were passed, members wore the usual badge of mourning, and on the day of burial the two Houses attended the funeral in a body. When the Thirty-ninth Congress convened on December 4, 1865, after the death of President Lincoln in the preceding April,[1] it desired "to express the deep sensibility of the Nation" by some "token of respect and affection" more elaborate than that shown upon the death of President Harrison, and accordingly a joint committee, additional to resolutions and emblems of mourning, arranged for a meeting of the two Houses to be held in the chamber of the House on February 12, the anniversary of the late President's birthday, to be addressed by George Bancroft, the distinguished historian. To this assemblage invitations were extended to the President and his Cabinet, the Justices of the Supreme Court, the representatives of foreign governments, to such officers of the army and navy as had received the thanks of Congress, to the Judges of the Court of Claims and of the Supreme

[1] April 15, 1865.

Court of the District of Columbia, to assistant heads of departments, heads of bureaus, the mayors of Washington and Georgetown, and to such eminent citizens as were then at the seat of government.

On the day set apart, promptly at twelve o'clock meridian, members of the Senate, preceded by their officers, entered the hall of the House and occupied the first four rows on either side of the main aisle, in front of members of the House, the President *pro tem* sitting at the Speaker's right. Thereafter the guests entered and occupied seats as follows: The President of the United States, in front of the Speaker's table; the Supreme Court Justices next to and on the right of the President; the Diplomatic Corps next to and on the left of the President; heads of departments on the left of the Diplomatic Corps; army and navy officers on the right of the Supreme Court Justices; Judges of the Court of Claims and of the Supreme Court of the District of Columbia in the rear of the Justices of the Supreme Court; governors of States and mayors in the rear of the Diplomatic Corps; and assistant heads of departments and heads of bureaus in the rear of the army and navy officers. The orator of the day occupied the clerk's desk. The audience being seated, the Marine Band, stationed in the vestibule, played appropriate dirges, after which the chaplain of the Senate offered prayer. The orator was then presented by the presiding officer of the Senate. The audience left the hall as it entered, except that special guests preceded the senators.

On February 27, 1882, a memorial service of similar character was held after the death of President Garfield on September 19, 1881, former Speaker Blaine being the eulogist. On February 27, 1902, a similar service was held after the death of President McKinley on September 14, 1901, the orator of the occasion being Secretary of State John Hay.

In paying tributes of respect to former Presidents at the time of their death, Congress has observed the early precedent of ignoring the event unless it occurred when the Senate and House were in session. Curiously enough only eight have died when the Congress was in session, and the record shows action taken only in the cases of six; namely, General Washington (1799), Mr. Madison (1826), Mr. John Quincy Adams (1848), Mr. Buchanan (1868), Mr. Fillmore (1874), and Mr. Hayes (1893). Mr. Tyler died on January 18, 1862, and Mr. Van Buren on July 24 of the same year, when Congress was in session, but Mr. Tyler was then within, and in sympathy with, the Confederate States. Although the eve of Mr. Van Buren's life was as peaceful as its noon and day had been stormy, Congress likewise, upon the report of his death, took no action. Six years afterward, upon the decease of Mr. Buchanan, the House tabled a resolution of commendation. Later in the day, however, it resolved "that as a mark of respect to one who has held such eminent public station, the Speaker is requested to appoint a committee of seven members to attend his funeral." [1] A wag said that the House approved the funeral!

[1] 40th Cong., 2d Sess., *Globe*, pp. 2810, 2817.

THE END

APPENDIX

APPENDIX

A

PRESIDENTS AND VICE-PRESIDENTS AND THE CONGRESSES COINCIDENT WITH THEIR TERMS

Presidents	Vice-Presidents	Service	Congresses
George Washington	John Adams	Apr. 30, 1789–Mar. 3, 1797	1, 2, 3, 4.
John Adams	Thomas Jefferson	Mar. 4, 1797–Mar. 3, 1801	5, 6.
Thomas Jefferson	Aaron Burr	Mar. 4, 1801–Mar. 3, 1805	7, 8.
Thomas Jefferson	George Clinton	Mar. 4, 1805–Mar. 3, 1809	9, 10.
James Madison	George Clinton (died Apr. 20, 1812)	Mar. 4, 1809–Mar. 3, 1813	11, 12.
James Madison	Elbridge Gerry (died Nov. 23, 1814)	Mar. 4, 1813–Mar. 3, 1817	13, 14.
James Monroe	Daniel D. Tompkins	Mar. 4, 1817–Mar. 3, 1825	15, 16, 17, 18.
John Quincy Adams	John C. Calhoun	Mar. 4, 1825–Mar. 3, 1829	19, 20.
Andrew Jackson	John C. Calhoun (resigned Dec. 28, to become U.S. Senator)	Mar. 4, 1829–Mar. 3, 1833	21, 22.
Andrew Jackson	Martin Van Buren	Mar. 4, 1833–Mar. 3, 1837	23, 24.
Martin Van Buren	Richard M. Johnson	Mar. 4, 1837–Mar. 3, 1841	25, 26.
William Henry Harrison	John Tyler	Mar. 4, 1841–Apr. 4, 1841	27.
John Tyler		Apr. 6, 1841–Mar. 3, 1845	27, 28.
James K. Polk	George M. Dallas	Mar. 4, 1845–Mar. 3, 1849	29, 30.

PRESIDENTS AND VICE-PRESIDENTS (continued)

Presidents	Vice-Presidents	Service	Congresses
Zachary Taylor	Millard Fillmore	Mar. 5, 1849-July 9, 1850	31.
Millard Fillmore	...	July 10, 1850-Mar. 3, 1853	31, 32.
Franklin Pierce	William R. King (died Apr. 18, 1853)	Mar. 4, 1853-Mar. 3, 1857	33, 34.
James Buchanan	John C. Breckenridge	Mar. 4, 1857-Mar. 3, 1861	35, 36.
Abraham Lincoln	Hannibal Hamlin	Mar. 4, 1861-Mar. 3, 1865	37, 38.
Abraham Lincoln	Andrew Johnson	Mar. 4, 1865-Apr. 15, 1865	39.
Andrew Johnson	...	Apr. 15, 1865-Mar. 3, 1869	39, 40.
Ulysses S. Grant	Schuyler Colfax	Mar. 4, 1869-Mar. 3, 1873	41, 42.
Ulysses S. Grant	Henry Wilson (died Nov. 22, 1875)	Mar. 4, 1873-Mar. 3, 1877	43, 44.
Rutherford B. Hayes	William A. Wheeler	Mar. 4, 1877-Mar. 3, 1881	45, 46.
James A. Garfield	Chester A. Arthur	Mar. 4, 1881-Sept. 19, 1881	47.
Chester A. Arthur	...	Sept. 20, 1881-Mar. 3, 1885	47, 48.
Grover Cleveland	Thomas A. Hendricks (died Nov. 25, 1885)	Mar. 4, 1885-Mar. 3, 1889	49, 50.
Benjamin Harrison	Levi P. Morton	Mar. 4, 1889-Mar. 3, 1893	51, 52.
Grover Cleveland	Adlai E. Stevenson	Mar. 4, 1893-Mar. 3, 1897	53, 54.
William McKinley	Garret A. Hobart (died Nov. 21, 1899)	Mar. 4, 1897-Mar. 3, 1901	55, 56.
William McKinley	Theodore Roosevelt	Mar. 4, 1901-Sept. 14, 1901	57.
Theodore Roosevelt	...	Sept. 14, 1901-Mar. 3, 1905	57, 58.
Theodore Roosevelt	Charles W. Fairbanks	Mar. 4, 1905-Mar. 3, 1909	59, 60.
William H. Taft	James S. Sherman	Mar. 4, 1909-Mar. 3, 1913	61, 62.
Woodrow Wilson	Thomas R. Marshall	Mar. 4, 1913-Mar. 3, 1917	63, 64.

B

SPEAKERS, CLERKS, AND SERGEANTS-AT-ARMS

Congress	Year	Speakers	Clerks	Sergeants-at-arms
1	1789	Fred. A. Muhlenburg, Pa....	John Beckley, Va....	Joseph Wheaton.
2	1791	Jonathan Trumbull, Conn...	" "	"
3	1793	Fred. A. Muhlenburg, Pa...	" "	"
4	1795	Jonathan Dayton, N.J...	" "	"
5	1797	" "	Jonathan W. Condy, Pa..	"
6	1799	Theodore Sedgwick, Mass.	John Holt, Pa...	"
7	1801	Nathaniel Macon, N.C.	John Beckley, Va..	"
8	1803	" "	" "	"
9	1805	" "	" "	Thomas Dunn, Md....
10	1807	Joseph B. Varnum, Mass...	Patrick Magruder, Md....	"
11	1809	" "	" "	"
12	1811	Henry Clay, Ky...	" "	"
13	1813	{ Langdon Cheves, S.C...	Thomas Dougherty, Ky...	"
14	1815	Henry Clay, Ky...	" "	"
15	1817	" " "	" "	"
16	1819	{ John W. Taylor, N.Y.	" "	"
17	1821	Philip P. Barbour, Va...	Matthew St.Clair Clarke, Pa.	"
18	1823	Henry Clay, Ky...	" "	"
19	1825	John W. Taylor, N.Y...	" "	John O. Dunn, D.C.

SPEAKERS, CLERKS, AND SERGEANTS-AT-ARMS (continued)

Congress	Year	Speakers	Clerks	Sergeants-at-arms
20	1827	Andrew Stevenson, Va......	Mathew St. Clair Clarke, Pa.	John O. Dunn, D.C.
21	1829	" " "	" " "	" " "
22	1831	" " "	" " "	" " "
23	1833	{ John Bell, Tenn......	Walter S. Franklin, Pa......	Thomas B. Randolph, Va.
24	1835	James K. Polk, Tenn......	" " "	Roderick Dorsey, Md.
25	1837	" " "	" " "	
26	1839	Robert M. T. Hunter, Va...	Hugh A. Garland, Va......	
27	1841	John White, Ky......	Matthew St. Clair Clarke, Pa	Eleazor M. Townsend, Conn.
28	1843	John W. Jones, Va......	Benjamin B. French, N.H..	Newton Lane, Ky.
29	1845	John W. Davis, Ind......	" " "	" " "
30	1847	Robert C. Winthrop, Mass..	Thomas J. Campbell, Tenn.	Nathan Sargent, Vt.
31	1849	Howell Cobb, Ga......	Richard M. Young, Ill......	" " "
32	1851	Linn Boyd, Ky......	John W. Forney, Pa......	Adam J. Glossbrenner, Pa.
33	1853	" " "	" " "	" " "
34	1855	Nathaniel P. Banks, Mass..	William Cullom, Tenn......	" " "
35	1857	James L. Orr, S.C......	James C. Allen, Ill......	" " "
36	1859	William Pennington, N.J...	John W. Forney, Pa......	Henry W. Hoffman, Md.
37	1861	Galusha A. Grow, Pa......	Emerson Etheridge, Tenn..	Edward Ball, Va.
38	1863	Schuyler Colfax, Ind......	Edward McPherson, Pa......	Nathaniel G. Ordway, N.H.
39	1865	" " "	" " "	" " "
40	1867	" " "	" " "	" " "
41	1869	James G. Blaine, Me......		

SPEAKERS, CLERKS, AND SERGEANTS-AT-ARMS (continued)

Congress	Year	Speakers	Clerks	Sergeants-at-arms
42	1871	James G. Blaine, Me.	Edward McPherson, Pa.	Nathaniel G. Ordway, N.H.
43	1873	" "	" "	" "
44	1875	{Michael C. Kerr, Ind. / Samuel J. Randall, Pa.	George M. Adams, Ky.	John G. Thompson, O.
45	1877	" "	" "	" "
46	1879	" "	" "	" "
47	1881	J. Warren Keifer, O.	Edward McPherson, Pa.	George W. Hooker, Vt.
48	1883	John G. Carlisle, Ky.	John B. Clark, Mo.	John P. Leedom, O.
49	1885	" "	" "	" "
50	1887	" "	" "	" "
51	1889	Thomas B. Reed, Me.	Edward McPherson, Pa.	Adoniram J. Holmes, Ia.
52	1891	Charles F. Crisp, Ga.	James Kerr, Pa.	Samuel S. Yoder, O.
53	1893	" "	" "	Herman W. Snow, Ill.
54	1895	Thomas B. Reed, Me.	Alexander McDowell, Pa.	Benjamin F. Russell, Mo.
55	1897	" "	" "	Henry Casson.
56	1899	David B. Henderson, Ia.	" "	" "
57	1901	" "	" "	" "
58	1903	Joseph G. Cannon, Ill.	" "	" "
59	1905	" "	" "	" "
60	1907	" "	" "	" "
61	1909	" "	" "	" "
62	1911	Champ Clark, Mo.	South Trimble	U. Stokes Jackson.
63	1913	" "	" "	R. B. Gordon.

C

DOORKEEPERS AND POSTMASTERS

Congress	Year	Doorkeepers	Postmasters
1	1789	Gifford Dalley.	
2	1791	" "	
3	1793	" "	
4	1795	Thomas Claxton.	
5	1797	" "	
6	1799	" "	
7	1801	" "	
8	1803	" "	
9	1805	" "	
10	1807	" "	
11	1809	" "	
12	1811	" "	
13	1813	" "	
14	1815	" "	
15	1817	" "	
16	1819	" "	
17	1821	Benjamin Birch, Md.	
18	1823	" " "	
19	1825	" " "	
20	1827	" " "	
21	1829	" " "	
22	1831	Overton Carr, Md.	
23	1833	" " "	
24	1835	" " "	
25	1837	" " "	William J. McCorm'·k, D.C.
26	1839	Joseph Follansbee, Mass............	" " "
27	1841	" " ...	" " "
28	1843	Jesse E. Dow, Conn.	" " "
29	1845	Cornelius S. Whitney, D.C............	John M. Johnson, Va.
30	1847	Robert E Horner, N.J.	" " "
31	1849	" " "	" " "
32	1851	Z. W. McKnew, Md.	" " "
33	1853	" " "	" " "
34	1855	Nathan Darling, N.Y.	Robert Morris, Pa.
35	1857	Robert B. Hackney, Va............	Michael W. Cluskey, Ga.

DOORKEEPERS AND POSTMASTERS (*continued*)

Con-gress	Year	Doorkeepers	Postmasters
36	1859	George Marston, N.H.	Josiah M. Lucus, Ill.
37	1861	Ira Goodnow, Vt....	William S. King, N.Y.
38	1863	" " "	" " "
39	1865	" " "	Josiah Given, O.
40	1867	Charles E. Lippincott, Ill...............	William S. King, N.Y.
41	1869	Otis S. Buxton, N.Y.	" " "
42	1871	" " "	" " "
43	1873	" " "	Henry Sherwood, Mich.
44	1875	John H. Patterson, N.J..............	" " "
45	1877	Charles W. Field, Ga.	" " "
46.	1879	" " "	" " "
47	1881	Walter P. Brownlow, Tenn.............	" " "
48	1883	James W. Winter-smith, Tex........	Lycurgus Dalton, Ind
49	1885	Samuel Donaldson, Tenn.............	" " "
50	1887	A. B. Hurd, Miss....	" " "
51	1889	Charles E. Adams, Md..............	James L. Wheat, Wis.
52	1891	Charles H. Turner, N.Y..............	Lycurgus Dalton, Ind.
53	1893	A. B. Hurd, Miss....	" " "
54	1895	William J. Glenn, N.Y.	Joseph C. McElroy, O.
55	1897	" " "	" " "
56	1899	" " "	" " "
57	1901	Frank B. Lyon, N.Y.	" " "
58	1903	" " "	" " "
59	1905	" " "	" " "
60	1907	" " "	Samuel A. Langum.
61	1909	" " "	" "
62	1911	Benjamin Vail.......	William M. Dunbar.

D

FATHERS OF THE HOUSE

Name	State	Born	Age on entering Congress	Age on becoming Father	Congresses served as Father	Total no. of terms served
William Findlay	Pa.	1751	40	56	12 to 14	11
Thomas Newton	Va.	1769	32	48	15 " 21	16
Lewis Williams	N.C.	1786	29	48	22 " 27	14
Dixon H. Lewis	Ala.	1802	27	41	28	8
John Quincy Adams	Mass.	1767	64	78	29 " 30	9
Linn Boyd	Ky.	1800	35	49	31 " 33	9
Joshua R. Giddings	O.	1795	42	61	34 " 35	11
John S. Phelps	Mo.	1814	31	45	36	10
Elihu B. Washburne	Ill.	1816	37	45	37 " 41	9
Henry L. Dawes	Mass.	1816	41	55	42 " 43	9
William D. Kelley	Pa.	1814	47	61	44 " 51	15
Charles O'Neil	Pa.	1821	42	70	52 " 53	15
Alfred C. Harmer	Pa.	1825	46	70	54 " 56	14
Henry H. Bingham	Pa.	1841	38	54	57 " 62	17
John Dalzell	Pa.	1845	42	66	62	18
Sereno E. Payne	N.Y.	1843	38	70	63	15
William A. Jones	Va.	1849	42	65	63	12

E

CHAIRMEN OF MOST IMPORTANT STANDING COMMITTEES FROM DATE OF FORMATION

Con-gress	Year	Ways and Means	Elections	Interstate Commerce
1	1789	Thomas Fitzsimons, Pa	George Clymer, Pa	
2	1791	" "	Samuel Livermore, N.H	
3	1793	" "	William Smith, S.C	
4	1795	William Smith, S.C	Abraham B. Venable, Va	Benjamin Goodhue, Mass.
5	1797	Robert G. Harper, S.C	Joshua Coitt, Conn	John Swanwick, Pa.
6	1799	Roger Griswold, Conn	Samuel W. Dana, Conn	Samuel Smith, Md.
7	1801	John Randolph, Va	John Milledge, Ga	
8	1803	" "	William Findlay, Pa	Samuel L. Mitchell, N.Y.
9	1805	Joseph Clay, Pa	" "	Jacob Crowninshield, Mass.
10	1807	George W. Campbell, Tenn	" "	Thomas Newton, Va.
11	1809	John W. Eppes, Va	" "	" "
12	1811	Langdon Cheves, S.C		" "
13	1813	John W. Eppes, Va	James Fisk, Vt	" "
14	1815	William Lowndes, S.C	John W. Taylor, N.Y	" "
15	1817	" "	" "	" "
16	1819	Samuel Smith, Md	" "	" "
17	1821	" "	John Sloane, O	" "
18	1823	Louis McLane, Del	" "	" "

CHAIRMEN OF STANDING COMMITTEES (*continued*)

Congress	Year	Ways and Means	Elections	Interstate Commerce
19	1825	Louis McLane, Del.	John Sloane, O.	Thomas Newton, Va.
20	1827	George McDuffie, S.C.	" "	Churchill C. Cambreleng, N.Y.
21	1829	" "	Willis Alston, N.C.	" "
22	1831	Gulian C. Verplanck, N.Y.	Nathaniel H. Claiborne, Va.	" "
23	1833	James K. Polk, Tenn.	" "	Jose B. Sutherland, Pa.
24	1835	C. C. Cambreleng, N.Y.	" "	" "
25	1837	" "	Andrew Buchanan, Pa.	Francis O. J. Smith, Me.
26	1839	John W. Jones, Va.	John Campbell, S.C.	Edward Curtis, N.Y.
27	1841	Millard Fillmore, N.Y.	William Halstead, N.J.	John P. Kennedy, Md.
28	1843	John J. McKay, N.C.	Lucius Q. C. Elmer, N.J.	Isaac E. Holmes, N.C.
29	1845	" "	Hannibal Hamlin, Me.	Robert McClelland, Mich.
30	1847	Samuel F. Vinton, O.	Richard W. Thompson, Ind.	Washington Hunt, N.Y.
31	1849	Thomas H. Bayley, Va.	William Strong, Pa.	Roberts H. McLane, Md.
32	1851	George S. Houston, Ala.	William S. Ashe, N.C.	David L. Seymour, N.Y.
33	1853	" "	Richard H. Stanton, Ky.	Thomas J. B. Fuller, Me.
34	1855	Lewis D. Campbell, O.	Israel Washburn, Me.	Elihu B. Washburne, Ill.
35	1857	{ J. Clancy Jones, Pa. / John S. Phelps, Mo. }	Thomas L. Harris, Ill.	John Cochrane, N.Y.
36	1859	John Sherman, O.	John A. Gilmer, N.C.	Elihu B. Washburne, Ill.
37	1861	Thaddeus Stevens, Pa.	Henry L. Dawes, Mass.	" "
38	1863	" "	" "	" "
39	1865	Justin S. Morrill, Vt.	" "	" "
40	1867	Robert C. Schenck, O.	" "	" "

CHAIRMEN OF STANDING COMMITTEES (continued)

Con-gress	Year	Ways and Means	Elections	Interstate Commerce
41	1869	Robert C. Schenck, O.	Halbert E. Paine, Wis.	Nathan F. Dixon, R.I.
42	1871	Henry L. Dawes, Mass.	George W. McCrary, Ia.	Samuel Shellabarger, O.
43	1873	" "	H. Boardman Smith, N.Y.	William A. Wheeler, N.Y.
44	1875	William R. Morrison, Ill.	John T. Harris, Va.	Frank Hereford, W.Va.
45	1877	Fernando Wood, N.Y.	" "	John H. Reagan, Tex.
46	1879	" "	William M. Springer, Ill.	" "
47	1881	William D. Kelley, Pa.	William H. Calkins, Ind.	Horace F. Page, Cal.
48	1883	William R. Morrison, Ill.	Henry G. Turner, Ga.	John H. Reagan, Tex.
49	1885	" "	" "	" "
50	1887	Roger Q. Mills, Tex.	Charles F. Crisp, Ga.	Martin L. Clardy, Mo.
51	1889	William McKinley, O.	Jonathan H. Rowell, Ill.	Charles S. Baker, N.Y.
52	1891	William M. Springer, Ill.	Charles T. O'Ferrall, Va.	George D. Wise, Va.
53	1893	William L. Wilson, W.Va.	" "	" "
54	1895	Nelson Dingley, Me.	Charles Daniels, N.Y.	William P. Hepburn, Ia.
55	1897	" "	Robert W. Taylor, O.	" "
56	1899	Sereno E. Payne, N.Y.	" "	" "
57	1901	" "	James R. Mann, Ill.	" "
58	1903	" "	" "	" "
59	1905	" "	" "	" "
60	1907	" "	" "	" "
61	1909	" "	Charles L. Knapp, N.Y.	James R. Mann, Ill.
62	1911	Oscar W. Underwood, Ala.	Timothy T. Ansbery, O.	William C. Adamson.
63	1913	" "	John D. Post, O.	" "

CHAIRMEN OF STANDING COMMITTEES (continued)

Congress	Year	Appropriations	Banking and Currency	Rivers and Harbors
39	1865	Thaddeus Stevens, Pa....	Theodore M. Pomeroy, N.Y...	
40	1867	" "	" "	
41	1869	Henry L. Dawes, Mass....	James A. Garfield, O....	
42	1871	James A. Garfield, O....	Samuel Hooper, Mass....	
43	1873	" "	Horace Maynard, Tenn....	
44	1875	Samuel J. Randall, Pa....	Samuel S. Cox, N.Y....	
45	1877	John D. C. Atkins, Tenn....	Aylett H. Buckner, Mo....	
46	1879	" "	" "	
47	1881	Frank Hiscock, N.Y....	William W. Crapo, Mass....	
48	1883	Samuel J. Randall, Pa....	Aylett H. Buckner, Mo....	
49	1885	" "	James F. Miller, Tex....	Albert S. Willis, Ky.
50	1887	" "	Beriah Wilkins, O....	" "
51	1889	Joseph G. Cannon, Ill....	George W. E. Dorsey, Neb....	Newton C. Blanchard, La.
52	1891	William S. Holman, Ind....	Henry Bacon, N.Y....	Thomas J. Henderson, Ill.
53	1893	Joseph D. Sayers, Tex....	William M. Springer, Ill....	Newton C. Blanchard, La.
54	1895	Joseph G. Cannon, Ill....	Joseph H. Walker, Mass....	{ Thomas C. Catchings, Miss.
55	1897	" "	" "	Warren B. Hooker, N.Y.
56	1899	" "	Marriott Brosius, Pa....	
57	1901	" "	Charles N. Fowler, N.J....	Theodore E. Burton, O.
58	1903	James A. Hemenway, Ind....	" " "	" " "
59	1905	James A. Tawney, Minn....	" " "	" " "

CHAIRMEN OF STANDING COMMITTEES (*continued*)

Congress	Year	Appropriations	Banking and Currency	Rivers and Harbors
60	1907	James A. Tawney, Minn......	Charles N. Fowler, N.J......	Theodore E. Burton, O.
61	1909	" " "	Edward B. Vreeland, N.Y......	DeAlva S. Alexander, N.Y.
62	1911	John J. Fitzgerald, N.Y......	Arsene P. Pujo, La........	Stephen M. Sparkman, Fla.
63	1913	" "	Carter Glass, Va............	"

Congress	Year	Military Affairs	Naval Affairs	Territories
17	1821	William Eustis, Mass........	Timothy Fuller, Mass........	
18	1823	James Hamilton, S.C........	B. W. Crowninshield, Mass.	
19	1825	" "	Henry R. Storrs, N.Y........	James Strong, N.Y.
20	1827	" "	Michael Hoffman, N.Y........	"
21	1829	William Drayton, S.C........	" "	James Clark, Ky.
22	1831	Richard M. Johnson, Ky	" "	John L. Kerr, Md.
23	1833	" "	Campbell P. White, N.Y.	Chilton Allen, Ky.
24	1835	" "	Leonard Jarvis, Me..........	John M. Patton, Va.
25	1837	James J. McKay, N.C........	Samuel Ingham, Conn........	"
26	1839	Cave Johnson, Tenn........	Francis Thomas, Md..........	John Pope, Ky.
27	1841	Edward Stanly, N.C........	Henry A. Wise, Va..........	" "

CHAIRMEN OF STANDING COMMITTEES (continued)

Congress	Year	Military Affairs	Naval Affairs	Territories
28	1843	Hugh A. Haralson, Ga.	Henry A. Wise, Va.	Aaron V. Brown, Tenn.
29	1845	"	Israel E. Holmes, S.C.	Stephen A. Douglas, Ill.
30	1847	John M. Botts, Va.	Thomas B. King, Ga.	Caleb B. Smith, Ind.
31	1849	Armisted Burt, S.C.	Fred. P. Stanton, Tenn.	Linn Boyd, Ky.
32	1851	William H. Bissell, Ill.	"	William A. Richardson, Ill.
33	1853	"	"	"
34	1855	John A. Quitman, Miss	Thomas S. Bocock, Va.	Galusha A. Grow, Pa.
35	1857	"	Samuel P. Benson, Me.	Alexander H. Stephens, Ga.
36	1859	Benjamin Stanton, O.	Thomas S. Bocock, Va.	Galusha A. Grow, Pa.
37	1861	Francis P. Blair, Jr., Mo.	Freeman H. Morse, Me.	James M. Ashley, O.
38	1863	Robert C. Schenck, O.	Charles B. Sedgwick, N.Y.	"
39	1865	"	Alexander H. Rice, Mass.	"
40	1867	James A. Garfield, O.	Frederick A. Pike, Me.	"
41	1869	John A. Logan, Ill.	Glenni W. Scofield, Pa.	Shelby M. Cullom, Ill.
42	1871	John Coburn, Ind.	"	John Taffe, Neb.
43	1873	"	"	"
44	1875	Henry B. Banning, O.	Washington C. Whitthorne, Tenn.	George C. McKee, Miss.
45	1877	"	Washington C. Whitthorne, Tenn.	Milton L. Southard, O.
46	1879	William A. J. Sparks, Ill.	Washington C. Whitthorne, Tenn.	Benjamin J. Franklin, Mo.
				Henry L. Muldrow, Miss.

CHAIRMEN OF STANDING COMMITTEES (*continued*)

Congress	Year	Military Affairs	Naval Affairs	Territories
47	1881	Thomas J. Henderson, Ill.	Benjamin W. Harris, Mass....	Julius C. Burrows, Mich.
48	1883	William S. Rosecrans, Cal....	Samuel S. Cox, N.Y.........	Luke Pryor, Ala.
49	1885	Edward S. Bragg, Wis......	Hilary A. Herbert, Ala......	William D. Hill, O.
50	1887	Richard W. Townsend, Ill. ..	" "	William H. Springer, Ill.
51	1889	Byron M. Cutcheon, Mich...	Charles A. Boutelle, Me....	Isaac S. Struble, Ia.
52	1891	Joseph H. Outhwaite, O....	Hilary A. Herbert, Ala......	Jos. E. Washington, Tenn.
53	1893	" "	Amos J. Cummings, N.Y.....	Joseph Wheeler, Ala.
54	1895	John A. T. Hull, Ia.	Charles A. Boutelle, Me....	Joseph A. Scranton, Pa.
55	1897	" "	" "	William S. Knox, Mass.
56	1899	" "	" "	" "
57	1901	" "	George E. Foss, Ill........	" "
58	1903	" "	" "	Edward L. Hamilton, Mich.
59	1905	" "	" "	" "
60	1907	" "	" "	" "
61	1909	" "	" "	" "
62	1911	James Hay, Va............	Lemuel Padgett, Tenn.....	Henry D. Flood, Va.
63	1913	" "	" "	William C. Houston, Tenn.

CHAIRMEN OF STANDING COMMITTEES (*continued*)

Congress	Year	Agriculture	Indian Affairs	Foreign Affairs
16	1819	Thomas Forrest, Pa........		
17	1821	Josiah Butler, N.H........	Samuel Moore, Pa........	John Russell, Mass.
18	1823	Stephen Van Rensselaer, N.Y.	John Cocke, Tenn........	John Forsythe, Ga.
19	1825	" " "	" "	" "
20	1827	" " "	William McLean, O........	Edward Everett, Mass.
21	1829	Ambrose Spencer, N.Y.....	John Bell, Tenn........	William S. Archer, Va.
22	1831	Erastus Root, N.Y........	" "	" " "
23	1833	Abraham Bockee, N.Y.....	Dixon H. Lewis, Ala.....	" " "
24	1835	" " "	John Bell, Tenn........	John Y. Mason, Va.
25	1837	Edmund Deberry, N.C.....	" " "	Benjamin C. Howard, Md.
26	1839	" " "	" " "	Francis W. Pickens, S.C.
27	1841	" " "	John Quincy Adams, Mass.	Caleb Cushing, Mass.
28	1843	" " "	Cave Johnson, Tenn.....	Charles J. Ingersoll, Pa.
29	1845	Joseph H. Anderson, N.Y.	Jacob Thompson, Miss....	
30	1847	Hugh White, N.Y........	Dan. M. Barringer, N.C.	Freeman Smith, Conn.
31	1849	Nat. S. Littlefield, Me....	Robert W. Johnson, Ark.	John A. McClernand, Ill.
32	1851	John G. Floyd, N.Y........	" " "	Thomas H. Bayley, Va.
33	1853	John L. Dawson, Pa......	James L. Orr, S.C........	" " "
34	1855	David P. Holloway, Ind...	Benjamin Pringle, N.Y...	A. C. Pennington, N.J.
35	1857	William G. White, Del....	Alfred B. Greenwood, Ark	Thomas L. Clingman, N.C.
36	1859	Martin Butterfield, N.Y...	E. Etheridge, Tenn......	Thomas Corwin, O.
37	1861	Owen Lovejoy, Ill........	Cyrus Aldrich, Minn.....	J. J. Crittenden, Ky.

CHAIRMEN OF STANDING COMMITTEES (*continued*)

Congress	Year	Agriculture	Indian Affairs	Foreign Affairs
38	1863	Brutus J. Clay, Ky	William Windom, Minn	Henry Winter Davis, Md.
39	1865	John Bidwell, Cal.	" "	Nathaniel P. Banks, Mass.
40	1867	R. E. Trowbridge, Mich.	" "	" "
41	1869	John T. Wilson. O.	Sidney Clarke, Kans.	" "
42	1871	" "	John P. C. Shanks, Ind.	Goodlove S. Orth, Ind.
43	1873	Charles Hays, Ala.	John T. Averill, Minn.	Thomas Swann, Md.
44	1875	John H. Caldwell, Ala.	Alfred M. Scales, N.C.	" "
45	1877	Augustus W. Cutler, N.J.	" "	Samuel S. Cox, N.Y.
46	1879	James W. Covert, N.Y.	" "	Charles G. Williams, Wis.
47	1881	Edward K. Valentine, Neb.	Dudley C. Haskell, Kans.	Andrew G. Curtin, Pa.
48	1883	William H. Hatch, Mo.	Olin Wellborn, Texas	Perry Belmont, N.Y.
49	1885	" "		James B. McCreary, Ky.
50	1887	" "	Samuel W. Peel, Ark.	Robert R. Hitt, Ill.
51	1889	Edward H. Funston, Kans.	B. W. Perkins, Kans.	James H. Blount, Ga.
52	1891	William H. Hatch, Mo.	Samuel W. Peel, Ark.	James B. McCreary, Ky.
53	1893	" "	William S. Holman, Ind.	Robert R. Hitt, Ill.
54	1895	James W. Wadsworth, N.Y.	James S. Sherman, N.Y.	" "
55	1897	" "	" "	" "
56	1899	" "	" "	" "
57	1901	" "	" "	" "
58	1903	" "	" "	Robert G. Cousins, Ia.
59	1905	" "	" "	

CHAIRMEN OF STANDING COMMITTEES *(continued)*

Congress	Year	Agriculture	Indian Affairs	Foreign Affairs
60	1907	Charles F. Scott, Kans.....	James S. Sherman, N.Y....	Robert G. Cousins, Ia.
61	1909	" "	Charles M. Burke, S.D....	James B. Perkins, N.Y.
62	1911	John Lamb, Va....	John H. Stephens, Tex....	William Sulzer, N.Y.
63	1913	Asbury F. Lever, S.C	" "	Henry D. Flood, Va.

Congress	Year	District of Columbia	Post Offices and Roads	Judiciary
10	1807	Philip Barton Key, Md....	John Rhea, Tenn....	
11	1809	John Love, Va....	" " "	
12	1811	Joseph Lewis, Jr., Va....	" " "	
13	1813	John Dawson, Va....	" " "	Charles J. Ingersoll, Pa.
14	1815	H. St. G. Tucker, Va....	Samuel D. Ingham, Pa....	Hugh Nelson, Va.
15	1817	John C. Herbert, Md....	" " "	" "
16	1819	Joseph Kent, Md....	Arthur Livermore, N.H....	John Sergeant, Pa.
17	1821	" " "	Francis Johnson, Ky....	" "
18	1823	" " "	" " "	" "
19	1825	" " "	Samuel D. Ingham, Pa....	Daniel Webster, Mass.
20	1827	Mark Alexander, Va....	" " "	" "
				Philip P. Barbour, Va.

CHAIRMEN OF STANDING COMMITTEES (*continued*)

Congress	Year	District of Columbia	Post Offices and Roads	Judiciary
21	1829	Gershom Powers, N.Y.	Richard M. Johnson, Ky	James Buchanan, Pa.
22	1831	Philip Doddridge, Va.	"	John Davis, Mass.
23	1833	Joseph W. Chinn, Va.	Henry W. Connor, N.C.	John Bell, Tenn.
24	1835	W. B. Shepard, N.C.	"	Samuel Beardsley, N.Y.
25	1837	James W. Bouldin, Va.	"	Francis Thomas, Md.
26	1839	William Cost Johnson, Md.	James J. McKay, N.C.	John Sergeant, Pa.
27	1841	Joseph R. Underwood, Ky.	George N. Briggs, Mass.	Daniel D. Barnard, N.Y.
28	1843	John Campbell, S.C.	George W. Hopkins, Va.	William Wilkins, Pa.
29	1845	Robert M. T. Hunter, Va.	"	George Rathbun, N.Y.
30	1847	John G. Chapman, Md.	William L. Goggin, Va.	Joseph R. Ingersoll, Pa.
31	1849	Albert G. Brown, Miss.	Emery D. Potter, O.	James Thompson, Pa.
32	1851	Orlando B. Ficklin, Ill.	Edson B. Olds, O.	James X. McLanahan, Pa.
33	1853	William T. Hamilton, Md.	"	Frederick P. Stanton, Tenn.
34	1855	James Meacham, Vt.	Daniel Mace, Ind.	George A. Simmons, N.Y.
35	1857	William O. Goode, Va.	William H. English, Ind.	George S. Houston, Ala.
36	1859	Luther C. Carter, N.Y.	Schuyler Colfax, Ind	John Hickman, Pa.
37	1861	Roscoe Conkling, N.Y.	"	John A. Bingham, O.
38	1863	Owen Lovejoy, Ill.	John B. Alley, Mass.	James F. Wilson, Ia.
39	1865	Ebon C. Ingersoll, Ill.	"	"
40	1867	"	John F. Farnsworth, Ill	"
41	1869	Burton C. Cook, Ill.	"	"
42	1871	H. H. Starkweather, Conn.	"	John A. Bingham, "

CHAIRMEN OF STANDING COMMITTEES (continued)

Congress	Year	District of Columbia	Post Offices and Roads	Judiciary
43	1873	Robert S. Hale, N.Y.	John B. Packer, Pa.	Benjamin F. Butler, Mass.
44	1875	Aylett H. Buckner, Mo.	John B. Clark, Mo.	J. Proctor Knott, Ky.
45	1877	A. S. Williams, Mich.	Alfred M. Waddell, N.C.	" "
46	1879	Eppa Hunton, Va.	H. D. Money, Miss.	" "
47	1881	Henry S. Neal, O.	H. H. Bingham, Pa.	Thomas B. Reed, Me.
48	1883	John S. Barbour, Va.	H. D. Money, Miss.	J. Randolph Tucker, Va.
49	1885	" "	James H. Blount, Ga.	" "
50	1887	John J. Hemphill, S.C.	" "	D. B. Culberson, Texas.
51	1889	William W. Grout, Vt.	H. H. Bingham, Pa.	Ezra B. Taylor, O.
52	1891	John J. Hemphill, S.C.	J. S. Henderson, N.C.	D. B. Culberson, Texas.
53	1893	John T. Heard, Mo.	"	" "
54	1895	Joseph W. Babcock, Wis	Eugene F. Loud, Cal.	D. B. Henderson, Iowa.
55	1897	" "	" "	" "
56	1899	" "	" "	George W. Ray, N.Y.
57	1901	" "	" "	John J. Jenkins, Wis.
58	1903	" "	J. Overstreet, Ind.	" "
59	1905	" "	" "	" "
60	1907	Samuel W. Smith, Mich.	" "	" "
61	1909	" "	John W. Weeks, Mass.	Richard W. Parker, N.J.
62	1911	Ben Johnson, Ky.	John A. Moon, Tenn.	H. D. Clayton, Ala.
63	1913	" "	" "	Edwin Y. Webb, N.C.

F

POLITICAL DIVISIONS OF THE HOUSE OF REPRESENTATIVES FROM 1789 TO 1915

Con-gress	Total Repre-sentatives	Dele-gates	Feder-alists	Demo-crats	Whigs	Repub-licans	Amer-icans	Inde-pend-ents	Na-tionals	Read-justers	Free Soil	Labor	Silver-ite	Popu-lists	Vacant	Pro-gres-sives
1	65		53	12												
2	69	1	55	14												
3	105		51	54												
4	105	1	46	50												
5	105		51	54												
6	105	1	57	48												
7	105		34	71												
8	141	3	38	103												
9	141	3	29	112												
10	141	4	31	110												
11	141	4	46	95												
12	182	3	36	105												
13	183	3	67	115												
14	185	3	61	122												
15	187	3	57	128												
16	213	3	42	145												
17	213	3	58	129												
18	213	3	72	141												
19	213	3	79	134												
20	240	2	85	128												
21	242	3		142	71											
22	242	3		130	83											
23	242	3		147	93											
24	242	2		144	98											
25	223	3		117	115			10								
26	225	3		103	132			6								
27	227	2		103	132			6								
28		1		142	81	1									1	
29				141	78		6								1	
30				108	115			4								

POLITICAL DIVISIONS (continued)

Congress	Total Representatives	Delegates	Federalists	Democrats	Whigs	Republicans	Americans	Independents	Nationals	Readjusters	Free Soil	Labor	Silverite	Populists	Vacant	Progressives
31	227	2		116	111						5					
32	233	4		140	88						4					
33	234	6		159	71											
34	234	7		83		108	43									
35	237	7		131		92	14									
36	237	5		101		113	23								2	
37	178	8		42		106	28									
38	183	9		80		103									1	
39	191	9		49		145										
40	193	8		73		143									1	
41	243	9		104		170									2	
42	243	10		88		139										
43	293	10		181		203		3	14						1	
44	293	8		156		107			9			3				
45	293	8		150		137			2							
46	293	8		130		128			2	2					1	
47	293	8		200		152		4								
48	325	8		182		119		1							1	
49	325	8		170		140		1								
50	325	4		156		151						2				
51	330	4		231		173										
52	333	4		220		88										
53	356	3		104		128							1	14		
54	357	3		131		245							5	9		
55	357			160		202							1	7		
56	357			150		187							1	9		
57	357			172		201								6	1	
58	386			136		208								4	4	
59	386			166		249									1	
60	391			169		223							1		2	
61	391			228		219									3	
62	391			228		160								1	2	
63	435					197		1							2	6

G

APPORTIONMENT OF MEMBERS BY STATES

States	Constitutional apportionment	First census, 1790	Second census, 1800	Third census, 1810	Fourth census, 1820	Fifth census, 1830	Sixth census, 1840	Seventh census, 1850	Eighth census, 1860	Ninth census, 1870	Tenth census, 1880	Eleventh census, 1890	Twelfth census, 1900	Thirteenth census, 1910
Alabama					3	5	7	7	6	8	8	9	9	10
Arizona														1
Arkansas						1	1	2	3	4	5	6	7	7
California								2	3	4	6	7	8	11
Colorado											1	2	3	4
Connecticut	5	7	7	7	6	6	4	4	4	4	4	4	5	5
Delaware	1	1	1	2	1	1	1	1	1	1	1	1	1	1
Florida							1	1	1	2	2	2	3	4
Georgia	3	2	4	6	7	9	8	8	7	9	10	11	11	12
Idaho											1	1	1	2
Illinois				1	1	3	7	9	14	19	20	22	25	27
Indiana				1	3	7	10	11	11	13	13	13	13	13
Iowa								2	6	9	11	11	11	11
Kansas									1	3	7	8	8	8
Kentucky		2	6	10	12	13	10	10	9	10	11	11	11	11
Louisiana				1	3	3	4	4	5	6	6	6	7	8
Maine				7	7	8	7	6	5	5	4	4	4	4
Maryland	6	8	9	9	9	8	6	6	5	6	6	6	6	6
Massachusetts	8	14	17	13	13	12	10	11	10	11	12	13	14	16
Michigan						1	3	4	6	9	11	12	12	13
Minnesota									2	3	5	7	9	10
Mississippi				1	1	2	4	5	5	6	7	7	8	8
Missouri					1	2	5	7	9	13	14	15	16	16
Montana											1	1	1	2

APPORTIONMENT OF MEMBERS BY STATES (continued)

States	Constitutional apportionment	First census, 1790	Second census, 1800	Third census, 1810	Fourth census, 1820	Fifth census, 1830	Sixth census, 1840	Seventh census, 1850	Eighth census, 1860	Ninth census, 1870	Tenth census, 1880	Eleventh census, 1890	Twelfth census, 1900	Thirteenth census, 1910
Nebraska									1	1	3	6	6	6
Nevada									1	1	1	1	1	1
New Hampshire	3	4	5	6	6	5	4	3	3	3	2	2	2	2
New Jersey	4	5	6	6	6	6	5	5	5	7	7	8	10	12
New Mexico														1
New York	6	10	17	27	34	40	34	33	31	33	34	34	37	43
North Carolina	5	10	12	13	13	13	9	8	7	8	9	9	10	10
North Dakota												1	2	3
Ohio			1	6	14	19	21	21	19	20	21	21	21	22
Oklahoma													5	8
Oregon								1	1	1	1	2	2	3
Pennsylvania	8	13	18	23	26	28	24	25	24	27	28	30	32	36
Rhode Island	1	2	2	2	2	2	2	2	2	2	2	2	2	3
South Carolina	5	6	8	9	9	9	7	6	4	5	7	7	7	7
South Dakota												2	2	3
Tennessee		1	3	6	9	13	11	10	8	10	10	10	10	10
Texas							2	2	4	6	11	13	16	18
Utah													1	2
Vermont		2	4	6	5	5	4	3	3	3	2	2	2	2
Virginia	10	19	22	23	22	21	15	13	11	9	10	10	10	10
Washington												2	3	5
West Virginia										3	4	4	5	6
Wisconsin							2	3	6	8	9	10	11	11
Wyoming												1	1	1
Total	65	106	142	186	213	242	232	237	243	293	332	357	391	435

INDEX

INDEX

Adams, George M., action as clerk, 24.

Adams, John, President, use of veto, 358.

Adams, John Quincy, opposes apportionment, 6; his lament, 7; as to members elect, 13; concerning Wise, 14; Rhett, 16; chairman of unorganized House, 17; father of the House, 35, Appendix D; chairman of Committee of the Whole, 48; opposes partisan committees, 67; resents an appointment, 68; on thanking Stevenson, 71; and Jones, 73; on use of sarcasm, 110; contributes to disorder, 114; funeral of, 153–54; refuses to vote, 158; encourages a disappearing quorum, 158; estimate of Randolph, 188–89; on Revolutionary soldiers, 215; fights for the right of petition, 215; revision of speeches, 291; power as a debater, 295; tribute to Prentiss, 318; condemns settlement of contested election cases, 319; reasons for Chase's acquittal, 349; on quarrel with Jackson, 350; blow at Buchanan, 350; his use of the veto, when President, 358.

Aiken, William, character of, 86; defeated for Speaker, 87.

Allison, William B., 305.

Alston, Willis, favors previous question, 187.

Ames, Fisher, orator and profound lawyer, 299; prepares rules for contested election cases, 314; basis of Statute of 1798, 314.

Ames, Oakes, connection with Crédit Mobilier, 150, and note.

Annals of Congress, number of volumes, 101; contents of, 101.

Apportionment, first law, 5; changes in ratio, 5; Webster's plan, 6; unfairness to New England, 6; Adams's denunciation of it, 6; Webster's system adopted, 7; large reduction, 7; rapid increase in numbers, 8; table of, 8.

Appropriations, alarming growth of, 250–52; plans to check waste, 254–55.

Archbold, Robert W., 341; impeachment of, 342; question of jurisdiction, 341–42.

Assaults in House, Grow and Keitt, 45, 125; Harper and Lyon, 111; John White, 115; John Bell, 116; Black and Giddings, 116; Rousseau and Grinnell, 138.

Atkins, John D. C., character of, 130.

Bacon, Ezekiel, character as floor leader, 124.

Bailey, Joseph W., relations with Reed, 114.

Baker, Edward D., his gifts as an orator, 303.

Bancroft, George, eulogy before Congress upon death of President Lincoln, 385.

Banks, Nathaniel P., Speaker, 32; character of, 86–87; election as Speaker, 87; appoints Campbell floor leader, 110; vivid picture of, 304.

Barbour, Philip P., made an Associate Justice of U.S. Supreme Court, 281; character of, 301.